COMPUTER SCIENCE, TECHNOLOGY AND APPLICATIONS SERIES

COMPUTER GAMES: LEARNING OBJECTIVES, COGNITIVE PERFORMANCE AND EFFECTS ON DEVELOPMENT

COMPUTER SCIENCE, TECHNOLOGY AND APPLICATIONS SERIES

Problem Solving with Delphi - CD included
Stephen John Sugden
2009. ISBN 978-1-60741-249-6

Mobile Computing Research and Applications
Kevin Y. Chen and H.K. Lee (Editors)
2009. ISBN 978-1-60741-101-7

Large Scale Computations, Embedded Systems and Computer Security
Fedor Komarov and Maksim Bestuzhev (Editors)
2010. ISBN: 978-1-60741-307-3

Performance Modelling Techniques for Parallel Supercomputing Applications
A. Grove and P.D. Coddington
2010. ISBN: 9781-60692-269-9

Data Mining and Management
Lawrence I. Spendler (Editor)
2010. ISBN: 978-1-60741-289-2

Biometrics: Methods, Applications and Analyses
Harvey Schuster and Wilfred Metzger (Editors)
2010. ISBN: 978-1-60876-412-9

Relational Databases and Open Source Software Developments
Jennifer R. Taylor (Editor)
2010. ISBN: 978-1-61668-436-5

Relational Databases and Open Source Software Developments
Jennifer R. Taylor (Editor)
2010. ISBN: 978-1-61668-468-6 (Online Book)

Computer Animation
Jaron S. Wright and Lloyd M. Hughes (Editors)
2010. ISBN: 978-1-60741-559-6

Java Software and Embedded Systems
Mattis Hayes and Isaiah Johansen (Editors)
2010. ISBN: 978-1-60741-661-6

Computer Games: Learning Objectives, Cognitive Performance and Effects on Development
Agustin Soria and Julián Maldonado (Editors)
2010. ISBN: 978-1-60876-658-1

Computational Mechanics Research Trends
Hans P. Berger (Editor)
2010. ISBN: 978-1-60876-057-2

Design and Performance of Biometric System
John T. Elsworth (Editor)
2010. ISBN: 978-1-60692-978-0

Design and Performance of Biometric System
John T. Elsworth (Editor)
2010. ISBN: 978-1-61668-524-9 (Online Book)

Peer-to-Peer Networks and Internet Policies
Diego Vegros and Jaime Sáenz (Editors)
2010. ISBN: 978-1-60876-287-3

Agent-Based Computing
Duarte Bouça and Amaro Gafagnão (Editors)
2010. ISBN: 978-1-60876-684-0

Biometrics, Privacy, Progress and Government
Rachel B. Jefferson (Editor)
2010. ISBN: 978-1-60741-098-0

3D Imaging: Theory, Technology and Applications
Emerson H. Duke and Stephen R. Aguirre (Editors)
2010. ISBN: 978-1-60876-885-1

Computer Communication for Metropolitan and Wide Area Networks
Matthew N. O. Sadiku and Sarhan M. Musa
2010. ISBN: 978-1-61668-024-4

Peer-to-Peer Storage: Security and Protocols
Nouha Oualha and Yves Roudier
2010. ISBN: 978-1-61668-199-9

Peer-to-Peer Storage: Security and Protocols
Nouha Oualha and Yves Roudier
2010. ISBN: 978-1-61668-462-4 (Online Book)

Persuasion On-Line and Communicability: The Destruction of Credibility in the Virtual Community and Cognitive Models
Francisco V. Cipolla-Ficarra
2010. ISBN: 978-1-61668-268-2

Persuasion On-Line and Communicability: The Destruction of Credibility in the Virtual Community and Cognitive Models
Francisco V. Cipolla-Ficarra
2010. ISBN: 978-1-61668-701-4 (Online Book)

Intuition and Computer Programming (WT)
Michael Weigend
2010. ISBN: 978-1-61668-330-6

Intuition and Computer Programming (WT)
Michael Weigend
2010. ISBN: 978-1-61668-813-4 (Online Book)

Semantic Web: Standards, Tools and Ontologies
Kimberly A. Haffner (Editor)
2010. ISBN: 978-1-61668-471-6

Semantic Web: Standards, Tools and Ontologies
Kimberly A. Haffner (Editor)
2010. ISBN: 978-1-61668-540-9

Logic of Analog and Digital Machines
Paolo Rocchi
2010. ISBN: 978-1-61668-481-5

Logic of Analog and Digital Machines
Paolo Rocchi
2010. ISBN: 978-1-61668-815-8

Computer Games: Learning Objectives, Cognitive Performance and Effects on Development

Agustin Soria
and
Julián Maldonado
Editors

Nova Science Publishers, Inc.
New York

For permission to use material from this book please contact us:
Telephone 631-231-7269; Fax 631-231-8175
Web Site: http://www.novapublishers.com

LIBRARY OF CONGRESS CATALOGING-IN-PUBLICATION DATA

Computer games : learning objectives, cognitive performance, and effects on development / Agustin Soria and Julián Maldonado.
p. cm.
Includes index.
ISBN 978-1-60876-658-1 (hardcover)
1. Computer games--Programming. 2. Computer games--Design. 3. Computer games--Research. 4. Video games--Design. I. Soria, Agustin, 1954- II. Maldonado, Julián.
QA76.76.C672C676 2009
794.8'1526--dc22

2009040474

Published by Nova Science Publishers, Inc. ✣ New York

CONTENTS

PREFACE

There is wide interest in the potential of 'serious' video games as vehicles for learning. Especially in the health education domain, there are now many reports of the use of video games intended to produce changes in players' knowledge, attitudes or behaviors that will transfer to 'real life' settings outside the context of the game. The authors of this book analyze the learning models implicit in health games described in the literature, and relates these to established learning models in order to illustrate the nature of the gaps between current game designs and relevant learning theory and technology. This analysis provides a systematic framework for identifying principles of game design that are soundly based both in theory and research evidence. Examples are provided from recent game designs. This book also reports on whether computer games can be put to good use for mathematics educational purposes for young teenagers. The authors believe that computer games can be used as a complement for making routine practice more varied, more enjoyable and more effective. In addition, digital epistemic games are computer-based games that mediate mental, intellectual, knowledge-oriented activities. This book presents a strategy for how to analyze digital epistemic games. Other chapters in this book investigate the relationship between video game play and dreams and the emergence of Massively Multiplayer Online Games (MMOGs) in the past decade.

Chapter 1 discusses Massively Multiplayer Online Games (MMOGs), which have emerged in the past decade as a new type of large-scale distributed application characterised by a huge real-time virtual world entertaining millions of players spread across the world, e.g., World of Warcraft counts over 6 million unique players daily. Today's MMOG operate as client/server architectures, in which the game server simulates a world via computing and database operations, receives and processes commands from the clients, and interoperates with a billing and accounting system. Based on the actions submitted by the players, the game servers compute the global state of the game world represented by the position and interactions of the entities, and send appropriate real-time responses to the players containing the new relevant state information. Depending on the game, typical response times to ensure fluent play must be between 100 milliseconds in online First Person Shooter (FPS) action games and 1-2 seconds for Role-Playing Games (RPG). A good game experience is critical in keeping the players engaged, and has an immediate consequence on the income of the MMOG operators.

Today, a single computer is limited at around 500 simultaneous and persistent network connections, and databases can manage the update of around 500 objects per second. To support at the same time millions of active concurrent players and many more other game entities, MMOG operators need to install and operate a large dedicated multi-server infrastructure, with hundreds to thousands of computers hosting the distributed load of each game. However, due to the dynamic character of MMOGs, both on the short and on the long term, the game providers have to over-provision their infrastructure, which leads to a low and inefficient resource utilisation and new providers finding it difficult to join the market. For example, the operating infrastructure of the Massively Multiplayer Online Role Playing Game (MMORPG) World of Warcraft has over 10,000 computers.

To alleviate this problem, the edutain@grid project funded by the European Union searches a Grid computing platform for inexpensive provisioning of resources to MMOGs based on a novel dynamic and on-demand allocation strategy. First of all, a load prediction service is in charge of projecting the future distribution of entities in the game world that will drive the resource allocation. For example, by timely foreseeing critical hot-spots (i.e. excessively populated area of interest generating a large number of interactions), one can dynamically provision additional servers on some new resources and take timely load balancing actions that transparently redistribute the game load before the servers become overloaded. Based on the entity distribution prediction and possible interactions, a load modelling service is using analytical methods for estimating the game server load. Finally, a resource allocation service is using the load information to provision the necessary resources that accommodate the player load while guaranteeing the real-time QoS constraints.

In Chapter 2 the authors will present a strategy for how to analyze digital epistemic games. Digital epistemic games are computer-based games that mediate mental, intellectual, knowledge-oriented activities. Mediate here suggests support, facilitate, transform, and enhance. Epistemic games can be used to improve players' problem solving, planning, information analysis, reasoning, critical thinking, and learning. Such games contain one or more cognitive tasks that players need to perform in order to advance or complete the game. Each game can be categorized and analyzed according to these underlying cognitive tasks. Some examples of cognitive tasks include the rearrangement of shapes, the linking of objects and ideas, the finding of paths through mazelike structures, and the matching of features and parts.

Traditionally, digital games have been categorized according to broad genres such as adventure, board, card, combat, educational, puzzle, strategy, and role-playing games. These genres categorize games based on their overall gameplay. As such, genres are intended to provide a prospective user with a general idea of what the gameplay experience will involve. Unfortunately, this type of taxonomy does not hint at the underlying cognitive tasks of the game.

Oftentimes, educators may want to use digital games to engage learners with certain cognitive tasks and to help them with the understanding of these tasks. Not knowing about the core structures of a game can therefore be troublesome. To address this problem, in this chapter the authors will analyze a number of existing games and categorize them according to their cognitive tasks. This analysis will help to display what educational and epistemic purposes these digital epistemic games can serve. As digital games continue to grow in popularity, it is important to know how to analyze games that serve the mind.

Chapter 3 examined how digital game playing patterns were related to depressed mood. Altogether 478 Finnish 10- and 13-year-old schoolchildren reported intensity of their digital game playing, game genres and game violence, motives for playing, play companions, depressive and anxiety symptoms and positive feelings. K-mean cluster analysis revealed six digital game playing patterns with significant gender but no age differences. Participants representing the task-oriented pattern had a significantly higher mean in depression and anxiety symptoms than the non-players or players representing sports and racing, and violent imagination patterns when sex and age were controlled. As hypothesized, depressed mood was associated with playing non-violent problem-solving type of games for ritualized purposes and social compensation but contrary to earlier results not with high intensity of playing. It is suggested that the problem-solving type of games may offer such rewarding and slightly effortful activity which is suitable for self-regulation of depressed mood.

There is wide interest in the potential of 'serious' video games as vehicles for learning. Especially in the health education domain, there are now many reports of the use of video games intended to produce changes in players' knowledge, attitudes or behaviors that will transfer to 'real life' settings outside the context of the game. Real progress in this exciting field may be seriously limited by the lack of evidentially-based and theoretically driven models for creating learning strategies that can be incorporated in game design. In particular, there has been little published discussion of how learning strategies should be used in game design to maximize the achievement of learning objectives that are transferable to criterion settings outside the game. Chapter 4 analyses the learning models implicit in health games described in the literature, and relates these to established learning models in order to illustrate the nature of the gaps between current game designs and relevant learning theory and technology. This analysis provides a systematic framework for identifying principles of game design that are soundly based both in theory and research evidence. Examples are provided from recent game designs.

In a series of studies Gackenbach and colleagues have been investigating the relationship between video game play and dreams. Three lines of inquiry have been pursued, cognitive factors, emotional content and bizarreness in dreams associated with video game play. The question across studies being does hard core video game play change these fundamental qualities of dreams in the player? It has been found that gamers report more lucid/control type dreams, higher dream bizarreness and unusual reactions to nightmares. These findings are summarized in Chapter 5.

In Chapter 6 the author suggests a family of computer games which modify (in fact generalize) some well-known games: such as Chess, Checkers, Go, Go-Moku, Reversi, etc. The main idea is simple: **do not wait for your turn**, move as soon as you wish and can. However, to realize a move you need to define it by your cursor. This takes time, since there are six main parameters of the game: handicap delay, move delay, cursor movement delay, and the same three parameters (which might take different values, yet) are defined for the opponent. These six parameters can be chosen in such a way that the Racing and Standard versions of a game become (almost) equivalent. On the other hand, if all delays are small enough then it becomes more important to make a fast move than clever one. In Racing games, speed and brains can be traded. Moreover, in general, whether a move is smart or not will depend on the parameters. Racing Chess, Go, and Go-moku were realized in the late 80s by Vladimir Oudalov and Andrei Vasiliev from Moscow. This program works on any IBM/PC compatible with CGA, EGA, VGA or Hercules. Although, this version can hardly be of any use now, since it works only with DOS and no "windows version" was ever written. Yet, if somebody will find such a task interesting then the following notes might help.

Chapter 7 investigates the use of an extended Ising spin glass prior in predicting financial time series. It introduces a probabilistic model consisting of a large number of computational agents (small neural networks and fuzzy logic systems) acting as nodes in a two-dimensional Ising spin glass. The research has been inspired partly by earlier applications of Minority Games (Lamper, D and Howison, S and Johnson, 2001, "Predictability of large future changes in a competitive evolving population", Advances in Condensed Matter and Statistical Physics) in predicting financial time series. In addition the chapter also investigates whether or not there are any benefits in using an intrinsic time scale when forecasting high-frequency foreign exchange time series. The method converts a constant frequency at which financial time series are sampled into a variable intrinsic trading frequency of real stock markets. This so-called intrinsic trading time may be more suitable when dealing with market models in which internal agents trade at fixed regular intervals.

Computer games constitute an important part of young teenagers' life in Sweden. Chapter 8 reports on our exploration of whether computer games can be put to good use for mathematics educational purposes for this age group. First, the authors discuss which positive role computer games could potentially play; in brief, the authors think that computer games can be used as a complement for making routine practice more varied, more enjoyable and more effective. Second, the authors describe a game that they have developed for practising the arithmetic of fractions. An important module of this game is built on our novel specification of how to automatically generate sensible problems of well-defined difficulty, which is the third point. Fourth, the authors report how the game has been evaluated by users (students and their teachers). Fifth, the authors present results of diagnostic tests given before and after playing this game, indicating a positive effect on learning. Last, the authors discuss what they have learned from this study.

In: Computer Games
Editors: A. Soria et al, pp. 1-51
ISBN: 978-1-60876-658-1

Chapter 1

EDUTAIN@GRID: A RESOURCE MANAGEMENT PLATFORM FOR MASSIVELY MULTIPLAYER ONLINE GAMES

Radu Prodan and Vlad Nae
Institute Of Computer Science, University Of Innsbruck, Austria

Abstract

Massively Multiplayer Online Games (MMOGs) have emerged in the past decade as a new type of large-scale distributed application characterised by a huge real-time virtual world entertaining millions of players spread across the world, e.g., World of Warcraft counts over 6 million unique players daily. Today's MMOG operate as client/server architectures, in which the game server simulates a world via computing and database operations, receives and processes commands from the clients, and interoperates with a billing and accounting system. Based on the actions submitted by the players, the game servers compute the global state of the game world represented by the position and interactions of the entities, and send appropriate real-time responses to the players containing the new relevant state information. Depending on the game, typical response times to ensure fluent play must be between 100 milliseconds in online First Person Shooter (FPS) action games and 1-2 seconds for Role-Playing Games (RPG). A good game experience is critical in keeping the players engaged, and has an immediate consequence on the income of the MMOG operators.

Today, a single computer is limited at around 500 simultaneous and persistent network connections, and databases can manage the update of around 500 objects per second. To support at the same time millions of active concurrent players and many more other game entities, MMOG operators need to install and operate a large dedicated multi-server infrastructure, with hundreds to thousands of computers hosting the distributed load of each game. However, due to the dynamic character of MMOGs, both on the short and on the long term, the game providers have to over-provision their infrastructure, which leads to a low and inefficient resource utilisation and new providers finding it difficult to join the market. For example, the operating infrastructure of the Massively Multiplayer Online Role Playing Game (MMORPG) World of Warcraft has over 10,000 computers.

To alleviate this problem, the edutain@grid project funded by the European Union searches a Grid computing platform for inexpensive provisioning of resources to MMOGs based on a novel dynamic and on-demand allocation strategy. First of all, a load prediction service is in charge of projecting the future distribution of entities in the game world that will drive the resource allocation. For example, by timely foreseeing critical hot-spots (i.e. excessively populated area of interest generating a large number of interactions), one can dynamically provision additional servers on some new resources and take timely load balancing actions that transparently redistribute the game load before the servers become overloaded. Based on the entity distribution prediction and possible interactions, a load modelling service is using analytical methods for estimating the game server load. Finally, a resource allocation service is using the load information to provision the necessary resources that accommodate the player load while guaranteeing the real-time QoS constraints.

1. Introduction

Entertainment industry including gaming is a huge growth sector worldwide. Massively Multiplayer Online Games grew from 10 thousand subscribers in 1997 to 6.7 million in 2003 and the rate is accelerating estimated to 60 million people by 2011. The release of World of Warcraft in 2005 saw a single game break the barrier of 4 million subscribers worldwide. The market size shows equally impressive numbers, estimated by the Entertainment Software Association (ESA) to 7 billion USD with an avid growth over 300% in the last 10 years. In comparison, the Motion Picture Association of America (MPAA) reports a size of 8.99 billion USD and the Recording Industry Association of America (RIAA) a size of 12.3 billion USD which stagnates (and even decreased by 2%) in the last 10 years. It is therefore expected that the game industry will soon grow larger than both movie and music market sizes.

Within the last ten years, online gaming has become a dominant component in the video game market. One by one, every genre on the market has been impacted and even redefined by the multiplayer network feature, completely transforming the players' experience. The period 2007-2011 is expected to be a truly turning point, as for the first time all the hardware devices released on the market will be connected online and even wireless-enabled. Whether it is a personal computer, a home console (Microsoft Xbox 360, Sony Playstation 3, Nintendo Wii) or a portable console (Sony PlayStation Potable, Nintendo DS, Gameboy), all the platforms will be online and distributed multiplayer parties can be played even across platforms.

The most widely employed architectural model for online games is client/server (White, Koch, Gupta, Gehrke, and Demers, 2007), which consist of a set of servers that are concurrently accessed by a number of users that dynamically interact with each other within a game session. Clients connect directly to the servers and send their play actions such as movements, shootings, collection of items, or chat. Based on the actions submitted by the players, the servers compute the global state of the game world represented by the position and interactions of the entities, store it into a persistent database, and send appropriate real-time responses to the players containing the new relevant state information, typically in a high-speed data stream. Depending on the type of game, the responses must be delivered promptly within a given time interval to ensure a good game experience for all participants, which is crucial for keeping the players engaged, and has an immediate consequence on the income of the game operators. Failing to deliver timely simulation updates leads to a degraded game experience and brings unhappiness to players that leave the game and close their accounts.

Typically, the load of one server increases dramatically with the number and density of the hosted players and their interaction within the simulated world. Today, a single computer is limited at around 500 simultaneous and persistent network connections, and databases can manage the update of around 500 objects per second (White, Koch, Gupta, Gehrke, and Demers, 2007). To support at the same time millions of *active concurrent players* and many more other game entities, Hosters need to install and operate a large dedicated multi-server infrastructure (Shaikh, Sahu, Rosu, Shea, and Saha, 2006), with hundreds to thousands of computers hosting the distributed load of each game (Bartle, 2003)(Müller and Gorlatch, 2006). However, due to the dynamic character of games, both on the short and on the long term, the resource providers have to over-provision their infrastructure, which leads to a low and inefficient resource utilisation and new providers finding it difficult to join the market. For example, the operating infrastructure of World of Warcraft has over 10,000 computers. To cope with an increasing demand in the number of players connected to extremely popular game sessions, techniques for parallelising and distributing the game load across multiple computational resources are currently being researched in the community (Glinka, Ploss, Müller-Iden, and Gorlatch, 2007)(Saha, Sahu, and Shaikh, 2003).

The most popular distributed games at the moment are the *Massively Multiplayer On-line Role Playing Games (MMORPG)* (MMORPG.COM). MMORPGs are adventure games offering a huge game world that can host a large number of participating clients that have a globally synchronised state. This game genre is characterised by a low rate of client state computations and updates which make them suitable for *static* distribution setups. Typically, an MMORPG game world (and its load) is statically distributed on different computing resources based on predefined game *zones*, where the transition between zones can only happen via well-defined *portals* (i.e. doors, teleportation, etc.). As the number of subscribing clients increases, the number of machines hosting separately different zones of the game session is supplemented.

The next generation of distributed online games, for which no massively multiplayer support exists yet, is the fast-paced *First Person Shooter (FPS)* action games. The FPS type of online games has very specific QoS demands in terms of client state computations and updates. For example, a typical FPS game client has to receive state updates from the server (showing the movements and actions of teammates and opponents) with a frequency of around 35 Hertz in order to offer a satisfactory experience. Considering the fast-paced nature of FPS games where, in contrast to the slow-paced MMORPGs, the load can dramatically change within a short time interval, proactive and more dynamic entity distribution and load balancing techniques are required.

We first present in Section 2 a model for a game ecosystem that describes the game operators, the resource providers, the application, and their integration. Extending on previous work where resources were provided by a single data centre (Doyle, Chase, Asad, Jin, and Vahdat, 2003)(Urgaonkar, Shenoy, Chandra, and Goyal, 2005), in our model the game resources are provided by multiple geographically distributed data centres (also called Hosters) with different lease policies. In contrast to previous client/server Internet applications (Doyle, Chase, Asad, Jin, and Vahdat, 2003)(Urgaonkar, Shenoy, Chandra, and Goyal, 2005)(Rolia, Zhu, Arlitt, and Andrzejak, 2004)(Urgaonkar, Pacifici, Shenoy, Spreitzer, and Tantawi, 2005)(Karve, et al., 2006) focusing on non-interacting user requests, our model is designed around the notion of player interactions within the same application instance.

In Section 3 we propose a service-oriented architecture for real-time MMOG management and resource provisioning based on a stack of five services: monitoring, load prediction, capacity management, and resource allocation. The monitoring service designed in Section 4 is in charge of collecting real-time metrics from the running game sessions, such as the number, position, and interactions of entities. Based on the monitoring information, a load prediction service presented in Section 5 estimates the future entity distribution in the game world, which is translated into resource load information using analytical methods by a capacity management service described in Section 6. Based on the estimated resource needs, a resource allocation service introduced in Section 7 provisions the correct amount of resources required and distributes the session accordingly such that the real-time QoS metrics are honoured at all times. Finally, Section 8 concludes the paper.

2. Model

In this section we present a model for the game ecosystem from the resource management perspective, in which a global network of data centres host services that execute many games at the same time. Our multi-game and multi-data centre model extends on previous work which focuses on either a single application (usually a Web service) and/or a single data centre (Rolia, Zhu, Arlitt, and Andrzejak, 2004)(Urgaonkar, Pacifici, Shenoy, Spreitzer, and Tantawi, 2005)(Ye and Cheng, 2006).

2.1. Game Application Model

Games are large-scale simulations of persistent *worlds* comprising various objects or *entities* that we classify in four categories:

- *avatars* are in-game representation of the participants;
- *bots* or *non-player characters* (NPC) are mobile entities that have the ability to act independently;
- *movable objects* (such as boxes or guns) are passive entities which can be manipulated but do not initiate interactions; and
- *immutable entities* or decor.

The architectural model employed for games is client/server (Bartle, 2003), with hosting companies maintaining the servers that simulate a distributed game world. The clients dynamically connect to a joint *game session* and interact with each other by sending play actions such as movements, shootings, operations on objects, or chat.

For the vast majority of games there is a similar computational model. The game server runs a large loop in which the state of all entities is first computed and then broadcasted to the clients. All entities within a specific avatar's *area of interest* (usually a surrounding zone) are considered to be interacting with the respective avatar (see Figure 1) and have an impact on its state. The more populated the entities' areas of interest are and the more interactions between entities exist, the higher the load of the underlying game server will be. Although inside the game loop there are some other computations to be performed (e.g. environment state update, game intelligence), the dominating part of the load L is determined by the entities' state computations and updates: $L = f(e_c, e_i)$, where e_c represents the entity count and e_i the number of entity interactions. We will present an analytical model for estimating the load of a game session (comprising processor, memory, and network load) based on entity count and interaction in Section 6.

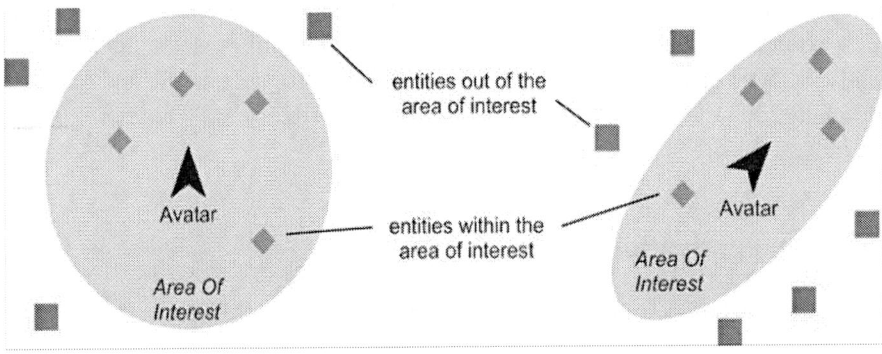

Figure 1. Area of interest.

In each loop iteration (also called tick), there are certain steps to be performed:

- processing events coming from the connected clients;
- processing the states of the active entities;
- processing state updates received from other servers.

Depending on the game, typical response times to ensure fluent play must be between 100 milliseconds in online FPS action games and 1-2 seconds for MMORPGs. A good game experience is critical in keeping the players engaged, and has an immediate consequence on the income of the game operators. Failing to deliver timely simulation updates leads to a degraded game experience and triggers player departure and account closing.

To ensure scalability and real-time response, a game session is distributed on multiple servers using three different techniques (see Figure 2), and each participant is mapped to an avatar on one of the servers, usually to one in its closest proximity to minimise latencies.

Spatial scaling of a game session is achieved through a conventional parallelization technique called *zoning* (Cai, Percival, Turner, and Lee, 2002), based on similar data locality concepts as in scientific parallel processing.

Zoning partitions the game world into geographical areas to be handled independently by separate machines. Zones are not necessarily of same shape and size, but should have an even load distribution that satisfies the QoS requirements. Today, zoning is successfully employed in slower-paced (compared fast-paced to FPS action games) MMORPG adventure games, where the transition between zones can only happen through certain portals (e.g. special doors, teleportation, accompanied on the screen by a load clock or some standard animation video) and requires an important amount of time. Typically, zones are started manually by the game operators based on the current load, player demand, or new game world and scenario developments.

The second technique called *replication* targets parallelization of game sessions with a large density of players located and interacting within each other's area of interest. Such situations are typical to fast-paced FPS action games in which players typically gather in certain hot-spot action areas that overload the game servers which are no longer capable of delivering state updates at the required rate. To address this problem, replication defines a novel method of distributing the load by replicating the same game zone on several CPUs. Each replicated server computes the state for a subset of entities called *active entities*, while the remaining ones, called *shadow entities* (which are active in the other participating servers), synchronised across servers. It was proven in previous research that the overhead ofsynchronised shadow entities is much lower than the overhead of computing the load produced by active entities (Müller and Gorlatch, 2006).

The third technique called *instancing* is a simplification of mirroring which distributes the session load by starting multiple parallel instances of the highly populated zones. The instances are completely independent of each other, which means that two avatars from different instances will not see each other, even if they are located at coordinates within their area of interest. This technique is relatively easy to implement based on the zoning technique and is mostly employed for MMORPGs.

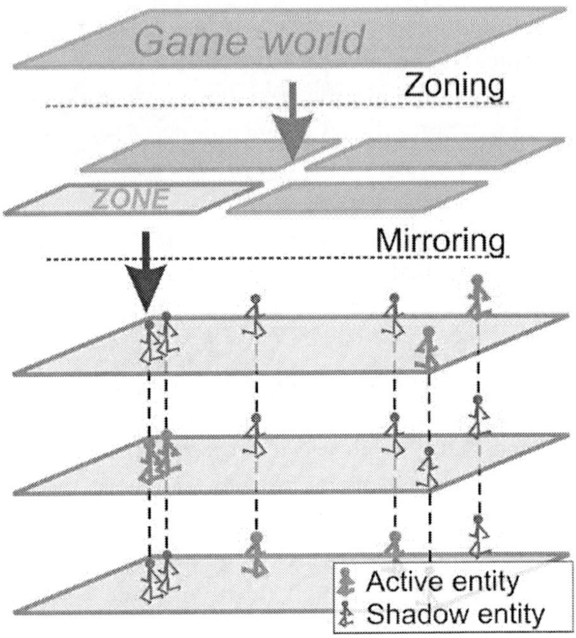

Figure 2. Zoning and mirroring.

2.2. Game Load Complexity Model

The load of a game depends not only on the number of active concurrent players, but also on the number and type of their interactions. The interaction type and count span a wide range depending on the game design. The number of interactions between the entities, and especially between the human players, may be very low (e.g. for puzzle games where a player interacts with the system after long periods of thinking), to low (e.g. for an MMORPG where small groups of people interact with a huge sparse environment), to very high (e.g., for an FPS action game where many players test their reaction time in a confined area).

Assuming the number of entities is n, the interaction complexity may range from $O(n)$ for games in which players are mostly solitary or the game does not need to make many state changes or compute complex environment reactions, to $O(n^2)$ for games in which many players acting individually are interacting, or to $O(n^3)$ for games in which groups of many players each are interacting. To reduce the computational load, most game simulate and send updates only for world regions representing *area of interest* of each avatar. When using such techniques, the interaction complexity may become $O(n \cdot log(n))$ from $O(n^2)$, and $O(n^2 \cdot log(n))$ from $O(n^3)$.

The lack of responsiveness may also be caused by high latency, independently from the data centre's server and bandwidth capacity. However, depending on the game design, games have different *latency tolerance* which has been investigated by previous research (Claypool, The effect of latency on user performance in Real-Time strategy games, 2005)(Claypool and Claypool, Latency and player actions in online games, 2006).

2.3. Game Hosting Model

We consider the hosting platform as consisting of Hosting centres scattered around the world, where each centre pools together resources that may serve several games simultaneously, each of them operated by a *Coordinator* (also called *game operator*). For simplicity, we assume that each hosting centre consists of a single computing resource, which can be a shared or distributed memory parallel machine owned by a so called *Hoster*. In this report we will use from here on the terms resource provider, Hoster, and data centre interchangeably.

The Coordinators submit requests to the Hosters by specifying the type, number, and duration for which the resources are desired. The resources considered in our work can be of four types: *CPU*, *memory*, input from the external network (*ExtNet[in]*), and output to the external network of a data centre (*ExtNet[out]*).

Depending on the data centre's service model (either best-effort or based on advance reservations) resource requests are queued or immediately fitted in the schedule, respectively. Once the available resources are matched against the requests, these resources are *allocated* to the game operators. From the Coordinator's point of view, we say that the resources have been *provisioned*. We use from here on the terms resource allocation and resource provisioning interchangeably. The allocated resources are reserved for executing the game servers for the entire duration of the game operator's request (task preemption or migration are not supported).

2.4. Complete Game Ecosystem Model

The game ecosystem comprises multiple Hosters and multiple Coordinators, where each Hoster may set a different space-time policy for its resources. The

Hosters handle simultaneously games of different genres and designs with different interactivity types and counts, and with different latency tolerance.

The relative success of each game is characterised by the number of registered players. Figure 3 displays the number of MMORPG players over time for the USA and European markets based on the survey of Carooe (Woodcock, 2008) for dates until June 2006, and on our own research afterwards. The chart shows that there are currently six games with more than 500 thousand players each. The total number of MMORPG players is well approximated by the exponential trend $\alpha \cdot e^{\beta x}$, where $\alpha = 7e\text{-}9$ and $\beta=0.028$ give a Pearson's coefficient of determination $R^2 = 0.974$[1]. Assuming the same rate of growth, we can estimate that there will be over 60 million players by 2011 in the US and EU markets alone. The large number of game players for each title, as well as for the game ecosystem as a whole, is one of the main motivations for our work.

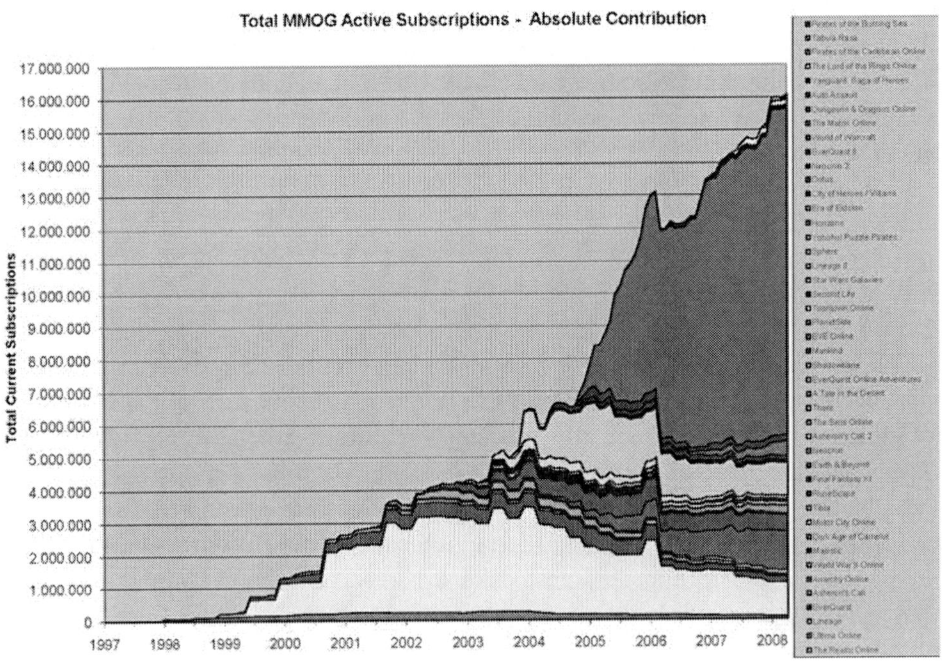

Figure 3. The number of MMORPG players over time.

[1]R2 values closer to 1 are better; R2 values higher than 0.95 give significant confidence in the match between the approximation and the empirical distribution.

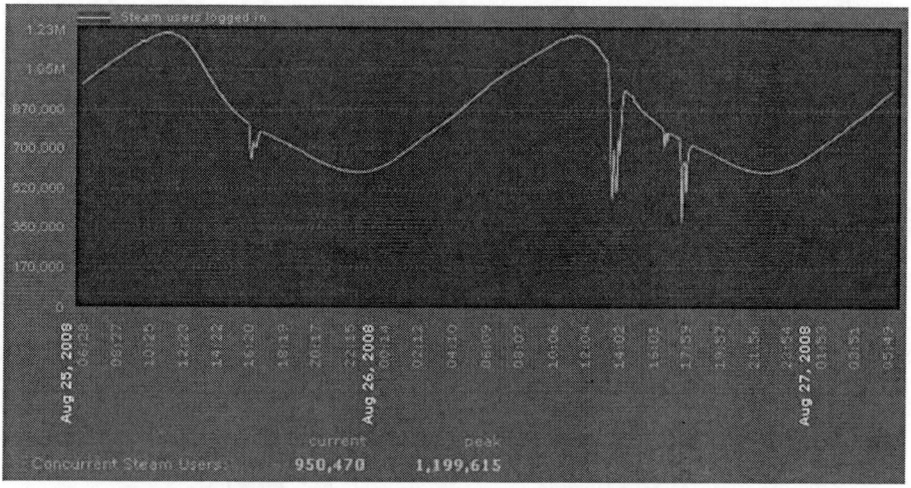

Figure 4. Online number of users logged in the Steam platform.

Not only the load of MMORPGs increases exponentially in long term, but is also highly dynamic during relatively short periods of times. Figure 4 for example displays the total number of users logged in the Steam platform (Steam), which is an online portal for building communities of people who play PC games of all kinds, comprising features such as finding online friends, organising groups, joining chats, hosting matches, and much more. We can see in the figure that the total number of online users dramatically varies over a period of ten hours, from 1.23 million people to about 550 thousand people based on the data collected on August 25-26, 2008. This high variation raises highly dynamic resource demands over a relatively short period of time, which is a challenge for an efficient resource management.

The Coordinators negotiate SLAs based on the load of the games they operate (either statically or dynamically computed), and the Hosters respond with offers based on their local time-space renting policy. The resource allocation is realised by a request-offer matchmaking mechanism based on three criteria that favour the Hoster. First, the number and the type of resources requested must match with the offer; when they do not match, an offer includes at least the requested amounts shall be returned. Second, depending on the game latency tolerance, the resources closest to the request are preferred. Third, to deal with data centre hosting policies, the finer grained resources with the shorter period of reservation time are preferred.

3. Architecture

To support this need, we designed a management middleware to coordinate the execution of games (especially FPS online games) in a distributed Grid environment that fulfils their scalability requirements (see Figure 5). A scalable game session is distributed across several servers that run on distributed resources provided by multiple *Hosters*. A real-time communication framework (Glinka, Ploss, Müller-Iden, and Gorlatch, 2007) provides the fundamental interfaces and protocols for parallelising and distributing the game session across multiple servers, as well as for transparent integration and migration of avatars and other entities between servers. By distributing the load of a session on multiple resources, a larger number of players can be accommodated.

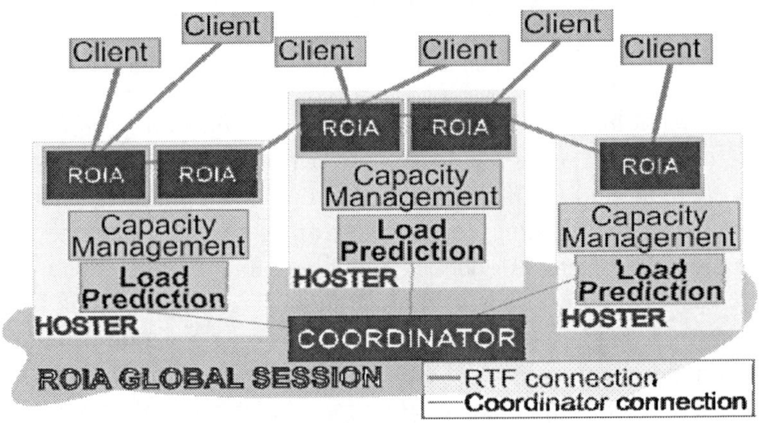

Figure 5. High-level management layer architecture.

Participants connect to a game session by means of a Coordinator that negotiates (in the business layer) with Hosters SLAs necessary for obtaining the required amount of resources that guarantees the QoS parameters. To ensure that they offer the correct amount of resources to honour the SLA, Hosters employ a stack of five services for translating the SLAs into QoS parameter that are maintained for the duration of the game execution through the following seven step protocol (see Figure 6):

- The monitoring service described in Section 4 observes the game instance and connects real-time metrics such as the number of entities, their position in the game world, or the network traffic;

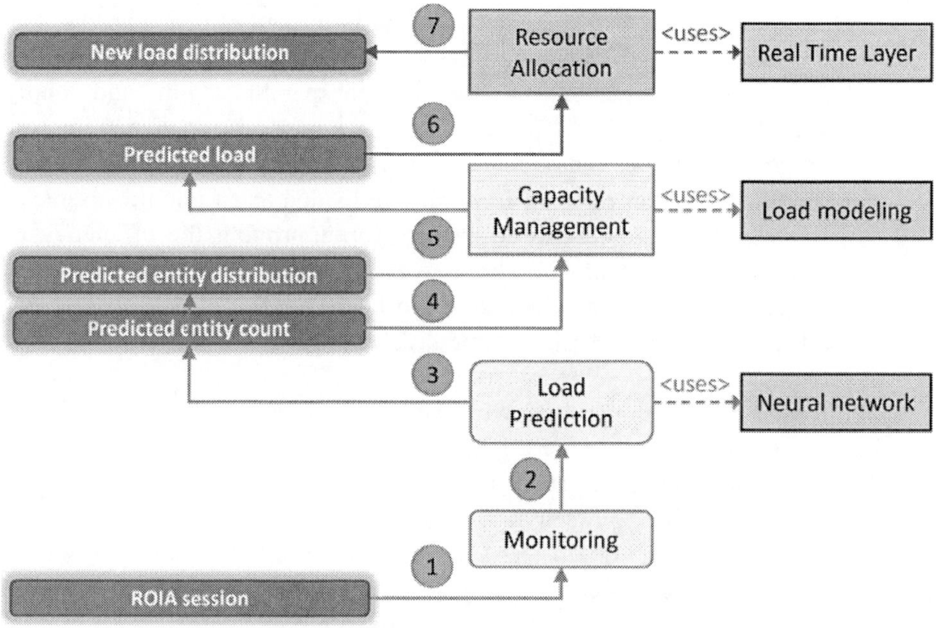

Figure 6. edutain@grid resource management method.

- Based on the monitoring information, a load prediction service estimates the future entity distribution (i.e. the coordinates of each entity) in the game world. The role of the load prediction is to foresee critical hotspots in the game session that congests the servers which can no longer send the state updates to the clients at the required rate which will result in serious lags. In addition, creating a new zoning or mirroring scheme is quite latency prone which has to be hidden such that, once the new parallelization scheme is established, the game play including the migration of entities is seamless. We will present in Section 5.3 a solution based on neural networks that outperforms related methods for a variety of simulated scenarios;
- The estimated load distribution is translated into load parameters by a capacity management service based on analytical modelling techniques for three types of resources: CPU, network, and memory. The predicted load is compared against the QoS thresholds and any eventual (predicted) violations are reported to the resource allocation service. An overloaded server will exhibit delays in broadcasting state updates to all connected clients who will experience lags or interruptions during their play;

- Depending on the QoS parameter which is in danger of being violated, the resource decides whether a new resource has to be provisioned by the Hoster and/or whether a new session parallelisation and entity distribution is required. Typical actions comprise supplementing the number of machines (and game servers) participating in a game session, migrating a portion of users from an overloaded to an idle processor, or even turning off underutilised servers for improving the efficiency of resource use. The Real-Time Framework (RTF) developed introduced in (Glinka, Ploss, Müller-Iden, and Gorlatch, 2007) is responsible for establishing the new parallelisation layout.

If the Hoster can no longer cope with the load it committed to host, it timely signals to the Coordinator that there is a critical user load that may saturate its underlying game servers. Upon such notifications, the Coordinator reacts at the business layer by triggering proactive load balancing actions that redistribute the user load among participating Hosters such that the QoS values are kept within the required limits. In such a case, SLA penalties are also issued in the business layer to the Hoster breaching its SLAs. Such a sample dynamic session scaling scenario based on real-time QoS parameters and load balancing actions is depicted in Figure 7.

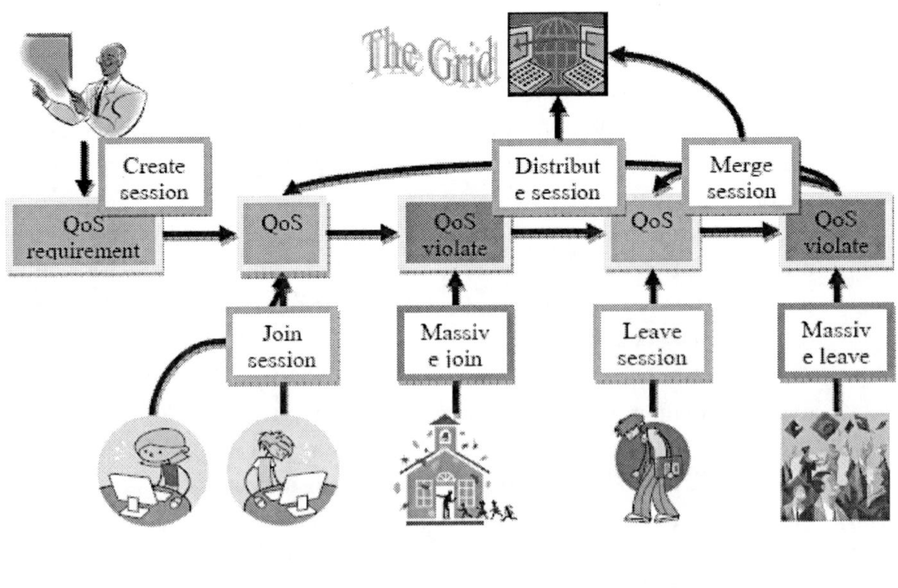

Figure 7. A typical session scaling and load balancing scenario.

4. Monitoring

The lowest-level service in the management layer is the monitoring service (see Figure 8) in charge of observing and collecting low-level information from the game session required by the other services for performing effective management of resources and preserving the negotiated QoS parameters.

4.1. Real-Time Metrics

We classify the real-time monitored metrics into three categories:

- *Host monitoring metrics* are basic, generic system parameters which do not depend on games such as operating system type (e.g. Unix, Windows, MacOS), machine uptime, CPU load, memory load, memory available, or inbound respectively outgoing bandwidth capacity and consumption. These metrics are collected directly from the machines through the Simple Network Management Protocol (SNMP) and do not require executing any game session. If there are running game sessions, they do not have to be connected to the monitoring module;
- *Process monitoring metrics* are game-specific parameters related to the execution of a single game process such as game loop saturation, or inbound respectively outgoing bandwidth consumption;
- *Game monitoring metrics* are process monitoring metrics extrapolated to the extent of an entire local game session comprising multiple distributed game processes, also collected through the HMI module underneath.

We can classify the game-specific process and session monitoring metrics into the following three categories:

- *Entity model parameters* are entity-centred and represent information related to internal game mechanisms (messages sent, messages received, etc.). Most of these parameters are only used to monitor online game games;
- *Client data parameters* include status information related to the end-user activity such as idle, spectator, or active;
- *World parameters* are used for monitoring game-specific information like entity positions to be used by the Capacity management and Resource allocation services.

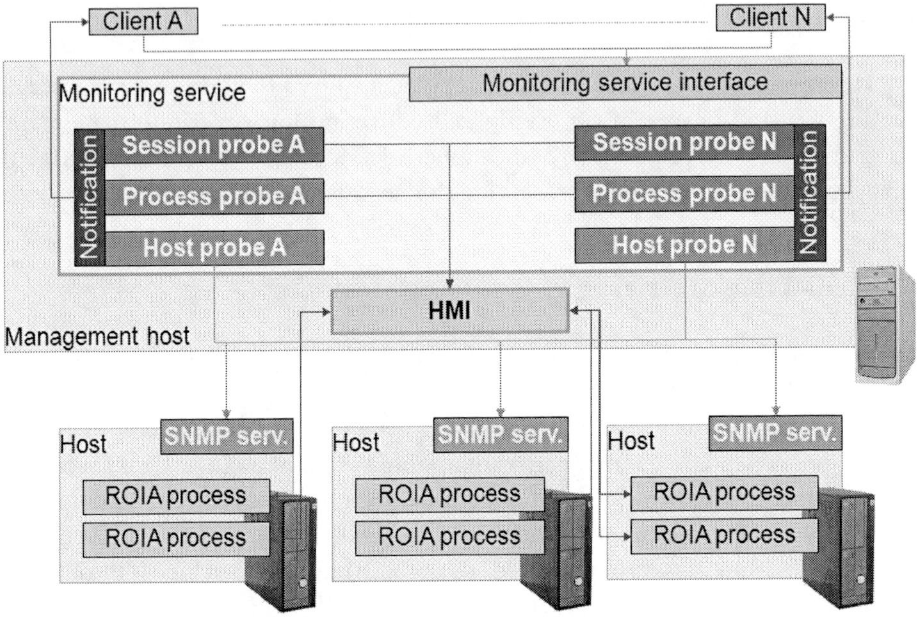

Figure 8. The monitoring service architecture.

4.2. Monitored Entities

The monitoring service is able to provide measurements of the previously mentioned metrics on three different entities. Not all metrics can be monitored for all entities; this condition is enforced in the monitoring service's implementation.

4.2.1. Host Entity

The host entity represents one any of the machines on which game processes can be run. These machines have to belong to the Hoster doing the monitoring and have to have a running SNMP server, through which the metrics are monitored.

4.2.2. Game Process Entity

A game process represents any RTF-based game which implements at least one of the monitoring profiles provided by the RTF framework. By default an RTF-based game implements at least the RTF network monitoring profile.

4.2.3. Game Local Session Entity

The latter, the game local session, is a super-entity comprised of a subset of game processes for which separate monitoring is done. The individual process monitoring results are reduced to single values representing the values for the corresponding local session metrics.

4.3. Monitoring Method

The monitoring service has several components: *the monitoring probes, the serialization probes* and *the notification dispatcher* (see Figure 8).

The active components are the monitoring probes, which carry out the actual monitoring data collection. Because the service can monitor different entities, the monitoring probes are profiled for each of these entities, resulting in three corresponding types of probes: process monitoring probe, local session monitoring probe and host monitoring probe.

Each monitoring probe can be attached to a serialization probe whose function is to buffer the monitoring data generated by the probe and eventually, at longer time intervals, serialize the data. The serialization can be done in two ways, either through a direct clear-text dump at a pre-specified location, or by pushing the data to the information service which will store it in its underlying database.

The notification dispatcher exists as a single instance regardless of the number of existing monitoring and serialization probes and of the service's number of clients. If clients requests notifications for their monitoring, they are registered with the notification dispatcher and, as a result, each time new monitoring data is generated by their probes, they will receive a notification.

The monitoring service's clients are the business layer components, the management portal and other internal management layer components (i.e. the load prediction service and the Hoster mapping service which continuously keeps track of the available hosts within the setup). Clients have different privileges, set at development time, which limit the range of metrics they have access to, or the right to serialize data.

Figure 9 presents the simple workflow the clients must follow in order to use the monitoring service:

Step 1. Choose the entity to monitor, select the needed metrics to monitor and the monitoring time interval and invoke the monitoring service with these parameters to start the monitoring process. Here, the monitoring probes are created and started;

Step 2. [optional] Request the serialization of the monitoring data. At this point the serialization probes are created and started;

Step 3. [optional] Request notifications for new monitoring data. Here, the client is registered with the notification dispatcher;

Step 4. Collect the existing monitoring data. This step has to be performed regularly, but not necessarily at the same time interval as the monitoring is taking place, due to the buffering mechanism provided by the monitoring service;

Step 5. [optional] Stop the notifications for new monitoring data. At this point the client is unregistered from the notification dispatcher;

Step 6. [optional] Stop the serialization of the monitoring data. At this point the client's serialization probes are destroyed;

Step 7. Stop the monitoring. Here, the client's monitoring probes are destroyed.

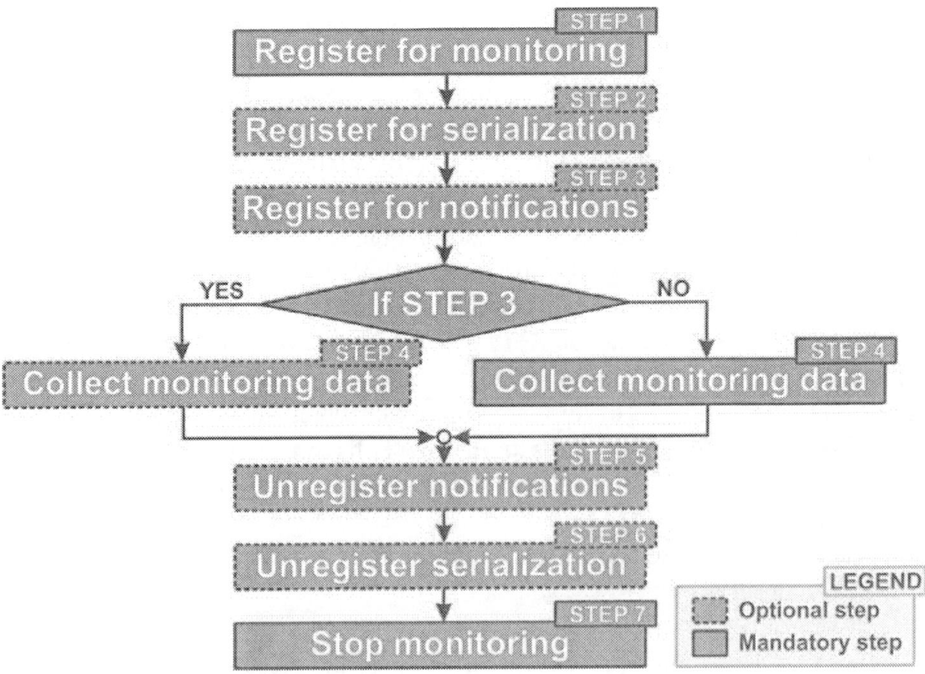

Figure 9. Monitoring service workflow for clients.

5. Load Prediction

One main challenge for our strategy described in Section 3 is finding a predictor with high accuracy and good performance. The subarea entity count predictor needs to be accurate for a variety of game workloads, or the overall game load prediction will be inaccurate. As the overall entity distribution is required for one global game load prediction, the predictor needs to be able to deliver tens of thousands of predictions per second. In the remainder of this section we address the problem of finding such a predictor.

5.1. Predictor Families

Two options are available for quantitative predictions in games: explanatory models and time series prediction. While explanatory models can deliver good accuracy with little computation, they are difficult to obtain for complex applications such as games, and are tightly-coupled to the application instance and sometimes to platform for which they have been constructed. With games relying on frequent and large updates to maintain interest among the players, the explanatory models quickly become not maintainable. Thus, our work is based on prediction algorithms that use historical values to discover patterns in the historical data series, and extrapolate these patterns into the future.

Many such prediction algorithms have already been proposed. Simple prediction algorithms like exponential smoothing and variants thereof are computationally inexpensive and can be applied in parallel on several data sets, but their predictive power is limited. More elaborated prediction algorithms like autoregressive (AR) models, integrated (I) models, moving average (MA) models, and combinations thereof like ARMA or ARIMA try to find the best prediction model for the given data set. Although their predictive power is higher, such methods are also more time consuming and resource intensive, thus being ill suited for highly dynamic games.

5.2. Prediction Method

The problem of predicting the game load reduces therefore to estimating two fundamental parameters: the number of entities managed by a game server and their spatial distribution within the world. The challenge in designing such a prediction service is that one physical game zone is in general too big and contains too much information (spatial position of over one hundred entities) for a prediction system to produce an accurate estimation of the future layout in real-time. This is particularly critical for fast-paced FPS action games where the game load can dramatically change within a short time interval and where fast prediction is an absolute requirement. We therefore apply once again the zoning technique (see Figure 10), which partitions one game zone in multiple subareas of reasonable size to be given as input to the prediction service. The subareas are small enough to be characterized by their entity count only. The overall entity distribution in the entire world consists of a map of entity counts for each subarea.

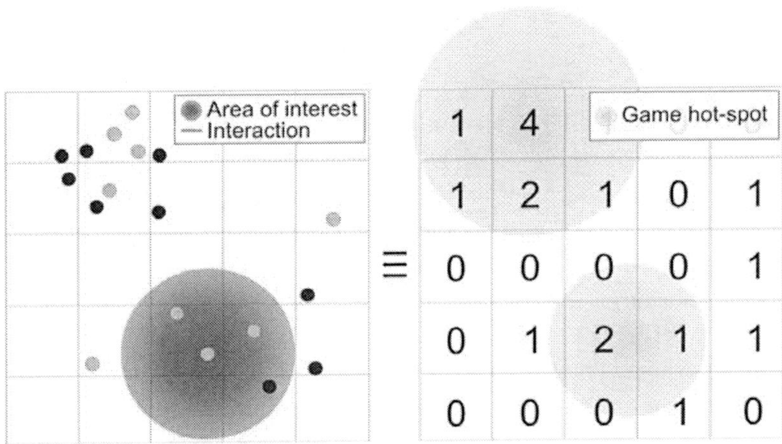

Figure 10. Subarea-based entity distribution.

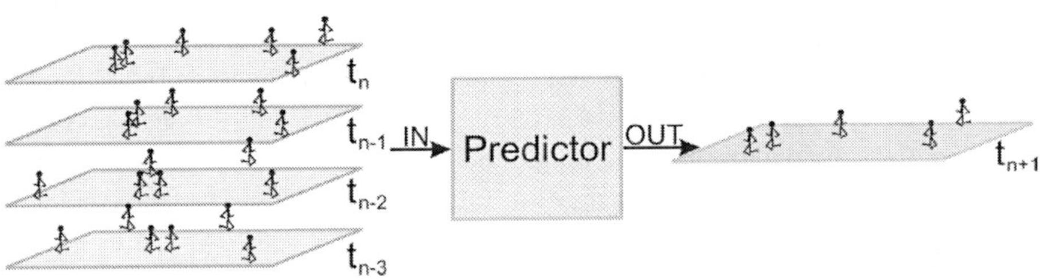

Figure 11. Load prediction system overview.

We use a prediction method based on historical information collected by tracing the execution of existing game servers. For each subarea, the prediction service uses as input the entity count at equidistant past time intervals, and delivers as output the entity count at the next time step (see Figure 11). The predicted entity count for the entire game world is the sum of all the subarea predictions.

5.3. Neural Network-Based Prediction

As an alternative to other prediction algorithms, we investigated in this work the use of neural networks (Haykin, 1994) that provide a robust approach to approximating real- or discrete-valued target functions. Low complexity neural networks are capable of approximating complex and noisy functions, provided that good input pre-processing is performed. Following the load prediction strategy introduced in Section 5.2, our neural network-based predictor uses one separate neural network for each game subarea which receives as input the entity count at equidistant past time intervals and delivers as output the entity count at the next time step, as displayed in Figure 12.

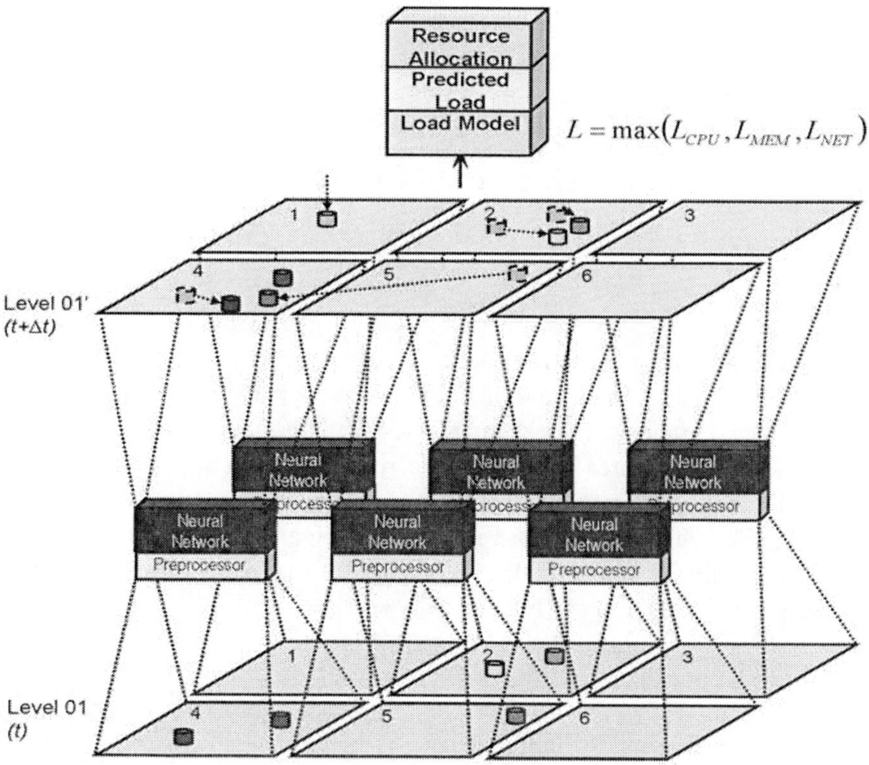

Figure 12. Neural network-based prediction architecture.

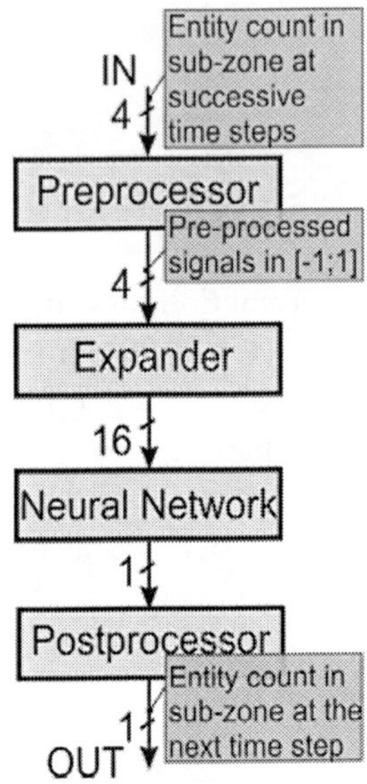

Figure 13. Neural network component design.

Each neural network consists of four important components: a pre-processing unit, a signal expanding unit, the actual neural network predictor, and a post-processing unit (see Figure 13).

5.3.1. Preprocessor

Since the raw entity count cannot be directly fed to the neural network, the pre-processor module transforms the discrete entity count values into correct neural stimuli (signals in the [-1,1] interval, as displayed in Figure 14). This process is not a simple value rescaling, but a transformation in which the entity position inside each subarea is weighted decreasingly from the centre towards the edges. Additionally, we also perform a certain overlapping between the subareas which alongside weighting offers a rough representation of the entities' location and movement direction, especially when an entity is about to migrate between two subareas.

5.3.2. Signal Expander

The signal expanding technique is used to help the neural network extract the relevant information from the pre-processed signal. This technique consists of applying simple transformations to the signals (e.g. distance, squaring, averaging) and feeding them along with the original signals to the neural network. The information contained in the original signals is presented in different ways, offering the neural networks a better chance of generalising the signal patterns.

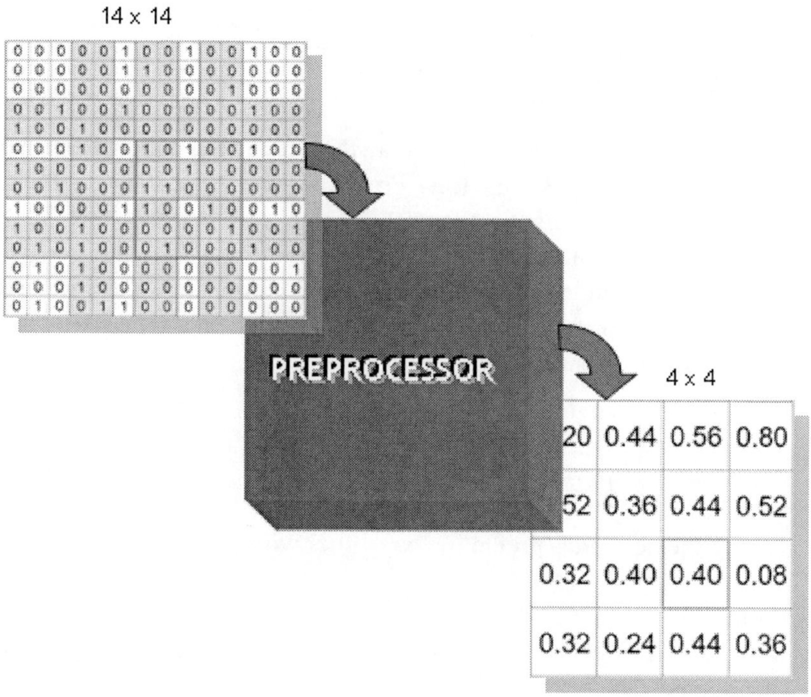

Figure 14. Entity count pre-processing example.

5.3.3. Neural Network

This unit is the actual predictor whose structure, size, and type can have various impacts on the prediction accuracy. The network has an input layer, a hidden layer, and an output layer, the latter consisting of a single neuron. Adding more hidden layers could help in some rare cases for generalising highly irregular signals, but could introduce more local minima during the training cycle. The neural network's inputs are the pre-processed and expanded signals coming from the expander unit, and the output consists of a stimulus in the [-1,1] interval representing the entity count at the next time step.

5.3.4. Postprocessor

The post-processing unit transforms the output stimulus generated by the neural network into a proper integer value representing the predicted entity count at the next time step.

5.3.5. Utilisation

A downside of neural networks is that they require a long offline training phase consisting of several sub-phases. First, the *data set collection* phase is a long process in which the game is observed by gathering entity count samples for all subareas at equidistant time steps. The *training* phase uses most of the previously collected samples as training sets, and the remaining as test sets. The training phase runs for a number of eras, until a convergence criterion is fulfilled. A training era consists of three steps:

- presenting all the training sets in sequence to the network;
- adjusting the network's weights to better fit the expected output (the real entity count for the next time step);
- testing the network's prediction capability with the different test sets.

Separating the training from the test sets is crucial for avoiding memorisation and ensures that the network has enough generalisation potential for delivering good results on new data sets.

5.3.6. Complexity Analysis

The computational complexity for training a symmetrical Hopfield neural network is in the order of $O(n^2 \cdot max\{w_{ij}\})$, where n is the total number of neurons, and $max\{w_{ij}\}$ is the maximum weight of all neurons. The computational complexity of using a Jordan-Elman network is in the same order of magnitude, as it only differs through the back-propagation links connected to context neurons instead of the input layer neurons (see Figure 18). By limiting the weights to non-exponential values, we are left with an $O(n^2)$ complexity which will not introduce relevant limitations to the network size for the training phase, since it is executed offline and only once for a game type and world combination. The prediction time equivalent to one network activation, however, may be affected and could require some size limitations since it is done in real-time.

To establish an upper bound on the number of neurons, let us consider 100 Jordan-Elman-based predictors for 100 different game subareas, each of them built with with hyperbolic tangent as transfer function. The computational demand C_{Act} for activation of all networks is:

$$C_{Act} = N \cdot (k + C_{\tanh}) + NC \cdot \left(\frac{N}{2} + C_{\tanh} \right),$$

where N is the number of neurons in the network (excluding the context neurons), k the number of weights, C_{tanh} is the number of floating point operations (FLOP) necessary to compute the *tanh* function, and NC is the number of context neurons. For simplicity reasons, let us further consider a fully interconnected network with the neurons evenly distributed between the first two layers, ignoring the single output layer neuron. The weights and the number of context neurons are $k = 2 \cdot \left(\frac{N}{2} \right)^2$ and $NC = \frac{N}{2}$, respectively. Using a common value of 100 FLOP for C_{tanh}, the computational demand for one activation becomes:

$$C_{Act} = \frac{N}{4} \cdot (2 \cdot N^2 + N + 600)$$

Assume we are running the predictor on a 2.13 Gigahertz Inter Core Duo processor with four floating point operations per cycle offering a theoretical peak performance of $8.52 \cdot 10^9$ FLOPS. Taking into account a realistic 80% efficiency and considering a maximum prediction time of five seconds (required by the dynamic nature of FPS game), this sets an upper limit for the network size at around 238 neurons which, as we will see in our experiments, is more than sufficient for our application.

5.4. Implementation

Given the novel way in which the networks are used by our prediction service and the fact that their performance is time critical, we did not use an already available neural network general-purpose software package, but implemented our own specialised packages. This also guarantees the necessary flexibility for future development.

The package contains implementations of diverse neural network types (feed-forward, recursive and also fuzzy logic networks). Although eventually only one type of network is used in the load prediction module, it was necessary to have the mentioned diversity in order to find the best configuration for the predictor (see Section 5.5).

The prediction module is accepting both offline and on-line inputs consisting of time-equidistant game world snapshots. The offline inputs are the results of game simulations generated with the FPS game simulator described in Section 5.5, while the online input is provided by the game pilot application running in the real-time layer. Some of the inputs are used in part for training the neural networks, the rest remaining for testing. After the training is complete each input is used to generate an output representing the predicted game world layout for the next time step. This is eventually converted to an *actual* load prediction by the resource allocation service.

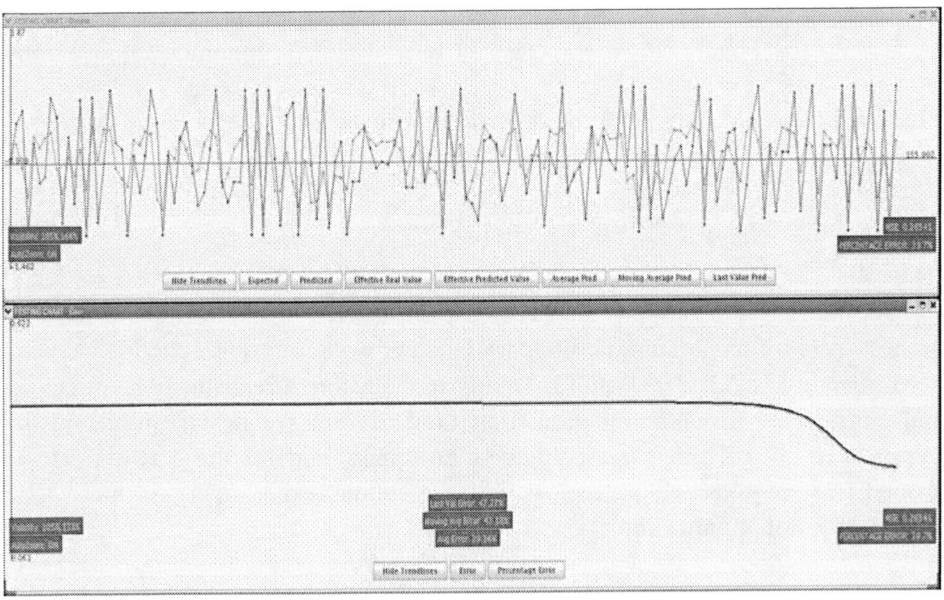

Figure 15. Neural network load prediction testing module.

In order to test the load prediction service, we developed a graphical interface which allows the interactive visualisation of the training process (see Figure 15). The two windows display the real and predicted values at consecutive steps using the training sets and respectively the error trend (either the mean squared error or the instantaneous error measured on the post-processed values). This application offers the possibility to stop and resume the training process at any point during the training process. It allows the visualisation of a wide range of signals at different measured at different locations inside the load prediction module (pre/post-processed inputs, pre/post-processed outputs). Also, it offers the possibility to compare the neural prediction against other fast prediction methods. An important contribution resulting from using this application is the fact that it helped us make an observation about the output of the neural network prediction module, namely that the shape of the output signal was similar to the one of the expected signal, but the amplitude was always smaller. This led to the introduction of a novel additional phase at the end of the classical training process: the *amplitude calibration*.

5.5. Distributed FPS Game Simulator

To validate our neural network-based predictor, we developed a distributed FPS game simulator supporting the zoning concept and inter-zone migrations of the entities using various entity interaction patterns (see Figure 16). We use this simulator for generating realistic load patterns such as entity interaction hot-spots or simply large numbers of entities managed by one game server. The entities in the simulation are driven by several Artificial Intelligence (AI) profiles which determine their behaviour during a simulation:

- *aggressive* determines the entity to seek and interact with opponents;
- *team player* causes the entity to act in a group together with its teammates;
- *scout* leads the entity for discovering uncharted zones of the game world (not guaranteeing any interaction);
- *camper* simulates a well-known tactic in FPS games to hide and wait for the opponent. Aggressive and team player profiles typically generate the highest rate of entity interactions, while scout produces the least dynamic profile

To also account for the mixed behaviour encountered in deployed games (Bartle, 2003), each entity has its own preferred profile, but can change the profiles dynamically during the simulation. We further tried to get as close as possible to real games by importing maps from a very popular FPS game (Counter Strike 1.6 (GameData, Inc.)).

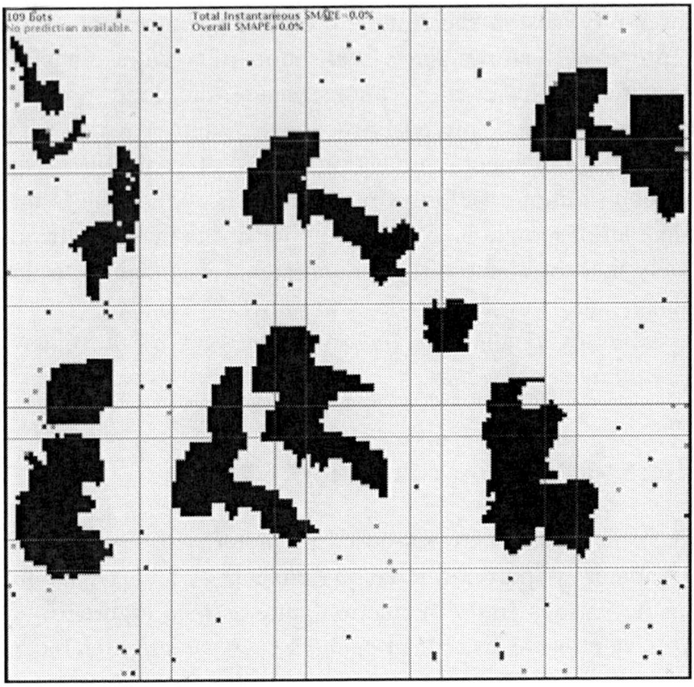

Figure 16. Game simulator snapshot.

5.6. Neural Network Tuning

As the neural networks are not deterministic, we carried out a significant number of experiments for tuning the parameters that influence the prediction accuracy: the signal expanding technique, the neural network type, and structure and the neural transfer function. The goal of our experiments is to minimise the prediction error:

$$PE = \frac{\sum_{i=1}^{N} \left| n_i^{(real)} - n_i^{(pred)} \right|}{\sum_{i=1}^{N} n_i^{(real)}},$$

where N is the total number of samples in the trace data set, and $n_i^{(real)}$ and $n_i^{(pred)}$ are the real, respectively predicted entity counts at time step i.

The challenge of the tuning process is caused by the fact that the variation of the accuracy with one parameter is not independent and not even coherent with its variation with another parameter. In conclusion, sequentially finding the best accuracy for every parameter is not possible and a guided exhaustive parameter study is necessary. In the following, we present only the main track of our experimental results, not mentioning the backtracking we have done for assessing the impact of altering one parameter on the others. The experiments presented are independent of each other or, in the worst case, have a very small impact on one another.

Using our game simulator introduced in Section 5.5, we generated eight different trace data sets with different characteristics by running 17 hours of simulations for each set and sampling the game state at every two minutes. In each simulation, we used a different configuration determined by four simulation parameters, which we vary by appropriately setting the predominant entity AI profiles usage (see Table 1). We first modelled peak hours in online gaming such as late afternoons or weekends. Then, we varied the entities' speed and inter-zone migration patterns to mimic two different dynamic profiles:

- *instantaneous dynamics* (typical to fast-paced FPS games) meaning a large difference in the entity interaction over a short period of time;
- *overall dynamics* (typical to MMORPGs) has a much more stable entity interaction load with large variations over a longer period of time.

Finally, we model the popularity of a game by setting the maximum peak load to different values.

We use this trace data for training the neural network until the process converges to a global minimum, as described in Section 5.3.5 and exemplified in Figure 17.

Table 1. Simulation trace data sets

Data set	Peak hours modelling	Peak load	Overall dynamics (17 h.)	Instantaneous dynamics (2 min.)
Set 1	No	+++++	+++++	+++++
Set 2	No	+++++	+++++	+++++
Set 3	No	+++++	+++++	+++++
Set 4	No	+++++	+++++	+++++
Set 5	Yes	+++++	+++++	+++++
Set 6	Yes	+++++	+++++	+++++
Set 7	Yes	+++++	+++++	+++++
Set 8	Yes	+++++	+++++	+++++

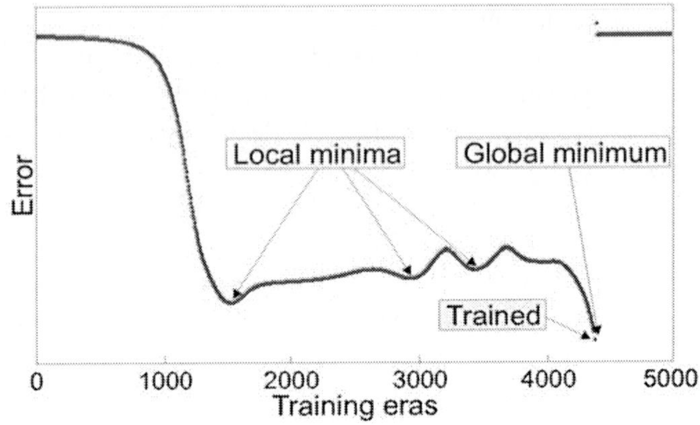

Figure 17. Sample prediction error during neural network training.

5.6.1. Network Type

The two main neural network types we experimented with are the classical feed-forward networks and the recurrent networks. In feed-forward networks the stimuli propagate only from the input layer towards the output layer, while in the recurrent networks there are also feedback loops towards a separate type of neurons called context neurons. From the feed-forward category, we experimented with a simple *multilayer perceptron (MLP)* and a modified three-layer perceptron, which has a different input layer consisting of fuzzy neurons intended to provide a different type of signal expansion. The recurrent network we use is a Jordan-Elman network (Haykin, 1994) (see Figure 18).

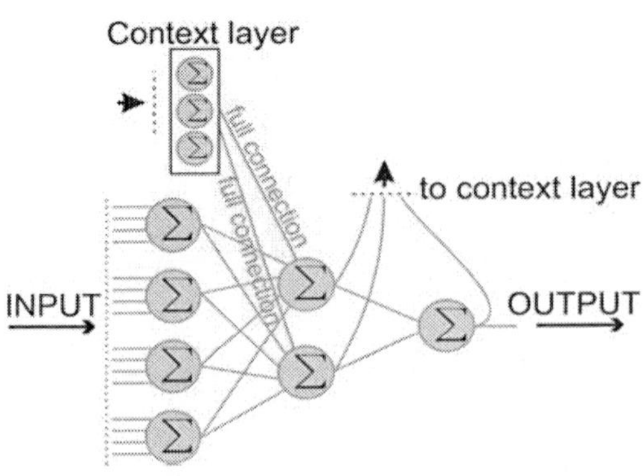

Figure 18. Jordan-Elman neural network.

Table 2. Experimental results for different network types

Network set-up				Prediction Error		
Input set	Structure	Transfer Function	Inputs [exp+raw]	MLP	Jordan Elman	Modif. MLP
Set 1	3,2,1	Sigmoid	6+3	34.86%	34.64%	36.73%
Set 1	5,2,1	Sigmoid	6+3	35.08%	34.86%	37.39%
Set 1	3,2,1	Sigmoid	3+3	34.86%	34.70%	40.00%
Set 1	5,2,1	Sigmoid	3+3	34.92%	34.70%	36.95%
Set 1	3,2,1	Linear	6+3	34.42%	33.33%	35.65%
Set 1	5,2,1	Linear	6+3	33.11%	33.77%	35.00%
Set 1	3,2,1	Linear	3+3	34.49%	33.18%	40.00%
Set 1	5,2,1	Linear	3+3	31.23%	33.83%	37.39%
Set 2	3,2,1	Sigmoid	6+3	28.90%	29.24%	29.11%
Set 2	5,2,1	Sigmoid	6+3	28.93%	29.24%	31.01%
Set 2	3,2,1	Sigmoid	3+3	30.15%	30.15%	34.49%
Set 2	5,2,1	Sigmoid	3+3	30.15%	30.47%	31.32%
Set 2	3,2,1	Linear	6+3	29.24%	29.55%	33.22%
Set 2	5,2,1	Linear	6+3	28.93%	28.93%	33.54%
Set 2	3,2,1	Linear	3+3	29.52%	29.20%	35.12%
Set 2	5,2,1	Linear	3+3	29.20%	29.52%	33.22%

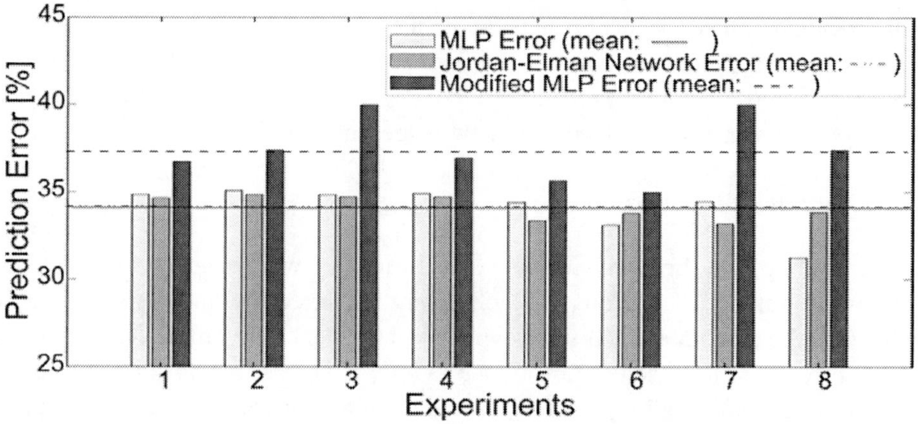

Figure 19. Network type experiments for data set 1.

As we previously mentioned, the parameters that influence the prediction accuracy are not independent. As a consequence, for each network type we present eight experiments varying most of the available parameters: the network structure, the transfer function, and the signal expansion technique. We present in Table 2 the results of these experiments on the input data sets 1 and 2 (see Table 1) since they model best dynamic FPS action games. In the modified MLP case, we used the fuzzy neuron input layer for expanding the input signals by varying their fuzzy domains.

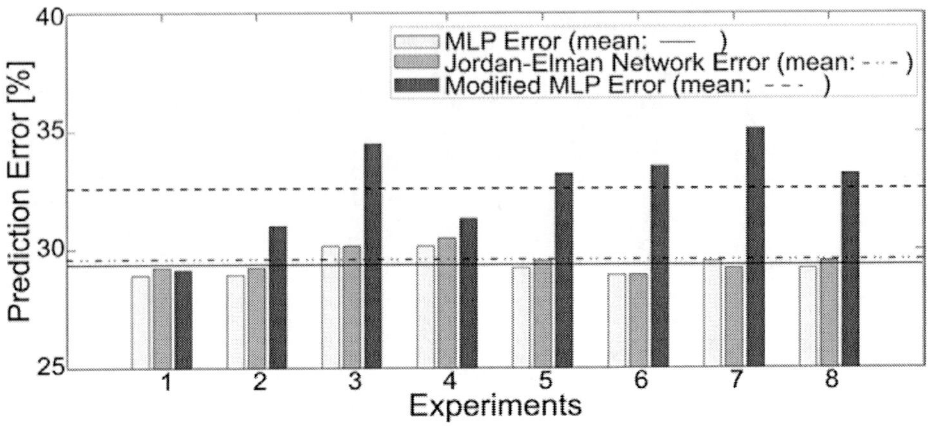

Figure 20. Network type experiments for data set 2.

A summary of the average prediction error for all network types can be found in Figure 19 and Figure 20. The simple MLP and the Jordan-Elman network performed well providing almost identical results, while the modified MLP struggled especially during the experiments with more fuzzy domains. Our conclusion is that the neural networks that best fit to our problem are the MLP and Jordan-Elman and, therefore, our next experiments will only take these two types into consideration.

5.6.2. Network Structure

In finding the best suited network structure, we focus on finding the appropriate number of neurons on each layer. We fixed the number of layers to three since the performance of these types of networks hardly improves with more layers. From a strictly scientific point of view, it is possible to add an infinite number of neurons on all layers, but this would add an increasing delay in making the prediction.

We therefore carried out a series of experiments using different three-layered network structures while maintaining all other relevant parameters fixed: classic MLP, full signal expanding, and linear transfer function (Haykin, 1994).

Table 3 demonstrates that the prediction does not improve when using networks with sizes one order of magnitude lower than the upper limit (good results were obtained with 15-20 neurons already). Figure 21 shows that the minimum prediction error is obtained for around 2-4 neurons in the second layer, while for the first layer we cannot make a similar assessment. Representing in Figure 22 the prediction error as a function of the number of neurons in both layers, we observe that the lowest error occurs if the network has twice as many neurons on the first layer than on the second layer. Taking into account these two observations, we conclude that the optimal network structure is *[6,3,1]* (representing the number of neurons on each layer). Obviously, similar structures will also produce comparably good results (e.g. *[9,3,1]*, *[8,4,1]*).

Table 3. Experimental results for different network structures

Experiment	Network structure [in,hidden,out]	Prediction error Data set 1	Prediction error Data set 3
1	3,1,1	34.70%	35.84%
2	5,1,1	34.92%	35.84%
3	15,1,1	34.92%	35.98%
4	20,1,1	34.92%	35.98%
5	30,1,1	34.49%	35.98%
6	3,2,1	33.40%	35.27%
7	5,2,1	32.92%	34.56%
8	15,2,1	33.83%	34.99%
9	20,2,1	33.83%	35.41%
10	30,2,1	34.49%	35.70%
11	3,5,1	34.27%	35.27%
12	5,5,1	33.18%	36.13%
13	15,5,1	32.97%	35.56%
14	20,5,1	34.05%	34.85%
15	30,5,1	34.27%	35.56%
16	3,10,1	33.62%	36.84%
17	5,10,1	37.09%	36.27%
18	15,10,1	34.27%	35.41%
19	20,10,1	33.83%	35.70%
20	30,10,1	34.05%	35.56%

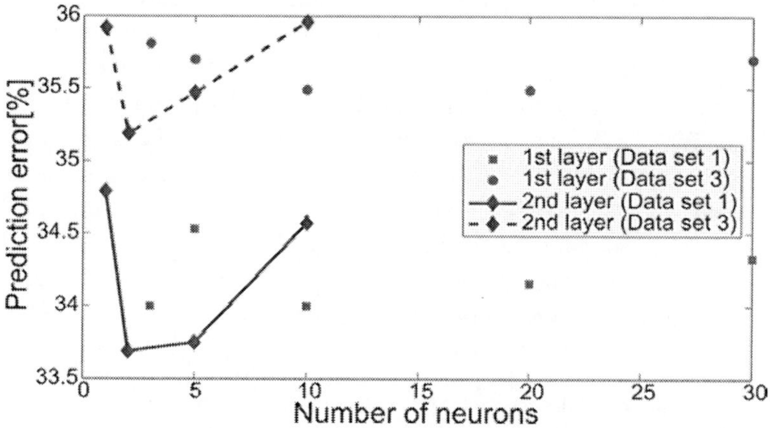

Figure 21. Prediction error for different first and second layer sizes.

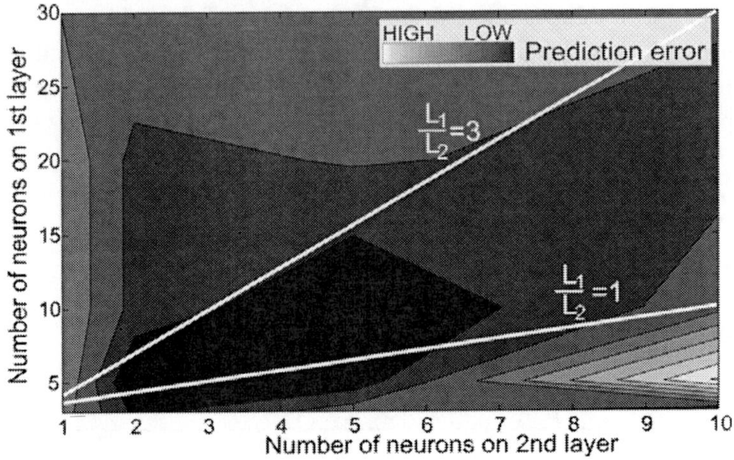

Figure 22. Prediction error map for variable first and second layer neurons.

5.6.3. Transfer Function

Extensive research has been done in the field of transfer functions for neural networks (Duch and Jankowski, 2001) (Katayama, Sakata, and Horiguchi, 2003). Unfortunately, there is no universal best transfer function, as the generalisation capabilities of the neural networks vary from case to case. For some simple systems using neural networks, the transfer function may not even matter in terms of performance, while for others this makes a big difference.

The transfer function represents the composition of two functions: the activation function which determines the total stimulus a neuron receives, and the output function which determines the total stimulus a neuron generates. We studied the behaviour of our system by using different transfer functions with three types of output functions: sigmoid, linear, and a modified Gaussian. The sigmoid transfers functions are known to best simulate the activity of a real neuron, but do not guarantee the best results. The computational demands of sigmoid neurons are also quite high. A much lighter alternative to the sigmoid function is the linear function which has the downside that for single layer networks does not guarantee training convergence. We modified the Gaussian function such that we only use the left lobe of the classical Gaussian bell, i.e.

$$G:[-1,1] \rightarrow [-1,1], G(x) = 2.1 \cdot e^{-\frac{(x-1)^2}{2 \cdot 0,86^2}} - 1,$$

where $\alpha = 2.1$, $\beta = 1$, and $\gamma = 0.86$.

In this batch of experiments, we fixed the previously determined parameters (i.e. network type and structure) at their best values. We use a classic MLP neural network with a *[6,3,1]* structure and ran experiments on input data sets 1, 2, and 3 with variable signal expanding. The results displayed in Table 4 confirm our original assumption that, even though the sigmoid functions give good results in most cases, they are not the best choice for all applications. The linear function performed best for all data sets and is closely followed by the modified Gaussian (see Figure 23) which performed worse for the data sets 1 and 3 characterised by higher overall dynamics. This leads us to the conclusion that, although the modified Gaussian gives good results for signals with high instantaneous dynamics, it cannot follow the overall trend of entity count over long time intervals.

Table 4. Experimental results for different transfer functions

Data set	Inputs [expanded+raw]	Prediction error Linear	Prediction error Sigmoid	Prediction error Gaussian
Set 1	4+2	32.53%	35.14%	32.97%
Set 1	9+3	32.75%	34.70%	33.18%
Set 1	12+4	33.62%	34.27%	33.62%
Set 2	4+2	29.84%	29.84%	29.52%
Set 2	9+3	29.37%	30.93%	29.06%
Set 2	12+4	28.61%	29.55%	29.24%
Set 3	4+2	32.71%	37.41%	34.85%
Set 3	9+3	35.27%	37.55%	36.41%
Set 3	12+4	36.54%	36.54%	35.83%

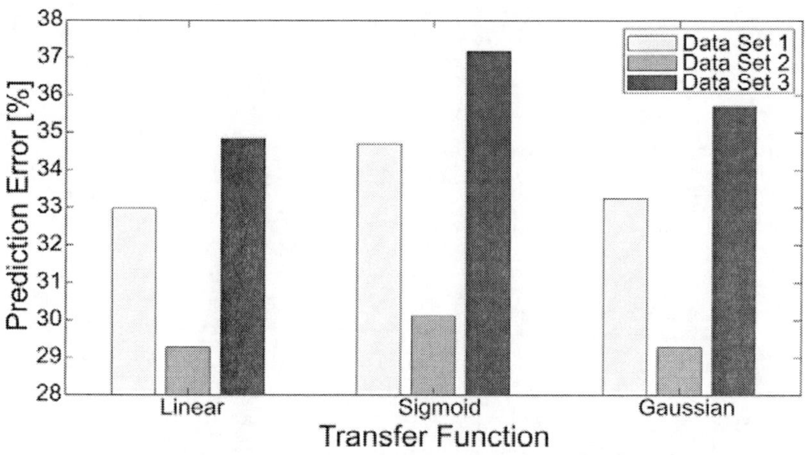

Figure 23. Transfer functions comparison for data set 1, 2, and 3.

5.6.4. Signal Expanding

Signal expanding is a type of signal pre-processing technique aimed at presenting the important information contained in the input signal in varied ways with the final purpose of improving the neural network's performance. Even simple functions such as difference and average can be applied to the raw input signals with good results. The improvement generated by this technique is most obvious in the case of noisy signals.

Table 5. Experimental results for signal expanding

Expansion level	Inputs [exp+raw]	Prediction error	Average error
	0+2	32.32%	
0	0+3	33.77%	33.09%
	0+4	33.18%	
	2+2	32.10%	
1	3+3	32.67%	32.72%
	4+4	33.40%	
	4+2	32.53%	
2	6+3	32.67%	32.94%
	8+4	33.62%	
	6+2	32.75%	
3	9+3	32.23%	32.72%
	12+4	33.18%	

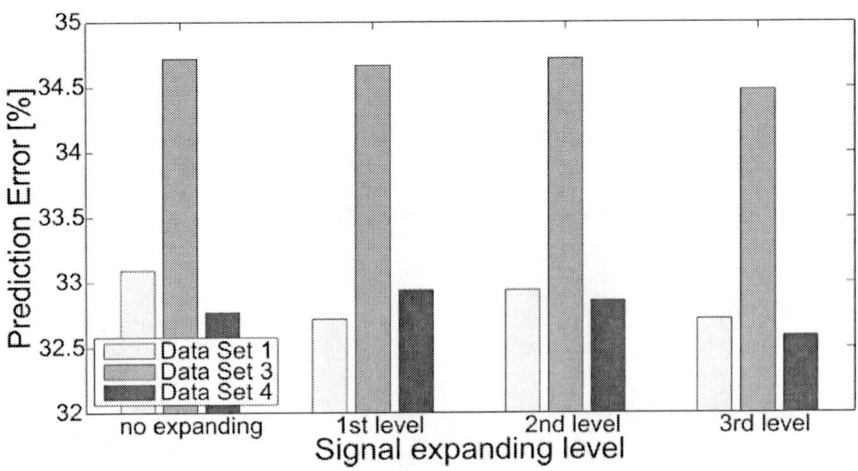

Figure 24. Signal expanding results for data sets 1, 3, and 4.

Regarding the functions we are using, as a first step we expand each value X_i from the input signal by subtracting it from the previous value:

$$EX_i^I = X_{i-1} - X_i,$$

which translates to the variation in entity count between all successive time steps. As a next level of expanding, we do an average of the input values in groups of three:

$$EX_i^{(II)} = \frac{X_{i-2} + X_{i-1} + X_i}{3},$$

which represents the average entity count in one subarea across each three successive prediction steps. As a final level of expanding, we apply the following formula:

$$EX_i^{(III)} = |X_{i-2} - X_i| - |X_{i-1} - X_i|,$$

which translates to an assessment of the dynamics of the last three signals.

The results for this batch of experiments displayed in Table 5 are not encouraging, the gain in performance being marginal even with the highest level of expanding. Nevertheless, the network shows some improvement in performance with the first and especially third level of expanding, as depicted in Figure 23.

5.7. Prediction Results

The final step of our experiments represents the evaluation of the quality of the results delivered by the neural network-based prediction compared to other methods. We use the best suited neural network architecture determined in the previous section, which is a standard fully connected MLP with a *[6,3,1]* structure, a linear transfer function, and a three level signal expansion.

We compared our system against other well-known fast prediction methods like average, moving average, last value, and three levels of exponential smoothing (Makridakis, Wheelwright, and Hyndman, 1998) (Wolski, 2003) on the eight input data sets described in Table 1. We selected these fast statistical methods for comparison since we observed them to be among the most accurate in highly dynamic systems like the Grid (Wolski, 2003), while fulfilling the time constraints of FPS action games where a high density of prediction intervals is essential.

The results displayed in Table 6 and Figure 25 show that, apart from producing better or at least equal predictions, the important quality of our system is its ability to adapt to various types of input signals. More precisely, we had in our data sets three major types of signals:

- signals with high instantaneous dynamic and medium overall dynamic (sets 2, 3, and 4) were best approximated by average;
- signals with low instantaneous dynamic (sets 6, 7 and 8) were best approximated by last value;
- signals with medium instantaneous and medium overall dynamics (sets 1 and 5) were best fitted by moving average and 50% exponential smoothing.

The drawback of these conventional methods is that it is not universally clear during a game play which of them should be applied as the real-time prediction method for the next time step. Moreover, as the dynamics of the game may change, for example during peak hours, the best prediction method may change too. Our neural network-based prediction successfully manages to adapt to all these types of signals and always delivers good prediction results.

Table 6. Comparison with other fast prediction methods

	Prediction Error						
Input data	Neural Network	Avg.	Moving Avg.	Last Val.	Exponential smoothing 25%	50%	75%
Set 1	**32.23%**	39.69%	39.25%	44.51%	40.04%	**37.83%**	39.60%
Set 2	**28.61%**	**30.79%**	34.60%	40.31%	34.19%	35.78%	36.74%
Set 3	**33.00%**	**37.98%**	39.40%	47.36%	38.34%	39.06%	41.92%
Set 4	**32.18%**	**34.48%**	39.78%	48.28%	42.90%	41.55%	43.97%
Set 5	**16.58%**	25.06%	**17.98%**	23.31%	19.85%	19.59%	20.27%
Set 6	**4.94%**	23.55%	8.13%	**5.08%**	10.89%	7.03%	5.66%
Set 7	**11.17%**	48.26%	18.88%	**11.84%**	20.50%	16.06%	12.53%
Set 8	**5.51%**	15.26%	8.45%	**5.66%**	12.96%	8.78%	5.90%

To compare our results, we calculate the *gain* of our prediction as follows:

$$Gain = \frac{\min\{PE_{other}\} - PE_{NN}}{\min\{PE_{other}\}},$$

where PE_{NN} denotes the prediction error of the neural network and $\min\{PE_{other}\}$ represents the minimum prediction error from set of other prediction methods (average, moving average, last value and the three exponential smoothing methods). We obtained the highest gains for signals with high instantaneous dynamics (sets 1 through 5) which represents the main characteristic of FPS games (see Figure 26). For data sets 6 through 8, characteristic to slow-paced MMORPGs, the best method other than our service was last value, which performed well leaving little margin for improvement. Nevertheless, our service performed better than the other methods, showing some gain in all cases.

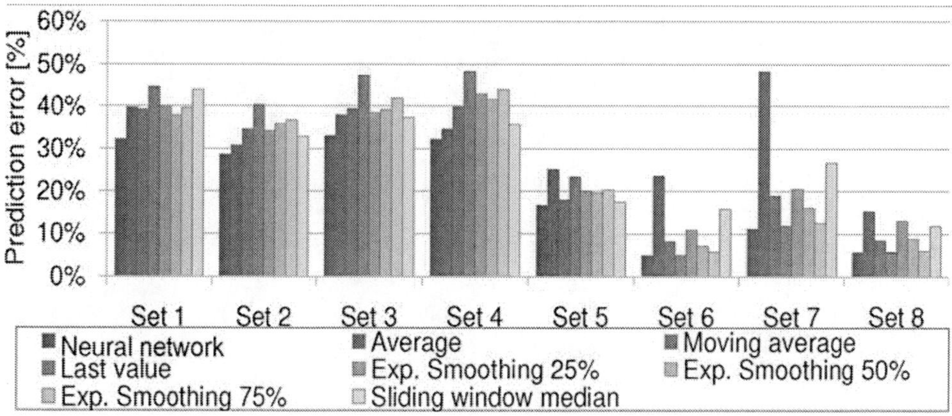

Figure 25. Prediction error for various prediction methods.

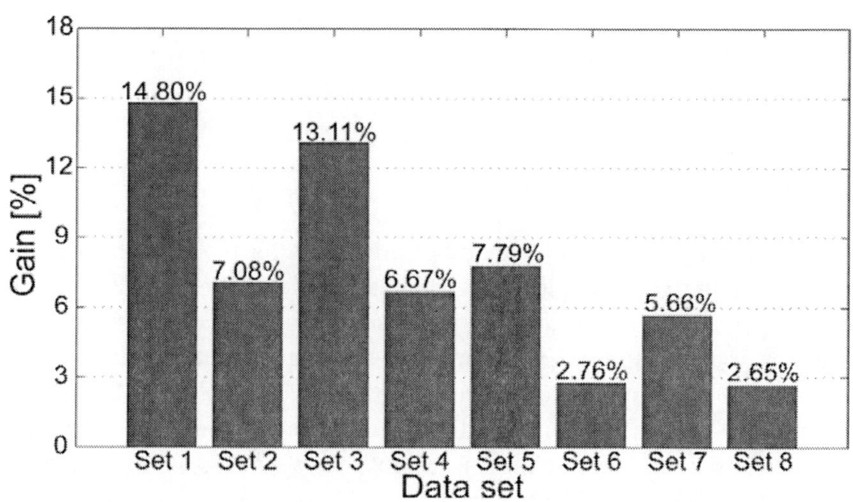

Figure 26. Neural network gain against next fastest prediction method.

Figure 27 depicts the duration of one prediction on a common off-the-shelf desktop with an Intel Core Duo E6700 (2.66 gigahertz) processor for the discussed prediction methods with the exception of the last value method which has no computational requirements. Although the neural predictor is the slowest of the presented methods, with average prediction duration of approximately 7 microseconds, it nevertheless fits into the fast prediction methods category, making it suited to its intended usage. Even with a few hundreds of sub-zones, the prediction time remains below one second which, considering a realistic prediction time step of about 30-300 seconds, leaves at least 97% of this time to the middleware for capacity management and load balancing decisions (i.e. creation of a new zone/instance, migration of players).

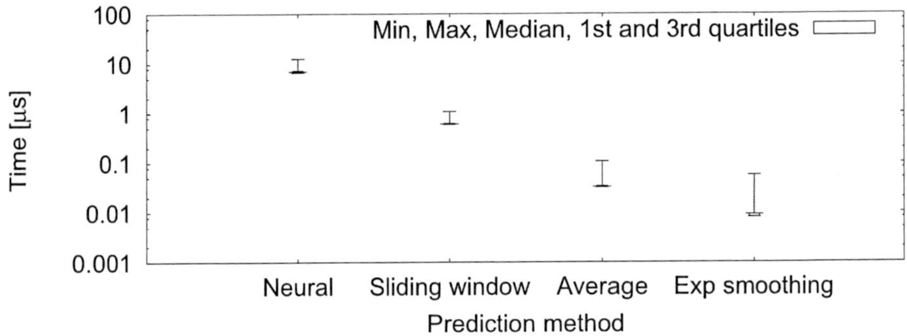

Figure 27. Statistical properties of the duration of one prediction for four prediction methods.

6. Capacity Management

In Section 5 we presented a method of prediction for the number of entities in all subareas of the game world zone handled by a specific host. To be able to make a proper resource allocation plans based on predicted loads for a certain time-interval in the future, it is first imperative to have an appropriate *number of entities – host load* mapping model.

Games are always pushing the limits in terms of hardware requirements. These applications are demanding on all resources with a strong emphasis on CPU utilisation, memory capacity, network (Internet) connection. There is no definite candidate amongst these for being the performance bottleneck for all (or at least most) of the games. Hence, these three parameters should be treated as equally potential threats for causing performance bottlenecks.

In our proposed method, we model all three parameters in order to adapt to an as wide range of games as possible. Still there is a strong emphasis on FPS and MMORPG game types, since they present the highest degree of interactivity (hence a more difficult resource allocation pattern).

6.1. Processor Load Model

As an important starting remark, we have to clarify the fact that modelling processor load for such applications with an extremely high degree of dynamicity is virtually impossible to achieve with a high level of detail. We define therefore a model with several simplifying hypothesis which will be mentioned along our presentation.

We first analyse the load model on one host in a distributed game session. Let us consider that N clients are connected to a distributed game session involving a total of H hosts provided by different Hosters. Inside the game world roam BE client-independent entities. On the host on which we are analysing the load, only AE entities are active (not shadows) and there are C clients connected.

The game intelligence is composed of a single big loop generically called the game loop. This is invariably true for all modern games, especially for the genres that we are studying. A game loop iteration is called a *tick* and in each tick there are certain steps that have to be done:

- processing events coming from the clients connected to the current host;
- processing state updates received from the other hosts for the shadow entities (client-independent and otherwise);
- processing the states of the active entities (client-independent and otherwise).
- In these steps, we can distinguish three basic time-consuming activities:
- computation of an interaction between two entities (t_i);
- receiving of an event message from one client (t_m); and
- update of one entity's state received or sent from or to another host (t_u).

In order to keep the complexity of this model at acceptable, we assume that user-independent entities do not interact amongst themselves, which is true in the majority of cases.

The CPU time spent for sending and receiving messages from the clients (active client-controlled entities) is:

$$t_M = C \cdot t_m.$$

The CPU time spent for processing the state updates from the other hosts can be expressed as:

$$t_U = (N - C) \cdot t_u + (BE - AE) \cdot t_u + AE \cdot t_u = (N - C + BE) \cdot t_u,$$

and the time t_I spent by the server for computing the interactions between the active entities is:

$$t_I = I \cdot t_i,$$

where I represents the total number of interactions involving the active entities. Obviously, the computation of interactions that do not involve active entities is allotted to other machines.

For quantifying the interactions between entities, we use a generic function $f(e_1, e_2)$ which has to be instantiated for each interaction type introduced in Section 2.2:

$$f(e_1, e_2) = \begin{cases} e_1 + e_2 & \text{for } O(n) \text{ interaction} \\ e_1 \cdot \log(e_2) & \text{for } O(n \cdot \log(n)) \text{ interaction} \\ e_1 \cdot e_2 & \text{for } O(n^2) \text{ interaction} \\ e_1^2 \cdot \log(e_2) & \text{for } O(n^2 \cdot \log(n)) \text{ interaction} \\ e_1^2 \cdot e_2 & \text{for } O(n^3) \text{ interaction} \end{cases},$$

where e_1 and e_2 are two classes of interacting entities.

Let IC denote the number of avatars interacting with any other entities (either avatars or NPCs). Furthermore, we define p_{ci} as the average number of interactions involving active avatars entities expressed as a percentage of IC. Analogously, we define p_{ei} as the average number of interactions involving active NPCs expressed as a percentage of BE. The total number of interactions is composed of the number of interactions between active avatars and the number of interactions between active avatars and NPC entities:

$$I = p_{ci} \cdot f(IC, IC) + p_{ei} \cdot f(IC, BE).$$

Consequently, the CPU time t_I for processing the interactions involving all active entities can be calculated as follows:

$$t_I = \left(p_{ci} \cdot f(IC, IC) + p_{ei} \cdot f(IC, BE)\right) \cdot t_i.$$

Approximating the time consumed for sending/receiving an event message as equal to the time needed to update the state of one entity ($t_m = t_u$), the total CPU time consumed in one tick is:

$$t_C = \left(N + BE\right) \cdot t_u + \left(p_{ci} \cdot f(IC, IC) + p_{ei} \cdot f(IC, BE)\right) \cdot t_i.$$

Furthermore, quantifying t_i with regard to t_u as:

$$t_i = p_{ui} \cdot t_u,$$

where p_{ui} is the ratio between the time necessary for one entity update and the time for computing one interaction (in percentage), the CPU time consumed in one tick becomes:

$$t_C = \left(N + BE + p_{ui} \cdot p_{ci} \cdot f(IC, IC) + p_{ui} \cdot p_{ei} \cdot f(IC, BE)\right) \cdot t_i.$$

Finally, considering t_{SAT} the tick saturation threshold, we can define the CPU load function as:

$$L_{CPU} = \frac{t_C}{t_{SAT}} = \frac{N + BE + p_{ui} \cdot p_{ci} \cdot f(IC, IC) + p_{ui} \cdot p_{ei} \cdot f(IC, BE)}{v},$$

where v is speed of the CPU expressed as an integer representing the number of t_u-long tasks it is able to perform in a t_{SAT}- long time interval.

6.2. Memory Load Model

The memory model is more or less straight forward since all the hosts involved in the mirroring process keep the entity-state records for all entities participating in the game session.

We begin by taking into account some game-dependent constants like the amount of memory needed to run the actual game engine with no game world loaded and no clients connected (m_{game}).

We also define m_{world} as being the amount of memory used for the game world being played and m_i as the amount of memory needed for each interaction taking place between two entities.

As for entity-related memory constants, let m_{cs} denote the amount of memory needed to store the state of one client-controlled entity, and let m_{es} be the amount of memory needed to store the state of a client-independent entity. The interactions do not have a significant impact in memory load, for most games m_i being very close to zero. Therefore, in order to keep the model simple, we assume that m_i is zero without introducing a significant error in the model.

Summing up all these data, the memory consumption for on a host taking part in a distributed game session will be:

$$M = N \cdot m_{cs} + BE \cdot m_{es} + m_{game} + m_{world}.$$

The memory load function can be expressed as:

$$L_{MEM} = \frac{M}{M_{machine}} = \frac{N \cdot m_{cs} + BE \cdot m_{es} + m_{game} + m_{world}}{M_{machine}},$$

where $M_{machine}$ represents the amount of memory available on the respective machine.

6.3. Network Load Model

There is significantly more research done in the game networking modelling area compared to the CPU load and memory load modelling ones. We use the network model presented in (42) which is developed especially for the system we are working with.

The model considers two functions:

$$D_{out} = C \cdot d_{cout} + (H-1) \cdot (C + AE) \cdot d_{update},$$

where d_{cout} represents the amount of data sent to a client, d_{update} represents the amount of data exchanged between hosts for updating a single entity's state, and:

$$D_{in} = C \cdot d_{cin} + (N - C + BE - AE) \cdot d_{update},$$

where d_{cin} represents the amount of data received from a client which define the incoming and outgoing bandwidth for a distributed game session.

In addition to this model, we define an overall (incoming and outgoing) network load function as the maximum of any of the two loads since the network connection is congested once one of the maxima is reached:

$$L_{NET} = \max\left(\frac{C \cdot d_{cout} + (H-1)\cdot(C+AE)\cdot d_{update}}{B_{out}}, \frac{C \cdot d_{cin} + (N-C+BE-AE)\cdot d_{update}}{B_{in}}\right).$$

6.4. General Load Model

Any of the monitored resources can be at one point in time the bottleneck of the entire system. Games can therefore be defined as a set of constants involved in all of the models previously described:

$$ROIA = \{(BE), (m_{cs}, m_{es}, m_{game}, m_{world}), (d_{cout}, d_{cin}, d_{update})\}.$$

Indeed, the *BE* value is not game-dependent, but rather game world and/or game style dependent. Still it is included amongst constants because we can consider a game running different game worlds and/or game styles as different games (from the point of view of the load model).

The overall load assessment is done as a simple maximum of all three loads:

$$L = \max(L_{CPU}, L_{MEM}, L_{NET}).$$

7. Resource Allocation

We designed and implemented our MMOG ecosystem within the edutain@grid project (Fahringer, et al., 2007), aiming to provide a platform for scalability, QoS provisioning, and user-friendly business models for real-time online interactive applications, with strong focus on MMOGs. edutain@grid is using as pilot a commercial FPS game application called Hunter developed by the Darkworks[2] game development company with the headquarters in Paris, France. Parallelisation of a game session according to the zoning, mirroring, and instancing techniques outlined in Section 2.1 is achieved by means of a generic

[2] http://www.darkworks.com/

portable library called Real-Time Framework (RTF) (Glinka, Ploss, Müller-Iden, and Gorlatch, 2007).

We used in our experiments an FPS demonstrator application that uses the open-source three-dimensional graphics engine (OGRE) (OGRE 3D: Open source graphics engine) for graphics and sound, and the RTF library for game session parallelization. Figure 28 and Figure 29 show two snapshots taken from a real game session parallelised across several severs. The resource testbed consists of two servers provided by the Amis Telecommunication Company located in Maribor, Slovenia and managed by one resource allocation service. The game world consists of two adjacent zones, handled in the beginning by two idle game servers. Clients connect to a game operator located at the University of Innsbruck, which processes their requests and arranges for the real-time connection the game servers. To stress the servers, we generated four waves of ten incoming clients, implemented as non-player characters (or bots) and modelled using the profiles described in Section 5.5.

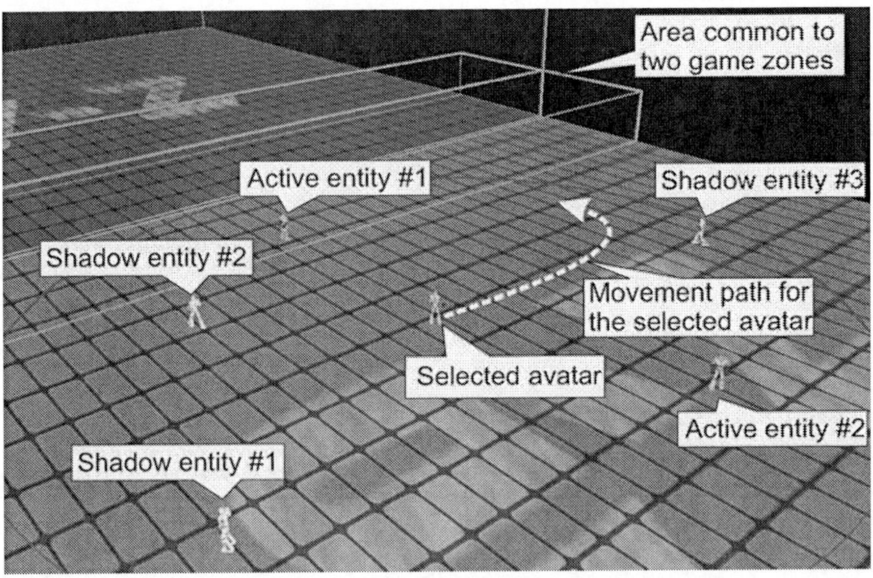

Figure 28. A snapshot from an online FPS game session with several participating avatars. The selected avatar represents the player that took the snapshot. The session is parallelised through zoning on two servers with a common area for hiding avatar migration latencies between servers. The two zones are further parallelised using replication: some of the entities close to the player are managed by the same server (the white active entities), while others are managed by another server (the light-green shadow entities).

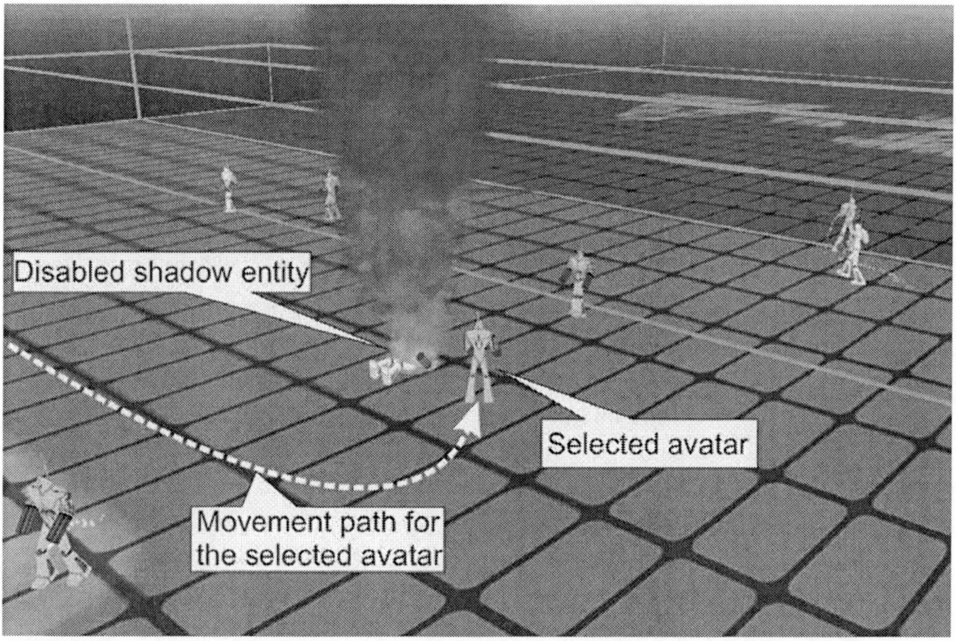

Figure 29. A snapshot from an online FPS game session with several participating avatars. The situation in the same game session some time after the previous snapshot was taken. The selected avatar has now moved close to another entity that has been disabled as a result of the real-time actions of other players, such as shooting.

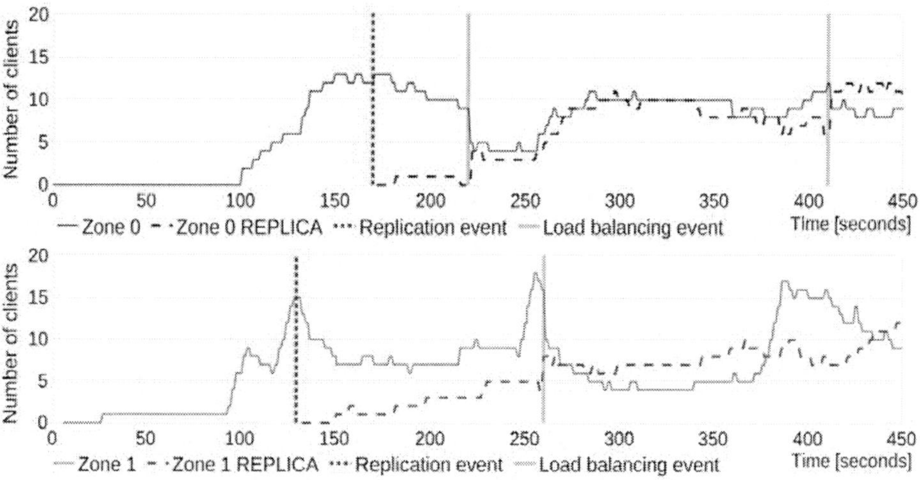

Figure 30. Number of clients connected over time in a distributed session.

Figure 30 displays the number of online players connected to a distributed game session in real-time. The four incoming player waves start at around seconds 95, 123, 253, and 384, respectively. The session load is evaluated at ten seconds interval and load balancing actions are triggered at intervals of at least 30 seconds to keep the overall session load below a preset threshold. At second 130, an overload is detected on the game server hosting zone 1, which triggers a replication action. A new server is started, connected to the overloaded one, and both servers start sharing the load. At second 170, another overload is detected at the server hosting the zone 0 and, as a result, another replication server is started. Since this newly created replica for zone 0 is not receiving enough clients, a load balancing action is triggered at second 220 by migrating clients to the new under-utilised zones. Another load balancing action is taken at second 260 on the servers running zone 1 as a result of an imbalance generated by a large number of clients connecting to one of the servers. The last similar measure, taken on the zone 0 servers at second 410, is caused by clients transiting from zone 1. A final load imbalance at second 380 which did not trigger a load balancing action since it did not exceed a preset threshold.

8. Conclusions

We presented the edutain@grid management infrastructure for real-time resource provisioning for MMOG. We first present a model for a game ecosystem that describes the game operators (also named Coordinators), the resource providers (also called Hosters or data centres), the application, and their integration. Extending on previous work where resources were provided by a single data centre (Doyle, Chase, Asad, Jin, and Vahdat, 2003) (Urgaonkar, Shenoy, Chandra, and Goyal, 2005), in our model the game resources are provided by multiple geographically distributed Hosters with different lease policies. In contrast to previous client/server Internet applications (Doyle, Chase, Asad, Jin, and Vahdat, 2003) (Urgaonkar, Shenoy, Chandra, and Goyal, 2005) (Rolia, Zhu, Arlitt, and Andrzejak, 2004) (Urgaonkar, Pacifici, Shenoy, Spreitzer, and Tantawi, 2005) (Karve, et al., 2006) focusing on non-interacting user requests, our model is designed around the notion of player interactions within the same application instance.

Afterwards, we introduced the overall service-oriented architecture of the management layer and a method for game resource provisioning based on the cooperation of five services: monitoring, load prediction, capacity management, resource allocation, and information services.

Motivated by the dynamic game workloads, we proposed a dynamic provisioning method in which the amount of needed resources is first predicted, and then obtained dynamically from data centres external to the game operator.

We presented the complete design of a monitoring service in charge of collecting real-time metrics from the game, such as the number, position, and interactions of entities required for driving the game session parallelisation with an efficient dynamic resource allocation.

We described a novel strategy for applying predictions to game player interaction that partitions the simulated world into small areas where real-time prediction is accurate, and aggregates the local estimations to get an overall prediction. We evaluated several classes of online predictors, from moving averages to simple neural networks and found that the simple neural networks have better accuracy than the studied alternatives for a variety of game workloads. To achieve this, we tuned one such algorithm for good accuracy and acceptable real-time performance.

We devised a capacity management method based on an analytical load model for three types of game resources (processor, memory, and network) that converted SLAs into QoS parameters and entity layout into load information. The model takes into account both the player interaction type and the player population size. By feeding real-time measurements or online predictions into the model, the Hosters and Coordinators can dynamically estimate the amount of resources needed to run their game.

References

Aron, M., Druschel, P., and Zwaenepoel, W. (2000). Measurement and Modeling of Computer Systems. *Cluster reserves: a mechanism for resource management in cluster-based network servers* (pp. 90-101). ACM SIGMETRICS.

Bartle, R. (2003). *Designing Virtual Worlds.* Indianapolis: New Riders.

Cai, W., Percival, X., Turner, S. J., and Lee, B.-S. (2002). 16th Workshop on Parallel and Distributed Simulation. *A scalable architecture for supporting interactive games on the Internet* (pp. 60-67). IEEE Computer Society.

Claypool, M. (2005). The effect of latency on user performance in Real-Time strategy games. *Computer Networks* , **49** (1), pp. 52-70.

Claypool, M., and Claypool, K. T. (2006). Latency and player actions in online games. *Communications of ACM* , **49** (11), pp. 40-45.

Doyle, R. P., Chase, J. S., Asad, O. M., Jin, W., and Vahdat, A. (2003). Symposium on Internet Technologies and Systems. *Model-Based Resource Provisioning in a Web Service Utility*. USENIX.

Duch, W., and Jankowski, N. (2001). 9th European Symposium on Artificial Neural Networks. *Transfer functions: hidden possibilities for better neural networks*, (pp. 81--94). Bruges, Belgium.

GameData, Inc. (n.d.). *Counter Strike*. Retrieved from http://www.counter-strike.com

Glinka, F., Ploss, A., Müller-Iden, J., and Gorlatch, S. (2007). NetGames. *RTF: A Real-Time Framework for Developing Scalable Multiplayer Online Games* (pp. 81-86). Melbourne, Australia: ACM Press.

Haykin, S. (1994). *Neural Networks: A Comprehensive Foundation* (2nd edition ed.). Prentice Hall PTR.

Iosup, A., Epema, D., Tannenbaum, T., Farrellee, M., and Livny, M. (2007). Inter-Operating Grids through Delegated MatchMaking. *Supercomputing* (pp. 1-12). ACM Press.

Karve, A., Kimbrel, T., Pacifici, G., Spreitzer, M., Steinder, M., Sviridenko, M., et al. (2006). 15th international conference on World Wide Web. *Dynamic placement for clustered web applications* (pp. 595-604). ACM.

Katayama, K., Sakata, Y., and Horiguchi, T. (2003). Layered Neural Networks with Non-Monotonic Transfer Functions. *Physica A: Statistical Mechanics and its Applications* , **317** (1-2), pp. 270--298.

Makridakis, S., Wheelwright, S., and Hyndman, R. (1998). *Forecasting Methods and Applications*. John Wiley and Sons, Inc.

MMORPG.COM. (n.d.). *Your Headquarters for Massive Multiplayer Online Role-Playing Games*. Retrieved 2008, from http://www.mmorpg.com/

Müller, J., and Gorlatch, S. (2006). Rokkatan: scaling an RTS game design to the massively multiplayer realm. *Computers in Entertainment* , **4** (3).

Rolia, J., Zhu, X., Arlitt, M. F., and Andrzejak, A. (2004). Statistical service assurances for applications in utility Grid environments. *Performance Evaluation* , **58** (2-3), pp. 319-339.

Saha, D., Sahu, S., and Shaikh, A. (2003). Workshop on Network and System Support for Games. *A Service Platform for Online Games* (pp. 180--184). Redwood City, CA, USA: ACM Press.

Shaikh, A., Sahu, S., Rosu, M. C., Shea, M., and Saha, D. (2006). On demand platform for online games. *IBM Systems Journal* , **45** (1), pp. 7-20.

Steam. (n.d.). *Welcome to Steam*. Retrieved June 2009, from http://store.steampowered.com

Urgaonkar, B., Pacifici, G., Shenoy, P. J., Spreitzer, M., and Tantawi, A. N. (2005). Measurement and Modeling of Computer Systems. *An analytical model for multi-tier internet services and its applications* (pp. 291-302). ACM SIGMETRICS.

Urgaonkar, B., Shenoy, P. J., Chandra, A., and Goyal, P. (2005). 2nd International Conference on Autonomic Computing. *Dynamic Provisioning of Multi-tier Internet Applications* (pp. 217-228). IEEE Computer Society.

White, W. M., Koch, C., Gupta, N., Gehrke, J., and Demers, A. J. (2007). Database research opportunities in computer games. *ACM SIGMOD Record* , **36** (3), pp. 7-13.

Wolski, R. (2003). Experiences with Predicting Resource Performance On-line in Computational Grid Settings. *ACM SIGMETRICS Performance Evaluation Review* , **30** (4), pp. 41--49.

Woodcock, B. S. (2008). *An Analysis of MMOG Subscription Growth.* Retrieved December 22, 2008, from http://www.mmogchart.com/downloads/

Ye, M., and Cheng, L. (2006). System-performance modeling for massively multiplayer online role-playing games. *IBM Systems Journal* , **45** (1), pp. 45-58.

In: Computer Games
Editors: A. Soria et al, pp. 53-84
ISBN: 978-1-60876-658-1

Chapter 2

A STRATEGY FOR ANALYZING DIGITAL EPISTEMIC GAMES

Robert Haworth[a] and Kamran Sedig[b]
[a]Department of Computer Science, The University of Western Ontario, Middlesex College, London, ON N6A 5B7
[b]Department of Computer Science and Faculty of Information and Media Studies, The University of Western Ontario, Middlesex College, London, ON N6A 5B7

Abstract

In this chapter we will present a strategy for how to analyze digital epistemic games. Digital epistemic games are computer-based games that mediate mental, intellectual, knowledge-oriented activities. Mediate here suggests support, facilitate, transform, and enhance. Epistemic games can be used to improve players' problem solving, planning, information analysis, reasoning, critical thinking, and learning. Such games contain one or more cognitive tasks that players need to perform in order to advance or complete the game. Each game can be categorized and analyzed according to these underlying cognitive tasks. Some examples of cognitive tasks include the rearrangement of shapes, the linking of objects and ideas, the finding of paths through mazelike structures, and the matching of features and parts.

Traditionally, digital games have been categorized according to broad genres such as adventure, board, card, combat, educational, puzzle, strategy, and role-playing games. These genres categorize games based on their overall gameplay. As such, genres are intended to provide a prospective user with a general idea of what the gameplay experience will involve. Unfortunately, this type of taxonomy does not hint at the underlying cognitive tasks of the game.

Oftentimes, educators may want to use digital games to engage learners with certain cognitive tasks and to help them with the understanding of these tasks. Not knowing about the core structures of a game can therefore be troublesome. To address this problem, in this chapter we will analyze a number of existing games and categorize them according to their cognitive tasks. This analysis will help to display what educational and epistemic purposes these digital epistemic games can serve. As digital games continue to grow in popularity, it is important to know how to analyze games that serve the mind.

Introduction

Digital games are now a noticeable part of popular culture and the digital game industry continues to grow, generating $11 billion USD in the United States alone last year (ESA, 2009). Due to this popularity, there is much speculation about whether digital games have any learning potential (De Aguilera and Mendiz, 2003; Kafai, 2006; Prensky, 2000; Van Eck, 2006). A variety of games have been examined in the context of learning or used in different training and learning situations, such as history (Squire, 2006), literacy (Gee, 2003), spatial reasoning (Crawford, 2003), organizational and memory strategies (Jacobs and Dempsey, 1993), and mathematics and science (Kafai, 1995; Randel et al., 1992). However, it would be incorrect to say that all games provide learning potential (Van Eck, 2006). Thus, this chapter only focuses on digital epistemic games, which are computer-based games that mediate mental, intellectual, knowledge-oriented activities. To mediate here suggests that games support, facilitate, transform, and enhance. Given this definition, digital epistemic games can be used to improve players' problem solving, planning, information analysis, reasoning, critical thinking skills and other related cognitive skills and abilities.

Digital epistemic games are not a specific category or genre of games, and are not limited to any specific game-playing platform. To determine whether a game is considered epistemic or not, it is best to determine what cognitive benefits the game provides. If a game provides very little cognitive benefit, or none at all, then it would not be considered an epistemic game. This chapter presents a strategy for analyzing digital epistemic games, thus allowing anyone to better determine what the cognitive benefits of a game are. This is of particular importance to educators who wish to integrate digital epistemic games into their learning material, since knowing what cognitive benefits a game provides will explain how the game can best supplement the learning material.

This chapter will first examine different methods of categorizing games, to determine whether and how these methods will help describe the cognitive benefits that different digital epistemic games can provide. Next, this chapter will examine patterns and describe a pattern-based strategy to categorize epistemic games, followed by a list of identified patterns. Lastly, the pattern-based strategy will be used to analyze several digital epistemic games, providing an example of how this strategy can be used by others.

Game Categorization

Taxonomies provide a structure for organizing objects, based on common properties, and for comparison or analysis of the organized objects. Different taxonomies or typologies exist to categorize digital games, each focusing on different common properties. Games are traditionally categorized according to genres, with a game placed into one genre or a sub-genre. However, there is some concern that the current genres used in the digital game industry are influenced by marketing and journalism (Järvinen, 2002; Elverdam and Aarseth, 2007), mainly due to a lack of consistency among the genres used (Alpert, 2007). Additionally, there is disagreement about how the genres categorize digital games. Some suggest genres categorize by the representational and aesthetic aspects of games (Novak, 2007; Caldwell, 2004), while others suggest the categorization is based on the gameplay elements and forms of interaction (Rollings and Adams, 2003; Apperley, 2006; Myers, 1990). Still others suggest the current genres involve the narrative, mood, and feel of the game (Elverdam and Aarseth, 2007).

Of these different interpretations of genres for categorizing games, categorizing by gameplay and forms of interaction are most likely to describe what cognitive skills the player will need to use. As an example, Crawford (1984) suggested dividing games into the two general categories of skill-and-action games, which focus on physical dexterity and reaction time, and strategy games, which focus on cognitive skills. This categorization would be somewhat useful, as any game in the strategy genre would be a digital epistemic game. However, Crawford's categorization is outdated so it is better to look at the more current genres used for categorization. Several of the more commonly used genres, with the interpretation that the genres categorize games by gameplay and by types of interaction, are shown in Table 1. Several specific genres, such as racing, are not included in the list as they can be considered sub-genres.

Table 1. Common game genres (Rollings and Adams, 2003; Alpert, 2007; Novak, 2007).

Action	Involves physical challenges and personal conflict, relying on hand-eye coordination, reaction time, and reflexive actions.
Adventure	Involves exploration, discovery, and solving puzzles or problems.
Puzzle	Involves one or a series of puzzles or logical challenges, often without much time pressure. These tend to be short in length.
Role-Playing	Involves one or more characters that progress and develop in various ways as the game advances, often coinciding with a story. These games also involve exploration, tactical conflict, and some logistical or economic conflicts.
Simulation	Involves replication of real-world scenarios or systems, such as vehicle simulations, sports games, or business and management simulations. The problems and goals of these games are similar to those of the replicated situation or system.
Strategy	Involves strategic, tactical, and logistical challenges requiring players to perform careful resource management. The depth and complexity of the challenges depend on the time constraints.

The puzzle genre from Table 1 seems to be the most likely category to locate epistemic games. However, there may also be epistemic games in the adventure genre. The remaining genres, with the possible exception of action, may also provide some degree of cognitive benefit. It is this "degree" which poses the biggest problem. Given that there are only vague notions of what cognitive skills are necessary, and no indication of the degree to which those skills are needed, categorization by genre does not provide the necessary information for an educator to properly select a game.

However, other taxonomies exist and could be examined. Wolf (2001) created a taxonomy based on types of interaction for gameplay and similar representational or thematic style, resulting in 42 different categories of which some may not be considered digital games. Although these categories differentiate between types of interaction, the focus is on how the game is played and not on what cognitive skills the game requires or teaches. Apperley (2006) suggests that games should be thought of as "belonging to several genres at once" rather than keep the restrictive view that games exist in one genre only. Although Wolf's taxonomy does not do this, it is also a combination of interactional style and representational style, suggesting that perhaps a multi-dimensional taxonomy would be better suited to categorize games.

Several multi-dimensional taxonomies are available, allowing games to be categorized based on a combination of properties rather than just one property. For example, rather than creating categories based simply on how the player interacts with the game, one dimension of the category could be interaction while another dimension could be how time affects the gameplay or how different narratives are used. Aarseth et al. (2003) developed a multi-dimensional taxonomy to describe games based on structural properties – space, time, player-structure, control, and rules – to understand in more detail how various games are similar or different at a structural or spatial level. Lewis et al. (2007) used multidimensional scaling techniques to compare the similarity of games on a 2-Dimensional map, in order to determine how players decide why a game is similar to another game. This map resulted in a categorization of games with respect to their aesthetics versus their mechanics. The Game Ontology Project (Zagal et al., 2005) is another framework that focuses more on analysis of games than just categorization, examining the various structural components of games and the relationships of these components. In contrast, the Game Design Rules (Falstein, 2002) focus on principles for better game design and the Game Design Patterns (Björk et al., 2003) identify common structural components of various games. These two frameworks provide an alternate methodology to examine the components of games and to better compare, analyze, and understand games. However, these frameworks can also be used for categorization (Björk and Peitz, 2007).

Epistemic Patterns

Although none of the categorizations described in the previous section organized games based on their epistemic utility, one deserves extra attention. The pattern-based approach to categorization used by Björk et al. (2003) focused on the structural aspects of digital games, but the same pattern-based approach can be used to categorize other aspects of games. Patterns are anything that repeat in a predictable and organized manner. As far as design is concerned patterns can be used as guidelines for the creation of, analyzation of, or solution to commonly occurring problems or features.

Patterns were first applied to design by Alexander et al. (1977) to examine common problems in architecture. By identifying architectural problems as patterns, solutions could be discussed that were known to work well against those problems. Thus, the patterns became useful as a problem-solving tool for designers. The idea of using patterns to identify common problems, and their solutions, has since been applied to a variety of other disciplines such as software design (Beck and Cunningham, 1987; Gamma et al., 1995; Buschmann et al., 1996; Fowler, 1997), human-computer interaction (Borchers, 2001), game design (Björk and Holopainen, 2005; McNaughton et al., 2004; Mor et al., 2006), and business (Sadtler et al., 2006). (For an in depth discussion of design patterns and their applications see Dearden and Finlay, 2006).

However, in many of those cases the patterns are used to solve design problems. The patterns this chapter will examine do not involve design problems, nor do they involve best practices or design decisions to avoid. This chapter uses the notion of a pattern as a commonly occurring idea or theme, specifically with regards to knowledge and learning. This chapter introduces epistemic patterns, which are patterns of thinking or patterns of coming to know something. When applied to games, these patterns determine what cognitive skills are utilized, learned, and improved in the completion of tasks in the game. Digital epistemic games can be analyzed to determine which epistemic patterns exist in the game. Knowing the epistemic patterns that a game contains will indicate what cognitive skills and knowledge the game will teach, as players will have to learn and use those skills and knowledge in order to advance further in the game.

From here a taxonomy can be created to categorize games based on what epistemic patterns they contain, as games are likely to contain more than one pattern. Since some patterns may not have as significant an impact in a game as others, patterns in a game may be primary patterns or supplementary patterns. Primary patterns are those that the game focuses upon or that exist regularly in the game. The patterns that are performed in addition to the primary patterns for given tasks, or that are not as pervasive in the game, are supplementary patterns. This taxonomy is more beneficial to educators, as they are able to identify what cognitive benefits a game contains and to what degree those benefits exist.

To identify these patterns, multiple games as well as large collections of puzzles were analyzed. The patterns are at an abstract level, keeping the detail of how the pattern exists in a game or puzzle at a minimum, and focus more on the cognitive and learning benefits the patterns provide than on how the patterns are used in games. This list of patterns is still a work in progress. More patterns may become apparent as more digital games and puzzles are examined, and as digital games are analyzed in more detail.

In the next section the patterns are listed and explained in detail. Multiple games are then examined to explain how the patterns are used in those games, and how the games can be categorized according to these patterns.

Pattern List

Arranging

The arranging pattern deals with changing the spatial positions of game objects or components of those objects. Arranging objects in space can lead to knowledge building, sensemaking, and improved problem solving (Ankerst et al., 1998; Kirsh, 1995; Kastens et al., 2008; Yang et al., 2003). Digital games that are designed with arranging can help players to understand underlying patterns, trends, and relationships between objects, (Ankerst et al., 1998), as well as help with organizational skills (Kirsh, 1995; Kastens et al., 2008).

The arranging itself is usually restricted in some manner, dependent on the game itself. For example, objects could be arranged only on a grid, obstacles could prevent objects from being arranged past them, physical laws such as gravity may be simulated to affect where the object ultimately ends up after the arrangement, and so on. There are a variety of purposes for arranging, such as placing objects in a specific way, sorting objects, or aligning objects to give insight into a bigger problem. Additionally, in games where a player manipulates a representative character – such as many action, adventure, and role-playing games – the act of simply moving that character around may not qualify as arranging. Moving a representative character is dealt with in the *searching* pattern.

Assigning

This pattern refers to the act of giving objects within the game meaning, properties, functionality, and so on. Assigning meaning or properties to objects within a game has the cognitive benefits of improving sensemaking, problem solving, and learning (MacKeracher, 2004; Renkl, 1997). By assigning meaning to objects or actions within the game, players are able to make sense of the game environment, the objects within it, and the relationships among the objects (MacKeracher, 2004). This is a more contextual example of making sense of anything in the world (MacKeracher, 2004) and supports more successful learning in general (Renkl, 1997).

Players may assign meaning to objects as they play the game, though this is usually not part of the game itself. However, changing the properties, functionality, and behavior of game objects is a part of the game, and the player is limited in what properties and functionality can be changed, added, or removed by the game itself. To be considered part of the assigning pattern, any changes that players make must advance the game in some manner and cannot be merely aesthetic changes. Although some games provide the option to change properties of objects for aesthetic purposes, by definition these changes do not advance the player further in the game.

Collecting

This pattern refers to gathering various objects for a specific purpose. Simply collecting objects may assist the cognitive development provided by other patterns, but collecting information about the game provides insight on how to organize and analyze information one collects (Kuhn and Ho, 1980). Often collecting is the goal of a game, where players must collect all of some object or a specific number of some object. In other cases collecting is simply a bonus, where players can collect all of some object and are given a bonus reward for doing so. When integrated within a digital game, collecting can be the motivation players have for trying to advance or the game can require players to figure out how they can collect all the necessary objects in order to advance further in the game.

Comparing

Comparing refers to examining objects to better understand their similarities and differences. This leads to matching similar objects, finding counterparts for objects, discovering the object that does not belong or is different, and so on. Comparison provides several cognitive benefits, such as learning, sensemaking, and problem solving (Gentner et al., 2007; Oakes and Ribar, 2005). Additionally, comparing is a key component of the problem solving process, organizing objects, and experimenting with objects (Smith and Medin, 1981). The complexity of similarity can be much greater than simple visual differences though, such as comparing the meanings of words or comparing two objects based on the relationship of their components. The comparing pattern often supplements other patterns, and is rarely an independent pattern in a game. For example, the comparison pattern would supplement the arranging or collecting pattern by requiring players to compare different objects in order to arrange or collect them.

Composing

This pattern refers to the act of bringing objects together and merging them into one larger object, although it can also be seen as creating new objects out of components. The cognitive benefits that composition provides focus on problem solving, planning, and learning (Abrahamson, 2006; Cox, 1999; Grossen and Carnine, 1990). Composing also facilitates analytical reasoning (Grossen and Carnine, 1990) and creativity with respect to creating new ideas (Cox, 1999). Merging objects to create a larger object may be the goal of the game, in which case this pattern is what motivates the player to advance through the game, but the merging of smaller objects may just be one part of the game.

Filtering

The filtering pattern allows players to change the amount of information, or type of information, displayed to them. The information is often provided in layers, allowing players to select and view what information is relevant. This decreases the perceptual and cognitive processing players need to perform in order to play the game, providing cognitive benefits such as reasoning, problem solving, decision making, and learning (Stolte et al., 2002; Kastens et al., 2008). Filters may be necessary in a game, as the information available to the player is too much to display all at once, or they may be optional, allowing players to decide how much information they want displayed.

Linking

This pattern involves connecting, joining, relating, or associating objects in some way, as well as understanding the connections and relationships between various objects. Linking aids in organization and incremental decision making (Foster and Stefik, 1986). In addition, linking provides the cognitive benefits of planning, learning, sensemaking, and problem solving (Peterson and Snyder, 1998; Faisal, et al., 2009). The relationships between objects may be obvious in a game, or explained in a manual or tutorial. Some games do not explain the relationships between objects, or make these relationships unclear, requiring players to understand how objects are connected in order to advance or complete the game.

Probing

The probing pattern involves examining, focusing on, and looking into game objects for more detailed information. Given that players cannot attend to all the information available to them at once (Ormrod, 1995) probing helps to focus their attention and process information more deeply, which is a significant requirement for learning (Hannafin and Hooper, 1993). Games provide probing to players in a variety of ways, such as zooming or panning a level in the game, inspecting individual game objects for information, and even requesting in-game help for specific objects or game concepts. Probing may be included in a game but it is not required in order to successfully complete the game. This is particularly noticeable if the player has already completed the game, as the player may already know whatever information probing could provide.

Searching

The searching pattern involves players finding objects within the game, finding information about the game or game objects, or finding a path through a portion of the game in order to advance. Searching is a directed activity, unlike simply wandering through the game world, as players are actively trying to understand the problem given to them and develop a solution for it (Bates, 1986). This pattern also provides the cognitive benefits of sensemaking and problem solving, as searching helps with acquiring new knowledge and updating existing knowledge (Rowley and Hartley, 2008). Finding a hidden object in a game may only be part of the solution, as players may need to overcome other obstacles in order to actually obtain the hidden object. As well, games may include searching as an optional task to provide hints or bonus rewards. Finding the exit in a maze-like environment, or finding a safe path through many obstacles in the game, are also examples of the searching pattern regardless of whether finding that path involves moving a representative character around the environment or not.

Selecting

The selecting pattern refers to choosing an object in the game and marking it, such as to keep track of the object or to remember it for further investigation later. Selecting usually precedes other related actions players may perform, such as selecting which object to arrange, and is usually connected to other patterns in a manner that enriches exploration and discovery (Yi et al., 2007). Some games involve objects that are always selected, or the game automatically selects objects for the player. These games may contain the selection pattern, depending on whether the selection involved helps the player keep track of the selected object or not.

Analysis of Games Using These Patterns

In order to better understand how these patterns are used in games, and how these patterns can be used to categorize games, several examples are shown below. Each example game is first described, to give a sense of what players do when they play the game. Then the patterns in the game are described to make it clear why the games contain those patterns. Although games often contain multiple patterns some are obviously more important than others. These patterns are denoted as primary patterns, in that they form the primary way of thinking or playing the game. Other patterns are supplementary, in that they supplement the other patterns or provide an aid to the thinking of the player but are not the primary task of the game. Not all games contain patterns that can be described in this manner. All the patterns in those games are primary, and thus there is no distinction between primary and supplementary. However even this distinction should be considered as a range, since the presence of the same pattern at the same level (primary or supplementary) in multiple games does not imply the pattern is equally utilized in them.

Adventures of Lolo[1]

The game Adventures of Lolo is broken down into many different levels that contain a variety of obstacles. To complete each level players collect all the heart objects. Once these hearts are collected a treasure chest that is somewhere on the level will open and the player must collect what is inside. Once the item inside the chest is collected the player exits through the door and proceeds to the next level. However, to collect all the hearts the player must avoid the many obstacles in the level. The obstacles come in different forms. There are objects that form walls, such as rocks and trees or a river, which the player must walk around. There are enemies that can defeat the player, and force the player to restart the level, as well as enemies that just block the player's path. Both of these enemies may stay in

[1] Copyright 1989 Hal Laboratory, Inc. All Rights Reserved. Adventures of Lolo is part of the Eggerland series, developed between 1985 and 2000 by Hal Laboratory, Inc.

one place, may wander the level in a set pattern, or may chase the player. For some enemies, the player is defeated upon entering their line of sight. There are also boxes that the player can push, but not pull, and otherwise act exactly as a wall.

In most levels the player has a limited number of magic shots, which allows the player to turn enemies into an egg. Shooting the egg will remove it from the level but the enemy will come back, within a few seconds, in the same location or sometimes a different location. Once the enemy has turned into an egg, the player can push it around the same as the player can push boxes around. To complete the game, players must recognize how to use the obstacles in the level to their advantage. For example, there may be a heart close to an enemy that defeats players as soon as players enter its line of sight. Players could get the heart by blocking the enemy's line of sight with a box or with an enemy that was turned into an egg. Although some levels require players to act quickly, possibly to avoid an enemy that is chasing them, players usually have plenty of time to figure out how to collect all of the hearts.

The Adventures of Lolo game contains the patterns of *arranging*, *collecting*, *linking*, and *searching*. First, since the goal of each level is to collect the hearts the *collecting* pattern plays a key role. *Collecting* provides the motivation and objective for each level, and occasionally provides another ability that the player needs to complete the level. The order in which objects are collected may matter, so it is not always possible for players to simply collect all the hearts however they want. Players use the *arranging* pattern in order to move objects around. *Arranging* provides the means for players to avoid obstacles, open new paths through the level, and collect the needed objects.

Searching is required for players to find the correct path through all the obstacles. Both *searching* and *arranging* are interconnected here, because to find the correct route players may need to move objects out of the way or move an object to prevent other enemies from stopping them. Players may also need to figure out the path to an object which, when moved, will open up a path elsewhere. Finally, *linking* is required in order for players to understand how the various objects on the level are interrelated. Players must recognize how enemies could be used in a beneficial way, how to use other obstacles to protect themselves, the order in which to collect the hearts to prevent players from becoming trapped, and so on. Without this understanding, players will not be able to complete any of the levels in the game.

For categorization purposes, Adventures of Lolo focuses on *arranging*, *linking*, and *searching* as primary patterns with *collecting* as a supplementary pattern.

Bejeweled[2]

The game Bejeweled consists of a grid of jewels, each jewel having one color out of a set of possible colors. Players must arrange these jewels such that there are three or more jewels of the same color in a horizontal or vertical line. However, players can only swap two adjacent jewels and are not allowed to move them in any other way. As well, players can only swap jewels if it creates a line of three or more jewels of the same color. When a line of jewels of the same color is created, the jewels disappear and all the jewels above that line in the grid are moved down, with new jewels of randomly chosen colors placed at the top.

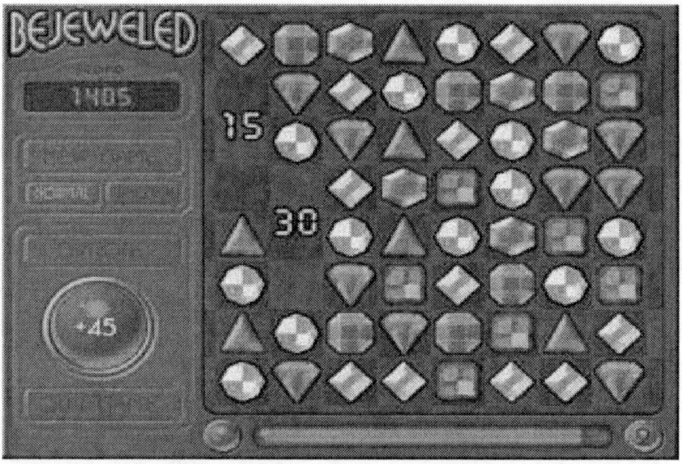

Figure 1. A game of Bejeweled in progress. Two vertical lines of jewels were simultaneously created, and the jewels were just removed from the board. Note that the jewels are of different shape as well as different color.

The primary pattern that exists in this game is *arranging*. This pattern provides the primary way for players to reach the objective of the game: by swapping the positions of the jewels in order to create lines of jewels of the same color. The *comparing* pattern is connected with the *arranging* pattern. Players *compare* the colors of jewels in order to determine which ones to *arrange*. The positions of the jewels are also compared, in order to determine if swapping two jewels will give the desired result.

This game also contains the *composing* pattern, which is the goal of the game. Players are not arranging the jewels blindly; they are arranging the jewels in order

[2] Copyright 2001 – 2007 PopCap Games, Inc. All Rights Reserved. Screenshot used with permission.

to *compose* a horizontal or vertical line. Lastly, this game contains the *selection* pattern, which is connected to how players swap jewels. Players must first select one jewel, which then becomes highlighted to indicate it is the one selected. Players then select another jewel that is adjacent to the selected one and the swap is performed.

For categorization purposes, this game contains *arranging* and *composing* as primary patterns with the *comparing* and *selecting* patterns as supplementary.

Blocksum[3]

The game of Blocksum focuses on a grid of squares. Blocks of varying sizes and shapes slowly rise from the bottom of the screen to fill up the grid. Each block contains a number, which is not necessarily related to its size. For example, a block could have the number two and be as large as two grid squares. However, a block could also have the number four and be one grid square in size. Players are able to combine individual blocks with adjacent ones, causing the new block to be the combined size and shape of the component blocks. As well, combined blocks have a number that is the sum of the numbers of the component blocks. Thus, combining a block with the number three and a block with the number four, both of which are one grid square in size, will create a block with the number seven that is two grid squares in size.

The purpose of the game is to combine blocks in order to eliminate them. Blocks are eliminated when they are adjacent to other blocks with the same number, provided there are at least as many adjacent blocks as the number on the blocks. For example, there must be at least three adjacent blocks each with the number three in order for the blocks to disappear. By removing blocks from the grid, players receive points and create space for the new blocks that continue to rise.

This description suggests that the main pattern of the game is *composing*. The *composing* pattern provides the goal of the game, since players advance by *composing* blocks. This pattern also describes how players actually play the game: by merging blocks together to form new ones. Players that wish to advance far in the game must plan ahead to determine which blocks to compose immediately and which blocks to leave for later in the game.

However, there are other patterns that exist in this game. The *searching* pattern plays a minor role, as players may need to search through the blocks to

---

[3] Copyright 2004 – 2006 Shintaro Sato, Ginger, XOR. http://infotech.rim.zenno.info/products/blocksum/en/.

find specific numbers. The *comparing* pattern is related to this. Players need to *compare* the numbers on the different blocks in order to determine which blocks they want to *compose*. The *selection* pattern is also required in order for players to select the blocks they will compose. All three of these patterns play a relatively minor role in the game, especially compared to the *composing* pattern.

Figure 2. An adaptation of the game Blocksum. The player's cursor is currently on a three block. Note the new blocks rising from below the green line. Also note that the size of the blocks do not always correspond to their number.

Thus, Blocksum can be categorized with the *composing* pattern as its primary pattern and with *comparing*, *searching*, and *selecting* as supporting patterns.

Bookworm[4]

This game provides players with a set of lettered tiles on a grid. Players need to find words within the set of tiles and select the tiles in order to spell out the word. When words are found, the tiles that compose that word are removed from

[4] Copyright 2003 – 2004 PopCap Games, Inc. All Rights Reserved. Screenshot used with permission.

the grid and new letters are added. Some tiles flash red and slowly burn the tiles below them. Should the burning reach the bottom of the grid, the game ends. These burning tiles add a sense of urgency and timing to a game that otherwise does not force any time constraints on the player.

Figure 3. A game of Bookworm in progress. The player has found and highlighted the word "star" and now just needs to submit it. The player could also select the 'E' below the 'R' to form "stare" instead.

The main pattern in this game is the *searching* pattern. The game requires that players continually search through all the letters to find words. Players can search for smaller words, or look for longer words to obtain a higher score. *Composing* also plays a significant role in this game, as players create the words by composing the individual letters together. The *selection* pattern provides a supporting role. Players must select the tiles in order to create words, and the tiles become highlighted whenever they are selected. As well, the order in which the tiles are selected is shown to better describe what word players are forming.

Bookworm can be categorized with *composing* and *searching* as primary patterns, and with the *selecting* pattern as supplementary.

Civilization IV[5]

This game is played on a large grid of tiles, with each tile representing a different type of terrain that provides different benefits. Players take on the role of guiding their civilization to victory in different ways such as culturally, diplomatically, economically, militaristically, or scientifically. Players do this by directing individual units around on the grid in order to explore, defend, or attack an opponent as well as build cities to provide a source of income and area of production for new units. Players must also manage their resources, to ensure they have a steady income and to provide enough funding for research to increase the effectiveness of their civilization.

Figure 4. The main game screen for Civilization 4. The city in the center provides information about its size (9), what it is building (stables), and any defenders (currently one archer). Special resources are highlighted and gridlines are turned on to ease distance calculations for the player.

[5] Sid Meier's Civilization IV: Beyond the Sword copyright 2005 – 2009 Firaxis Games and Take-Two Interactive Software. All Rights Reserved. Screenshots courtesy of Firaxis Games and Take-Two Interactive Software, Inc and used with permission.

One of the primary patterns in this game is the *arranging* pattern. Players arrange units around on the grid to further various goals. However, players do not normally need to find a route for their units as the game always shows the shortest route to the grid destination the player selects. Given that exploration plays an important role, especially early in the game, *searching* is another important pattern that exists. Players must search through the world to find good locations to build, to find their opponents, and to find other bonuses that may be hiding.

In order to move any unit around on the grid, the player must select the unit. The *selection* pattern can be seen when the player selects a unit, as the unit becomes marked to remind the player about which unit is currently selected. Players can direct the selected unit around, but the unit can also be assigned specific instructions.

Players can choose to have a unit automatically explore the map, to try to build roads between their cities, defend a location, and so on. This is an example of the *assigning* pattern.

Figure 5. The same location as in Figure 4, except an economic filter was turned on. Each tile now shows what economic bonuses it provides at a glance, so players do not have to examine each tile to see what is provided. In contrast to Figure 4, the filter to show special resources was turned off.

To build a city in the best location players must take into account what resources are close by, how far away the resources are from the city, what benefits the terrain around the city gives, and if there are any strategic advantages to the location. The same tiles that contain this information also contain cities the player has built and units that the player controls, as well as cities and units of the opposing players. Thus, the *comparing* pattern is used here. Players compare various tile locations in order to determine the optimal location for a city. Players also compare the strength of their civilization with the strengths of their opposing civilizations in areas such as military strength, scientific progress, financial prowess, and so on.

Figure 6. The same location as in Figure 4, but all the filters are turned off except the terrain filter. Now the player only sees the underlying terrain and its improvements, such as roads and the city. The player's units, economic information about game tiles, and the grid are all hidden.

When all the terrain information is displayed it can be very difficult to see where different units are, particularly opposing units. The *filtering* pattern is available in this game through various filters the player can turn on and off. By using these filters, players are able to see the information they require when they want it and can turn off extra information when it begins to clutter the screen. *Probing* can provide extra information that may or may not be available through the filters. Players can probe individual units for extra information, such as probing an archer unit to investigate what other units it could upgrade to. Players can also probe their own cities to get extra information about its production, its resources and income, and so on. The probing functionality is also linked with the in-game help, so that players who require more information on how to use a certain unit can easily access that information.

Thus, Civilization 4 contains the *arranging*, *assigning*, *comparing*, *filtering*, *probing*, *searching*, and *selecting* patterns. No individual pattern is a primary pattern in this game, as the patterns compliment each other and are interconnected. In order to achieve the best score, players should take advantage of the various features each pattern gives – particularly the *comparing*, *filtering*, and *probing* patterns – but the game can be played without significantly considering the *assigning*, *filtering*, and *probing* patterns.

The Incredible Machine[6]

The Incredible Machine is broken down into a large number of puzzles, with each puzzle requiring some different goal. Each puzzle is a Rube Goldberg-inspired machine, which is a complex-looking machine with various parts that performs a simple task such as catching a falling ball or lighting a candle. Some of the pieces create the structure of the machine, such as walls, and are static. Other pieces are more dynamic, such as the freely moving tennis ball or balloon, and react to other pieces as well as cause other pieces to react to them.

For example, a tennis ball could fall on a mouse cage. This causes the mouse inside the cage to start running on a wheel. The wheel is attached to a conveyor belt, which will start to move a bowling ball off the edge of the belt. The bowling ball falls and lands on an incline, causing it to roll down off the bottom of the screen.

Players have access to specific pieces that they need to position somewhere on the level, connect to other existing pieces, and then run their machine to see what happens. If the pieces are attached correctly, the puzzle will be solved. Otherwise, players will have to rearrange the pieces and try again. Due to this, one of the primary patterns of the game is *arranging*. Players need to arrange the game pieces in the correct manner to solve the puzzle. The pieces that are already placed on the

[6] Copyright 1993 – 2002 Activision Blizzard, Inc. and its subsidiary Activision, Inc. All Rights Reserved.

level only form a partial solution. Players cannot arrange those pieces, but must take them into account when placing and arranging the remaining pieces.

Linking is another important pattern in the game. Players need to understand the connection between the various pieces of the game in order to utilize them. For example, one level could contain a cannon and the objective is to put a cannon ball in a basket on the other side of the cannon. Even if the cannon is fired, the cannon ball will move in the direction opposite to the goal. Players need to identify the connection between the cannon and objects that will move a cannon ball, such as an incline or conveyor belt. Players also need to recognize what can be used to fire the cannon, such as a flashlight to generate light and a magnifying glass to focus the light onto the fuse of the cannon. *Linking* is also used when connecting the various pieces of the game. For example, a balloon could be floating freely or it could be connected to a rope that is connected to a gun. When the balloon flies into the air, it will pull the trigger of the gun and fire it.

Other supplementary patterns exist as well in this game, such as *collecting*, *selecting*, and *searching*. The *collecting* pattern exists as a goal in several levels. Players may need to collect a certain number of objects in some manner, such as collecting three basketballs in a bin at the top of the screen. The *selecting* pattern is connected to the arranging pattern, since players must select the object to arrange before it can be moved. The object being moved is always highlighted but when no object is selected, the mouse can be positioned over other objects. Positioning the mouse over an object that can be moved will highlight it, notifying the player that the object can be arranged. Players use the *searching* pattern to plan routes for objects through the level. For example, if a player needs to move a basketball from the top of the screen to the bottom, that player will need to find what paths the basketball can take depending on what obstacles are placed in the way. This task of finding routes through a level is often central to deciding how to arrange the given objects.

For categorization purposes, The Incredible Machine contains *arranging* and *linking* as primary patterns and *collecting*, *selecting*, and *searching* as supplementary patterns.

Legend of Zelda: Ocarina of Time[7]

In this game players direct their representative character through a variety of different environments. Some of these areas are very open and are connected in an

[7] Copyright 1998 – 2007 Nintendo Company, Ltd. All Rights Reserved.

obvious fashion, such as a road leading from a town towards the highlands. Other areas are dungeons or temples and are much more restrictive, containing different puzzles and obstacles that players must try to pass. Throughout the game are numerous different enemies that players must defeat, often by finding and exploiting the enemies' weakness.

Although navigating throughout the environments in the game is usually straightforward, navigating through several of the dungeon levels is often more difficult. It is in these dungeon areas that *searching* is necessary. In one dungeon, for example, walls of fire impede the player's movement but these walls are not visible until the player almost walks into them. Thus, players must walk carefully to see whether a hidden wall exists and try to determine how to reach their destination using this technique. Note that in the areas outside the dungeons it is not necessary to search for paths, as the areas contain very open spaces with the only obstacles being easy to avoid and the paths often clearly marked. Players may also need to search areas for special hidden items, either to advance in the area or as a bonus. Thus, the *collecting* pattern exists in the game. Although in each dungeon area there is one major item the player must find and collect, the game also involves a large number of bonus items that the player can collect but does not need to. For example, one of the major collectable items in the game is a golden token. Early in the game these tokens are hidden in rather obvious places, such as in an alcove by the exit door. Later in the game, they are hidden inside boxes or placed behind walls that the player must break through with a bomb. Searching becomes a key activity then if the player wants to collect all of these items

Linking is one of the primary patterns in this game, with players constantly required to understand how different objects are related. For example, one dungeon shows a locked door, two unlit torches beside the door, and one lit torch elsewhere in the room. Players must make the connection that the torches should be lit, and a hint in the game suggests that the torches are related to the locked door. In order to light the torches, players must again make the connection that by holding a wooden stick close to the torch, it will catch on fire and can be used to light other torches. Once players have discovered this, further puzzles involving the torches are made harder by increasing the difficulty of lighting the torches. Since it is assumed the player knows about lighting the torches, the difficulty then becomes reaching the torches before the player's stick is extinguished. The burning stick could be extinguished by water falling on the player, an enemy knocking the player down, or the stick becoming completely burnt. Also, players may need to perform other actions before they can reach the desired torch, such as first moving a ladder into place.

Arranging is also used in the game for many puzzles. Several dungeon areas involve large blocks that the player can stand on. However, the player can also push and pull these blocks along specific tracks. The player must figure out where to move the blocks in the area in order to open a path to the exit, or in order to reach a higher room. As another example, one dungeon is filled almost entirely with water. The player can swim but cannot dive very far, so it is advantageous to drain some of the water from the dungeon in order to reach other rooms. However, draining the water affects the entire dungeon and many of the rooms in the dungeon contain blocks that float on top of the water. By changing the water level the player will rearrange these blocks and open new paths, while closing others. Players need to consider which room they can get to with the water at what height in order to complete the dungeon.

The patterns of *arranging*, *linking*, and *searching* are often interrelated. For example, in one dungeon the player must cross a pool of water. The player can swim across, but the other side of the pool is too high to climb out of. Instead, the player must make the connection – hence *linking* – that firing a magic arrow will temporarily freeze part of the water and create a platform. However, the player can only create a limited number of these frozen platforms and the platforms do not last forever. Thus, the player must figure out how to *arrange* the ice platforms to discover the route to the other side of the pool.

For categorization, the Legend of Zelda: Ocarina of Time contains *arranging*, *linking*, and *searching* as primary patterns and *collecting* as a supplementary pattern.

Myst[8]

The purpose of the game Myst and its sequels is to investigate the worlds presented in each game. Players must examine objects in the world, try to understand the purpose of the objects, and use that knowledge to complete the various puzzles that arise. The main patterns that exist in this game are *linking* and *searching*. Players must search each of the areas to find clues. Then, players must understand what the clues explain and connect that with the objects around them. However, understanding how different objects work through experimenting with them is sometimes allowed. By *probing* objects in this manner, players are able to gain a better understanding of the meaning and purpose of those objects.

---

[8] Myst™ is the sole property of Cyan Worlds Inc. Copyright 1993/2005 Cyan Worlds, Inc. All Rights Reserved. Screenshots used with permission.

Figure 7. This shows the planetarium's star screen in Myst, where the player enters the date and time using sliding bars on the right to receive a star map on the left.

Figure 8. In this image, the library book is shown to help the player match up the stars shown in the planetarium with a symbol. With the star map from figure 7, the player has found the insect symbol.

For example, in the original Myst game players could visit a planetarium that showed the position of stars at various times of the year. Players could view the star positions for any night of the year, but the purpose of doing so was not clear unless the players read a book in the library that mentioned the position of stars. Players then had to make the connection between the star maps in the library book, the planetarium, and a clue about the correct dates. By choosing the correct dates, the players were given symbolic clues that they then needed to connect with symbols shown on another part of the island. Making that connection allowed them to proceed to the next area of the game.

Thus, Myst is categorized as containing *linking* and *searching* as its primary patterns and *probing* as a supplementary pattern.

Pacman[9]

In this game, players direct their representative character through a maze. Four ghosts chase the player through this maze, and the player must try to avoid the ghosts while attempting to collect all the pellets scattered throughout the maze. There are bonus items that players do not have to collect but are awarded a bonus if they do. There are also power pills that, when collected, allow players to eat the ghosts chasing them. Again, the power pills are not necessary to collect but provide a temporary advantage if players choose to collect them.

Searching is one of the main patterns in this game. Players must find their way through the maze in each level, trying to avoid the constantly moving ghosts, in order to collect all the pellets. The other main pattern in this game is *collecting*. In order to advance in the game, players collect the pellets that are all throughout the level. There are other objects players can collect as well, such as the power pills, but these are not required in order to complete the level. For categorization purposes, Pacman contains *collecting* and *searching* as primary patterns.

Step-By-Step[10]

This game is broken down into multiple different levels. Each level contains several round tiles, in different layouts, that players must walk over. The tiles disappear after the player walks on them a certain number of times, with the exact number depending on the color of the tile. For example, blue tiles disappear after

---

[9] Copyright 1980 – 2007 Namco Bandai Games, Inc. and its subsidiary Namco. All Rights Reserved.

[10] Developed by Manfred Kopp, released under the GNU Public License version 3.

the player walks on them once, green tiles after the player walks on them twice, and so on. The game involves finding a path from the starting location that covers every tile of the level the exact number of times needed to remove the tiles. Since tiles disappear after the player walks on them, each level contains at least one tile that does not disappear. This type of tile is where players must end their route.

This game is almost entirely the *searching* pattern, as players need to find the correct path through each level. Although the correct path may initially seem obvious, it becomes much more difficult once certain tiles must be walked over multiple times. Players must carefully plan their path or else they may become stuck. The *comparing* pattern provides a supporting role in this game. Players compare the colors and types of different tiles to aid in the planning of their route through the level. As no other patterns are used in the game, Step-By-Step is categorized by *searching* as its primary pattern and *comparing* as its supplementary pattern.

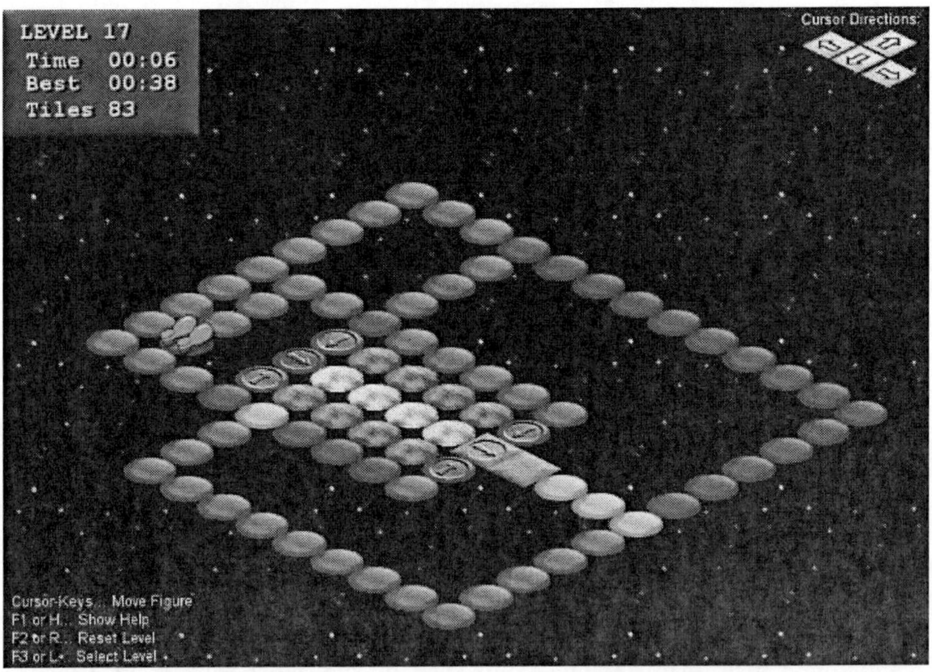

Figure 9. A level in Step-By-Step. Note the yellow tiles, which take three steps to remove, and the tiles with arrows, which force the player to move in that direction.

Tetris[11]

This game involves a single screen with a grid of squares. Blocks of specific shapes and sizes appear at the top of the grid and automatically move down to the bottom of the grid, at a constant speed depending on how far in the game the player has progressed. Players can arrange the falling block by moving it to the left or right, and by rotating it clockwise, but they cannot move any other block. To help the player decide where to arrange the falling block, the next block that will appear is shown on the side of the screen. Whenever the player fills every grid square in a horizontal line, that line of blocks disappears and the player is awarded points. If no new blocks can be added to the central topmost squares of the grid, the game is over and the player has lost. Some versions of the game have a maximum "level" at which the player can reach and win, while others have no winning level and players keep playing to achieve a high score.

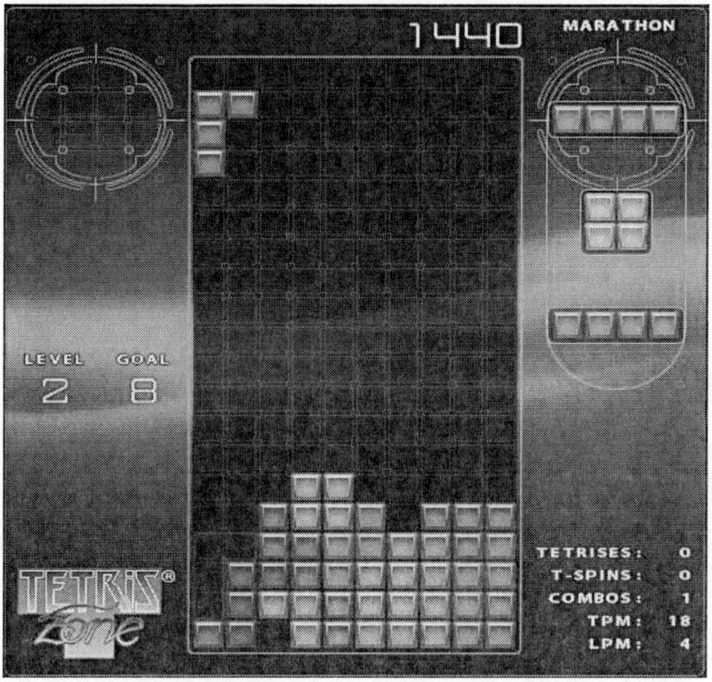

Figure 10. A screenshot from a game of TetrisZone in progress. The blue L-shaped block on the left is the block currently being arranged. Note that the next three blocks that will appear are shown on the right rather than next one block.

[11] Copyright 1985 – 2009 Tetris Holding, LLC. All Rights Reserved.

The primary pattern used in Tetris is the *arranging* pattern. Players must rotate and position the falling block in the best location in order to advance. This can be especially difficult when players are given a block that is not currently useful, and the block must be arranged such that it is used later in the game. This game also uses the *composing* pattern. When players arrange the blocks to form a horizontal line across the grid, the players have composed a row of blocks. *Composition* provides the goal of the game, with *arranging* providing the method by which players accomplish that goal. Thus, Tetris is categorized with both *composing* and *arranging* as its primary patterns.

Conclusion

This chapter presented a strategy for analyzing digital epistemic games, based on ten epistemic patterns. Categorizing games based on broad genres, such as action or adventure, does not provide enough indication about what cognitive benefits the games provide, if any. Taxonomies other than genres exist, but these categorize games in ways that are also not beneficial towards explaining their cognitive benefits. Thus, a categorization based on the presented patterns was discussed. By organizing games based on the epistemic patterns, the cognitive benefits that the games provide become apparent. Thus, these patterns help with choices about which game to use for different educational purposes. This pattern-based strategy is still incomplete, with the potential for other patterns to be discovered. Further research is needed to determine the complete set of patterns as well as a framework for applying these patterns to the design of digital epistemic games.

References

Aarseth, E., Smedstad, S. M., and Sunnanå, L. (2003). A multi-dimensional typology of games. *Proceedings of the* **1***st Digital Games Research Association International Conference,* Utrecht, The Netherlands. 48 – 53.

Abrahamson, D. (2006). Mathematical representations as conceptual composites: Implications for design. *Proceedings of the Twenty Eighth Annual Meeting of the North American Chapter of the International Group for the Psychology of Mathematics Education,* Mérida, Yucatán, México: Universidad Pedagógica Nacional, **2**, 464 - 466.

Alexander, C., Ishikawa, S., and Silverstein, M. (1977). *A pattern language: Towns, buildings, construction.* New York: Oxford University Press, USA.

Alpert, F. (2007). Entertainment software: Suddenly huge, little understood. *Asia Pacific Journal of Marketing and Logistics,* **19**(1), 87 - 100.

Ankerst, M., Berchtold, S., and Keim, D. A. (1998). Similarity clustering of dimensions for an enhanced visualization of multidimensional data. *Proceedings of the IEEE Symposium on Information Visualization 1998,* 52 - 60.

Apperley, T. H. (2006). Genre and game studies: Toward a critical approach to video game genres. *Simulation and Gaming,* **37**(1), 6 - 23.

Bates, M. J. (1986). An exploratory paradigm for online information retrieval. *Proceedings of the* **6***th International Research Forum in Information Science,* London. 91 - 99.

Beck, K., and Cunningham, W. (1987). Using pattern languages for object-oriented programs. *Workshop on the Specification and Design for Object-Oriented Programming (OOPSLA-87),* Florida.

Björk, S., and Holopainen, J. (2005). *Patterns in game design.* Hingham, Massachusetts: Charles River Media.

Björk, S., Lundgren, S., and Holopainen, J. (2003). Game design patterns. *Proceedings of the 1st Digital Games Research Association International Conference,* Utrecht, The Netherlands. 180 - 193.

Björk, S., and Peitz, J. (2007). Understanding pervasive games through gameplay design patterns. *Proceedings of the 3rd Digital Games Research Association International Conference,* University of Toyko, Japan.

Borchers, J. O. (2001). A pattern approach to interaction design. *AI and Society,* **15**(4), 359 - 376.

Buschmann, F., Meunier, R., Rohnert, H., Sommerlad, P., and Stal, M. (1996). *Pattern-oriented software architecture: A system of patterns.* New York: John Wiley and Sons.

Caldwell, N. (2004). Theoretical frameworks for analysing turn-based computer strategy games. *Media International Australia Incorporating Culture and Policy,* **110**, 42-51.

Cox, R. (1999). Representation construction, externalised cognition and individual differences. *Learning and Instruction,* **9**(4), 343 - 363.

Crawford, C. (1984). *The Art of Computer Game Design.* Berkeley, CA: Osborne/McGraw-Hill.

Crawford, C. (2003). *Chris Crawford on Game Design.* Thousand Oaks, CA: New Riders Publishing.

De Aguilera, M., and Mendiz, A. (2003). Video Games and Education (Education in the Face of a "Parallel School"). *Computers in Entertainment,* **1**(1), 10 - 23.

Dearden, A., and Finlay, J. (2006). Pattern languages in HCI: A critical review. *Human-Computer Interaction,* **21**(1), 49 - 102.

Elverdam, C., and Aarseth, E. (2007). Game classification and game design: Construction through critical analysis. *Games and Culture,* **2**(1), 3 - 22.

Entertainment Software Association (ESA). (2009). *Essential Facts about the Computer and Video Games Industry.* Retrieved June 12, 2009 from http://www.theesa.com/facts/pdfs/ESA_EF_2009.pdf

Faisal, S., Attfield, S., and Blandford, A. (2009). A classification of sensemaking representations. *Proceedings of CHI 2009, A Workshop on Sensemaking,* Boston, United States.

Falstein, N. (2002). Better by Design: The 400 Project. *Game Developer Magazine,* **9**(3), 26.

Foster, G., and Stefik, M. (1986). Cognoter: Theory and practice of a colab-orative tool. *Proceedings of the 1986 ACM Conference on Computer-Supported Cooperative Work,* Austin, Texas. 7 - 15.

Fowler, M. (1996). *Analysis patterns: Reusable object models.* Boston, MA: Addison-Wesley Professional.

Gamma, E., Helm, R., Johnson, R., and Vlissides, J. (1995). *Design patterns: Elements of reusable object-oriented software* Addison-Wesley Professional.

Gee, J. P. (2003). *What video games have to teach us about learning and literacy.* New York: Palgrave MacMillan.

Gentner, D., Loewenstein, J., and Hung, B. (2007). Comparison facilitates children's learning of names for parts. *Journal of Cognition and Development,* **8**(3), 285 - 307.

Grossen, B., and Carnine, D. (1990). Diagramming a logic strategy: Effects on difficult problem types and transfer. *Learning Disability Quarterly,* **13**(3), 168 - 182.

Hannafin, M. J., and Hooper, S. R. (1993). Learning principles. In M. Fleming, and W. H. Levie (Eds.), *Instructional message design: Principles from the behavioral and cognitive sciences* (2nd ed., pp. 191 - 231). Englewood Cliffs, NJ: Educational Technology Publications.

Jacobs, J. W., and Dempsey, J. V. (1993). Simulation and gaming: Fidelity, feedback, and motivation. In J. V. Dempsey, and G. C. Sales (Eds.), *Interactive instruction and feedback* (pp. 197 - 227). Englewood Cliffs, NJ: Educational Technology Publications.

Järvinen, A. (2002). Halo and the anatomy of the FPS. *Game Studies,* **2**(1) Retrieved April 18, 2009 from http://www.gamestudies.org/0102/jarvinen/

Kafai, Y. B. (1995). *Minds in play: Computer game design as a context for children's learning*. Hillsdale, NJ: Lawrence Erlbaum Associates.

Kafai, Y. B. (2006). Playing and making games for learning: Instructionist and constructionist perspectives for game studies. *Games and Culture,* **1**(1), 36 - 40.

Kastens, K. A., Liben, L. S., and Agrawal, S. (2008). Epistemic actions in science education. *Proceedings of the International Conference on Spatial Cognition VI: Learning, Reasoning, and Talking about Space,* Freiburg, Germany. 202 - 215.

Kirsh, D. (1995). The intelligent use of space. *Artificial Intelligence,* **73**(1-2), 31 - 68.

Kuhn, D., and Ho, V. (1980). Self-directed activity and cognitive development. *Journal of Applied Developmental Psychology,* **1**(2), 119 - 133.

Lewis, J. P., McGuire, M., and Fox, P. (2007). Mapping the mental space of game genres. *Proceedings of the 2007 ACM SIGGRAPH Symposium on Video Games,* San Diego, CA. 103 - 108.

MacKeracher, D. (2004). *Making Sense of Adult Learning* (2nd ed.) University of Toronto Press.

McNaughton, M., Cutumisu, M., Szafron, D., Schaeffer, J., Redford, J., and Parker, D. (2004). ScriptEase: Generative design patterns for computer role-playing games. *Proceedings of the 19th International Conference on Automated Software Engineering,* Linz, Austria. 88 - 99.

Mor, Y., Winters, N., Cerulli, M., and Björk, S. (2006). Literature review on the use of games in mathematical learning, part I: Design. In *Report of the Learning Patterns for the Design and Deployment of Mathematical Games project.*

Myers, D. (1990). Computer Game Genres. *Play and Culture,* **3**, 286 - 301.

Novak, J. (2007). *Game development essentials: An introduction* (2nd ed.) Delmar Cengage Learning.

Oakes, L. M., and Ribar, R. J. (2005). A comparison of infants' categorization in paired and successive presentation familiarization tasks. *Infancy,* **7**(1),85 - 98.

Ormrod, J. E. (1995). *Human Learning* (2nd ed.). Englewood Cliffs, NJ: Prentice Hall.

Peterson, A. R., and Snyder, P. J. (1998). Using mind maps to teach social problems analysis. *Paper Presented at the 48th Annual Meeting of the Society for the Study of Social Problems,* San Francisco, CA.

Prensky, M. (2000). *Digital game-based learning*. New York, NY: McGraw-Hill.

Randel, J. M., Morris, B. A., Wetzel, C. D., and Whitehill, B. V. (1992). The effectiveness of games for educational purposes: A review of the research. *Simulation and Gaming,* **23**(3), 261 - 276.

Renkl, A. (1997). Learning from worked-out examples: A study on individual differences. *Cognitive Science: A Multidisciplinary Journal,* **21**(1), 1 - 29.

Rollings, A., and Adams, E. (2003). *Andrew Rollings and Ernest Adams on Game Design.* New Riders Games.

Rowley, J. E., and Hartley, R. J. (2008). *Organizing knowledge: An introduction to managing access to information* (4th ed.) Ashgate Publishing, Ltd.

Sadtler, C., Aggarwal, A., Cotignola, D., Grewal, S., Hood, P., Shrimali, S., et al. (2006). *Patterns: Implementing self-service in an SOA environment* (2nd ed.) International Business Machines Corporation.

Smith, E. E., and Medin, D. L. (1981). *Categories and Concepts.* Cambridge, MA: Harvard University Press.

Squire, K. (2006). From content to context: Videogames as designed experience. *Educational Researcher,* **35**(8), 19 - 29.

Stolte, C., Tang, D., and Hanrahan, P. (2002). Polaris: A system for query, analysis, and visualization of multidimensional relational databases. *IEEE Transactions on Visualization and Computer Graphics,* **8**(1), 52 - 65.

Van Eck, R. (2006). Digital game-based learning: It's not just the digital natives who are restless. *Educause Review,* **41**(2), 16 - 30.

Wolf, M. J. P. (2001). Genre and the video game. *The Medium of the Video Game* (pp. 113 - 134) University of Texas Press.

Yang, J., Peng, W., Ward, M. O., and Rundensteiner, E. A. (2003). Interactive hierarchical dimension ordering, spacing and filtering for exploration of high dimensional datasets. *Proceedings of the IEEE Symposium on Information Visualization, 2003,* Seattle, WA. 105 – 112.

Yi, J. S., ah Kang, Y., Stasko, J. T., and Jacko, J. A. (2007). Toward a deeper understanding of the role of interaction in information visualization. *IEEE Transactions on Visualization and Computer Graphics,* **13**(6), 1224 - 1231.

Zagal, J. P., Mateas, M., Fernández-Vara, C., Hochhalter, B., and Lichti, N. (2005). Towards an ontological language for game analysis. *Proceedings of the 2nd Digital Games Research Association International Conference,* Vancouver, Canada. 3 - 14.

In: Computer Games
Editors: A. Soria et al, pp. 85-110
ISBN: 978-1-60876-658-1

Chapter 3

PATTERNS OF DIGITAL GAME PLAYING IN EARLY ADOLESCENCE: RELATIONS TO DEPRESSED MOOD

Marjut Wallenius*[1,*]*, Raija-Leena Punamäki*[1]*,
***Clas-Håkan Nygård*[2] *and Arja Rimpelä*[2]**
[1] Department of Psychology, University of Tampere and Research Unit of Pirkanmaa Hospital District, Tampere University Hospital
[2] Tampere School of Public Health, University of Tampere, Finland

Abstract

The study examined how digital game playing patterns were related to depressed mood. Altogether 478 Finnish 10- and 13-year-old schoolchildren reported intensity of their digital game playing, game genres and game violence, motives for playing, play companions, depressive and anxiety symptoms and positive feelings. K-mean cluster analysis revealed six digital game playing patterns with significant gender but no age differences. Participants representing the task-oriented pattern had a significantly higher mean in depression and anxiety symptoms than the non-players or players representing sports and racing, and violent imagination patterns when sex and age were controlled. As hypothesized, depressed mood was associated with playing non-violent problem-solving type of games for ritualized purposes and social compensation but contrary to earlier

* E-mail address: marjut.wallenius@elisanet.fi. Phone: 358 3 355 111; fax: 358 3 3551 7345. Please address correspondence to Marjut Wallenius, Department of Psychology, FIN - 33014 University of Tampere, Finland.

results not with high intensity of playing. It is suggested that the problem-solving type of games may offer such rewarding and slightly effortful activity which is suitable for self-regulation of depressed mood.

Keywords Children; Adolescents; Digital game playing; Depressed mood

Introduction

For children and adolescents, digital game playing is one of the first ways to make contact with information and communication technology. Digital gaming is a natural part of everyday life especially for the majority of western school-aged children and adolescents, particularly for boys (Christakis, Ebel, Rivara, and Zimmerman, 2004; Ho and Lee, 2001). Durkin and Barber (2002) show that digital games can be a positive feature of healthy adolescence. Findings on traditional media show that mood management and seeking cognitive and emotional balance are some of the main uses and gratifications (Bryant and Zillmann, 1984; Zillmann, 1988). Likewise, digital games seem to have the potential to serve such emotion-regulation purposes. The interactive nature of playing and the active role of the player render digital games very effective in eliciting experiences and excitement (Griffiths and Hunt, 1998) and thus altering mood states (Bryant and Davies, 2006). In this research we are interested in the different patterns of digital game playing and their association with depressed mood among children and adolescents. With digital games we refer to games played on the computer, Internet, television or game consoles.

Digital Game Playing and Emotion Regulation

In general, by emotion regulation individuals aim at regaining a desired emotional state. They use various ways and strategies to influence their mood and feelings toward the preferred direction by making 'changes in the input to the emotional system' (Hoeksma, Oosterlaan, and Schipper, 2004, p. 355). These regulating processes include both inner homeostatic mechanisms and interaction with social and physical environment (Dodge and Garber, 1991). In children's and adolescents' self-regulation the self-initiated, goal-oriented and effortful—though not necessarily conscious—nature is emphasized as a distinction from an external intervention, such as an adult giving consolation to an adolescent (Eisenberg and Spinrad, 2004).

During child development new and more complex uses of environmental objects and interactions with other people emerge to regulate emotional states (Diener and Mangelsdorf, 1999). Because emotions emerge in transaction with the environment, selecting the environments being entered allows children and adolescents an effective way of regulating emotions. Avoiding a situation where an undesired emotion is likely to become activated, or choosing the one in which desired emotions will be likely, is conceptualized as an affect-dependent stimulus arrangement (Zillmann and Bryant, 1985) and nichepicking (Campos, Frankel, and Camras, 2004). Nichepicking offers an individual the possibility of emotional self-regulation at the very outset. Research provides evidence that entering a particular place is followed by mood change (Kerr and Tacon, 1999; Staats, Gatersleben, and Hartig, 1997). Digital games can be seen as virtual environments which children and adolescents can choose and which, therefore, can serve their emotional regulation. We suggest that digital games as virtual environments are able to serve an emotion regulation function when a child or adolescent is in a depressed mood.

Games as virtual environments offer special features. The visually realistic scenes, interactive nature of playing, and active role of the player provide a child or adolescent possibilities to become immersed (Csikszentmihalyi, 1988) in the new worlds, identify with the game characters, and find electronic friendships (Selnow, 1984). The many uses and gratifications offered by digital games make playing a pleasurable and meaningful experience in and of itself and in this sense the resulting emotions are based on hedonics (Campos et al., 2004). The mere immersion in gaming activity helps push external attention away from the inner states, and thus decreases negative feelings (Pennebaker and Brittingham, 1982). In this study we examine which kind of pattern of playing digital games is associated with depressed mood. The patterns of game playing are represented by the intensity of playing, game genres, motives for playing, game violence, and game companions.

Patterns of Playing Digital Games and Depressed Mood

Intensity of playing. Some research is available on the association between digital gaming and psychological distress. Results are discrepant with some showing neutral associations (Estalló, Masferrer, and Aguirre, 2001) while according to others, gamers are rated even lower in anxiety or depressed mood than non-gamers (Durkin and Barber, 2002). Yet, very intensive playing (Durkin and Barber, 2002), which may even reach features of addiction (Liu, Su, and He,

2001), has been related to negative mood. Adolescents who are both problem gamblers and high-frequency digital game players use these activities as a means of managing their mood states as well, aiming at, e.g., higher arousal or relaxation (Wood, Gupta, Derevensky, and Griffiths, 2004). On the basis of earlier results we hypothesize that higher levels of depressed mood are associated with more intensive digital game playing.

Game genres. Prior results show that engaging in a pleasant, rewarding activity that requires some effort is an effective technique to regulate mood, whereas passive distracting behaviour, such as watching television is less successful (Fichman, Koestner, Zuroff, and Gordon, 1999). One reason may be that effortful and pleasant activity has been found to have high intervention potential to interrupt cognitive rehearsal or rumination that are typical of depressed mood (Bryant and Davies, 2006). As suggested by Bryant and Davies (2006) digital games may have high intervention potential because the interactive nature of games demands both tactile and cognitive engagement of the player. Accordingly, we hypothesize that higher levels of depressed mood are associated with selecting game genres which have higher intervention potential, that is, games demanding higher levels of effort and interactivity.

Digital games are usually directed at male cultures, and girls and women read them differently, from the subject positions of their own world (Yates and Littleton, 1999). The established social norms and sex-role expectations make it more acceptable for males than for females to play and to use game-playing situations as a means of social interaction (Lucas and Sherry, 2004). Therefore, it is important to study if there are gender differences in e.g. game genres selected for emotion regulation purposes. Because the male culture is over-represented in digital games, girls have limited possibilities to find games not directed at males.

Motives for playing. Depressed children may lack effective strategies, such as problem solving or cognitive restructuring, to ameliorate the negative affect (De Cuyper, Timbremont, Braet, De Backer, and Wullaert, 2004). On the contrary, depressed individuals are prone to use dysfunctional emotion-focused coping, like passive avoidance, denial or escape (Min'er and Dejun, 2001; Silk, Steinberg, and Morris, 2003). Research on TV viewing suggests that people use similar emotion-focused coping strategies also as everyday means of managing mood states. For instance, people select certain types of TV programmes to escape depressed mood (Kubey and Csikszentmihalyi, 1990; Potts and Sanchez, 1994) and loneliness (Perse and Rubin, 1990). Interestingly, the mere amount of exposure time to TV viewing is not related to depression (Potts and Sanchez, 1994). We may expect that motives for digital game playing among children and adolescents in depressed mood reflect similar escaping, compensatory and emotion regulation purposes as was found concerning TV viewing

The two main orientations to playing digital games, instrumental and ritualized (Wallenius, Rimpelä, Punamäki, and Lintonen, in press), resemble the motivational structures found among users of traditional media (Rubin, 1993, 1994). Instrumental motives refer to active and purposive orientation where the content of the games, playing activity and skill development as well as social communication around games are important (Wallenius et al., in press). These motives indicate that gaming is pleasurable in itself, and the emotional significance of the situation is based on hedonics (Campos et al., 2004). Ritualized motives, instead, stem from the current undesirable status of the individual, and reveal striving for mood management (e.g. escape worries, fill empty time) and improvement of one's own condition to a more pleasurable one (e.g. recover) (Wallenius et al., in press). Thus, adolescents' ritualized digital game playing motives reflect emotion regulation by means of emotion-focused coping (Lazarus, 1993) through nichepicking (Campos et al., 2004) when an adolescent moves into a virtual environment where desired emotions are more likely. We hypothesize that higher levels of depressed mood are associated with higher levels of ritualized motives for playing digital games.

Game violence. Mood and psychological well-being may influence both motives to select gaming over other possible activities and to select playing a specific game genre, but it may also influence the way individuals respond psychologically to the content of a specific game. Message-behavioural affinity refers to the degree of similarity between communication content and a person's affective state, suggesting that similar affective content has less potential to alter the person's mood (Bryant and Davies, 2006). Congruently, Zillmann and Bryant (1985) proposed that persons have the lowest preference for content with similarity to their negative mood. The majority of the most popular games among children and adolescents contain violent acts designed to inflict injury or death to another character (Smith, Lachlan, and Tamborini, 2003). No research is available on how depressive or anxious children interpret the violent content of digital games. In general, human beings show aversive reaction to violence (Bartholow, Bushman, and Sestir, 2006). We suppose that depressive and anxious children and adolescents regard violent content as aversive and unable to alter their negative mood, and consequently avoid playing them. Thus, we hypothesize that higher levels of depressed mood are associated with playing non-violent games.

Game companions. When playing digital games the adolescents have the possibility to be in parasocial (Rubin, Perse, and Powell, 1985) but computer-mediated and impersonal interaction with game charactersis (Sproull and Kiesler,

1991). On the other hand, the game playing situation may be social in nature when adolescents play with e.g. friends or family members. Earlier results show that game players do not differ or they have even more intensive friendships than non-players (Colwell, Grady, and Rhaiti, 1995; Durkin and Barber, 2002). Other results show, however, that digital game playing is related to poor friendship quality among girls (Punamäki, Wallenius, Hölttö, Nygård, and Rimpelä, in press). We also know that depression is strongly associated with perceived social isolation (Hawthorne, 2008). Thus, we hypothesize that although digital game playing has the potential to be social in nature, higher levels of depressed mood are associated with not many game companions and seeking social compensation in digital game playing.

The Current Study

In the present study, we were interested in examining how the patterns of digital game playing are associated with depressed mood among 10- and 13-year-old children and adolescents. The age groups 10 and 13 were selected on the basis of developmental salience in transition from middle childhood to adolescence during which important changes in depression and emotion regulation occur (Steinberg and Morris, 2001; Twenge and Nolen-Hoeksema, 2002). Depressive symptoms become increasingly prevalent during adolescence, especially among girls after the age of 13 years (Galambos, Leadbeater, and Barker, 2004). The period of adolescence sets new challenges for emotion regulation.

A person-oriented approach using clustering-by-cases method is a useful tool for examining 'naturally occurring' gamer groups. Clustering-by-cases aims at identifying groups of individuals who share similar features within a particular group, but who differ from other groups according to the criteria variables. Several variables are simultaneously considered when forming groups. Moreover, clustering-by-cases analysis also provides information about how big a proportion of the sample belongs to a particular group.

The research tasks we addressed included the following:

1) To identify digital game playing patterns among children and adolescents according to intensity (frequency and duration), game genres, motives, game violence, and game companions.
2) To examine how digital game playing patterns are associated with depressed mood (depressive and anxiety symptoms and positive feelings).

We hypothesized that there are differences between the patterns of digital game playing according to the level of depressed mood. More specifically, we hypothesized that higher levels of depressed mood are associated with a) more intensive digital game playing, b) game genres demanding higher levels of effort and interactivity, c) higher levels of ritualized motives for playing, d) playing non-violent games, and e) fewer game companions and seeking social compensation in digital game playing.

Methods

Participants

A total of 689 schoolchildren (323 in the 4th and 366 in the 7th grade) from seven schools (5 primary and 2 secondary schools) in a major city in Finland were asked to participate in a classroom survey in spring 2004. Of the 478 children participating 222 were in the 4th grade (mean age = 10.27, SD = 0.47) and 256 in the 7th grade (mean age = 13.28, SD = 0.46) and 54.4% (260) were girls and 45.6% (218) were boys. There were no age group differences between boys and girls, χ^2 (1, 478) = 1.31, p = .86. The participation rate was thus 69.4%, and the dropouts were due to refusals and unwillingness to provide informed consent on the part of either the parents or the schoolchildren. The mean response rate was 68.7% among the 4th graders (70.7% among girls and 66.4% among boys) and 69.9% among the 7th graders (75.3% among girls and 64.7% among boys). The response rate varied between schools from 39% to 92%. Attrition analysis to compare characteristics of participants and dropouts was not possible, because no socio-economic records were available.

Study Procedure

Data were gathered as part of a wider survey which also contained questions not relevant for this study. Before data collection the approval of the Ethical Committee of Pirkanmaa Hospital District (Code Nr. R04013) was acquired. Permission was also obtained from the school principals. At each school an information meeting was held, usually for each participating class separately, where the purpose of the study was explained and an information letter was delivered both for the schoolchildren and their parents. Written consents for the participation were obtained from all children willing to participate, and their parent/guardian. Because of the great number of questions in the whole survey, the participants were asked to complete the questionnaire in two parts, given with a one-week interval in between. Each session took place in the classroom during a lesson, lasted about one hour, and was preceded by instructions of one of the researchers who also remained present for any inquiries.

Measures

Intensity of digital game playing. Earlier findings show that the validity of self-reported estimates of time use is moderately high when compared to the diary method (Greenberg, Eastin, Skalski, Cooper, Levy, and Lachlan, 2005; van der Voort and Vooijs, 1990). To measure *game frequency* participants were presented with three similar question patterns on a) playing TV or console games and b) playing computer or Internet games. In the first pattern, participants reported how often they generally play on a 5-point scale from (0) never, (1) less than once a week, (2) on 1-2 days a week, (3) on 3-5 days a week to (4) almost every day. A mean variable was constructed using the frequency of playing TV or console games and computer or Internet games.

Second, participants reported the *game time* they generally play digital games *during school days* and, third, *during weekend days* according to the following alternatives: (0) not at all, (1) less than an hour, (2) 1-2 hours, (3) 3-4 hours and (4) more than 4 hours a day. A mean variable was constructed using the times of playing TV or console games and computer or Internet games.

Digital game genres. Participants were asked what kind of computer, Internet, TV or console games they usually play of the following categories: (a) Platform (running and jumping on platforms), (b) Adventure (fantasy settings in which the player can escape to other worlds and take on new identities), (c) Sports (simulate sports such as golf, ice hockey), (d) Simulation (realistic simulation of activities such as flying), (e) Strategy (quite demanding and often violent games such as war games where the player has to develop strategies and tactics), (f) Action, fighting, shooting (involve physical violence, shooting and killing), (g) Racing (simulates motor sports like Formula 1 racing), (h) Role-playing (a kind of adventure where the player assumes the roles of characters and determines their action) , (i) Puzzle (brainteaser that requires active thinking), (j) Edutainment (involve learning new information or inventing new ways to use information), (k) Dance mat (requires physical exercise to the beat of music), (l) Games in which a video camera is used, and (m) Others (e.g. Ermi and Mäyrä, 2003). The participants were requested to answer each category using the response alternatives: (0) not at all, (1) sporadically, (2) often, and (3) very often.

A principal component analysis with varimax rotation revealed four principal components with eigenvalues greater than 1.0, and accounting for 60% of the variance. The first principal component represented imagination games like action, adventure, and role playing games; the second represented mainly sports and racing games; the third represented task performance games like puzzles, platform and edutainment games; and the last principal component represented games requiring additional equipment, such as a dancing mat or video camera. Cronbach's alpha coefficients were .73, .58, .56, and .53, respectively. Separate analyses by gender and age resulted in extraction of the same four components. Based on the analysis of all responses, the principal component scores were calculated for later analysis using the regression method.

Digital game playing motives. Reasons to play digital games were asked with the question "What is most important for you in game playing" and measured by a list of 13 possible motives compiled from previous research on digital game playing motives (Ermi and Mäyrä, 2003; Wallenius et al., in press) and modified for the present study (e.g. "In games I experience humour and have fun", "I play to recover and to relax", and "In games, I can use and develop my game skills, speed, and smartness"). For each item in the list, respondents rated the importance of that motive on a 4-point scale from (0) not at all important, (1) slightly important, (2) quite important to (3) very important.

A principal component analysis with oblimin rotation was chosen because we expected the motive components to correlate. This procedure revealed three principal components with eigenvalues greater than 1.0, and accounting for 61% of the variance. The first principal component was interpreted to represent instrumental motives (e.g. experience new, meet game characters, possibility for control and power, build and create, humour and fun, topics for conversation), the second social compensation motives (e.g. not to feel so lonely, experience success), and the third ritualized motives (e.g. pass the time, recover, escape) (see Rubin, 1993, 1994). Cronbach's alpha coefficients were .87, .63, and .69, respectively. The correlation between the first and second principal component was .32, and between the second and third .45. Separate analyses by gender and age resulted in extraction of the similar three components. Based on the analysis of all responses, the principal component scores were calculated for later analysis using the regression method.

Violence in games. Participants indicated how often the games they play contain violence (such as killing, fighting, attacks, kicking) on a 4-point scale from (0) not at all, (1) sporadically, (2) often to (3) very often (cf. Slater, Henry, Swain, and Andersson, 2003).

Game companions. With whom games were usually played was indicated by selecting all the suitable options from: (0) do not play at all, (1) alone, (2) with father, (3) with mother, (4) with sister, (5) with brother, (6) with buddy or friend, and (7) with some other person.

Depressed mood. Depressed mood was assessed by depressive and anxiety symptoms. Six items indicating depressiveness were derived from Child Depression Inventory (CDI; Kovacs, 1992), and include items such as 'I am sad', 'I cry easily and often' and 'I feel that nobody cares about me'. Five items indicating anxiety and fears were from Screen for Anxiety Related Emotional Disorders (5-item SCARED; Birmaher, 1999) and included items such as 'I fear that something bad will happen to me', 'Many things bother me', and 'I fear that I will fail'. The participants estimated how well the descriptions fitted them on a 5-point scale: (0) not at all, (1) somewhat, (2) quite well, (3) well, and (4) very well. The depressiveness and anxiety scales have been validated in a Finnish intervention study among children in depressive families (Solantaus and Toikka, 2005). A mean variable of depressed mood was formed, and it had sufficient internal consistency of Cronbach's alpha .79.

Positive feelings. Positive feelings and experiences were measured by six items derived from the resources scale by Rutter and Graham (1966). Items were e.g. 'I am as competent as others', 'I am satisfied with myself', and 'Many things make me glad and I laugh easily'. The participants estimated how well the descriptions fitted them on the same 5-point scale. A mean variable of positive feelings was formed (Cronbach's alpha .83).

Results

Descriptive Results

Of all the 478 participants 41 (8.6%; 13 girls and 1 boy age 10, and 24 girls and 3 boys age 13) did not play digital games. In addition, 49 game players, mainly girls and 13-year-olds (16 girls and 2 boy age 10, and 27 girls and 4 boys age 13) did not answer the game motive questions. These non-respondents played digital games seldom (M = .91; SD = .65) and short times only (M = .45; SD = .67), which explains why motives for playing digital games were unimportant to them. Thus, 388 digital game players (180 girls and 208 boys) were included in the final analysis.

Table 1 shows the means and standard deviations for each of the variables and the percentage rates of game companions for girls and boys in both age groups. To examine sex and age differences a 2 (sex) x 2 (age-group) multivariate analysis of variance (MANOVA) was performed on all the variables except for play companions. The results based on Wilk's Lambda yielded a significant main effect for sex ($F [12, 373] = 44.85$, $p < .001$) and age group ($F [12, 373] = 14.41$, $p < .001$). No sex x age group interactions were found.

Univariate analysis further indicated that boys played digital games more often ($F [1, 384] = 122.93$, $p < .0001$) and spent more time in playing ($F [1, 384] = 120.83$, $p < .0001$) than girls. Among the different game genre components, boys ($F [1, 384] = 104.40$, $p < .0001$) and 13-year-olds ($F [1, 384] = 16.97$, $p < .0001$) showed a preference for games involving imagination. Boys also preferred sports and racing ($F [1, 384] = 103.82$, $p < .0001$), whereas girls ($F [1, 384] = 18.55$, $p < .0001$) and 10-year-olds ($F [1, 384] = 12.58$, $p < .0001$) played more task-performing games. Both instrumental ($F [1, 384] = 61.68$, $p < .0001$), ritualized ($F [1, 384] = 18.90$, $p < .0001$) and social compensation ($F [1, 384] = 18.44$, $p < .0001$) motives were more important for boys than for girls. Social compensation motives were more important to the younger ($F [1, 384] = 25.44$, $p < .0001$) participants and ritualized motives ($F [1, 384] = 32.65$, $p < .0001$) to the older ones. Violent games were played more by boys ($F [1, 384] = 199.84$, $p < .0001$) than girls and by the older children ($F [1, 384] = 32.99$, $p < .0001$) more than the younger children.

Regarding game companions, we found that children and adolescents played digital games mainly with peers and friends or alone. The second most frequent companions were brothers and sisters, and the least frequent father or mother. The 13-year-olds played alone more than the younger ones. A greater amount of girls (32%) than boys (19%) reported playing only alone regardless of age.

Table 1. Means and Standard Deviation of Variables and Percentage Rates of Game Companions by Sex and Age

	Girls				Boys			
	10 years		13 years		10 years		13 years	
Variable	M	SD	M	SD M	SD	M		SD
Intensity of playing1								
Game frequency a	1.44	0.87	1.31	0.75	2.30	0.88	2.36	0.87
Game time a	0.88	0.61	0.81	0.47	1.56	0.74	1.61	0.75
Game genres2								
Imagination a, b	-0.55	0.61	-0.26	0.57	0.29	1.05	0.74	1.08
Sports a	-0.43	0.64	-0.45	0.66	0.51	0.99	0.48	1.12
Task performance a, b 0.42 Equipment		1.03 1.14	0.11 0.11	0.91 1.18	0.03 0.16	1.07 1.09	-0.36 -	0.89
b 0.13 Game motives2							0.30	0.56
Instrumental a -0.42		0.87	-0.37	0.88	0.40	1.01	0.30	0.95
Social compensation a, b -0.03		0.87 0.95	-0.40 0.09	0.81 0.96	0.50 -0.04	1.09 0.96	-0.10	0.99
Ritualized a, b -0.54							0.42	0.89
Game violence1 a, b 0.28		0.56	0.56	0.75	1.23	0.90	1.87	0.87
Depressive and anxiety symptoms1, a,		0.58 0.77	0.92 2.72	0.64 0.86	0.56 2.74	0.49 0.84	0.68	0.51
b 0.82 Positive feelings1 2.91							2.74	0.72
Game companions 3		%		%	%		%	
Alone		42		40	55		53	
Father or mother		5		12	4		4	
Brother or sister		34		32	34		24	
Peer or friend		54		65	44		68	
Other person		1		5	4		4	

Note. n (10-year-old girls) = 94, n (13-year-olds girls) = 86, n (10-year-old boys) = 96, n (13-year-old boys) = 112. [1] Range 0-4, except for game violence 0-3. [2] Regression score. [3] The column sums are more than 100 because respondents could mention several persons.

In all cases, a higher score indicates a higher level of the variable. a = sex difference significant at $p < .01$, b = age difference significant at $p < .001$.

For later analysis the respondents were classified in three categories: those who only played alone, those who also played with family members, and those who also played with peers or friends.

With regard to depressive and anxiety symptoms girls (F [1, 384] = 19.47, p < .0001) showed higher levels than boys and 13-year-olds (F [1, 384] = 4.02, p < .05) higher levels than10-year-olds (Table 3). Concerning positive feelings, no sex or age differences were found.

Digital Game Playing Patterns

To identify the different digital game playing patterns among children and adolescents a cluster analysis was used. We submitted the standardized scores measuring intensity of playing and game violence, and the game motive and game genre principal component scores to *k*-means cluster analysis. This non-hierarchical data analysis technique uses an iterative algorithm to partition individual cases into a pre-specified number (*k*) of clusters, in a manner that maximizes between-cluster differences and minimizes within-cluster variance in the scores used (Breckenridge, 1989). We examined four-, five- and six-cluster solutions, retaining the last for further analysis. The six-cluster solution was chosen to capture nuances in the profiles while still maintaining sufficiently large cell-sizes for meaningful analysis.

Descriptive data of each cluster on the ten clustering variables are presented in Table 2. The table also gives the contribution of each variable to the cluster solution (F-values). The six clusters identified were as follows. Due to the small number of members in *Equipment* cluster 3 (n = 7) this cluster was excluded from the analyses.

Cluster 1 participants (34 %) represented the *Low-intensity* pattern. They played least of all, only short periods every now and then. They did not play much of any of the game genres, and violent games less than any other group. They had no special motivation to play.

Cluster 2 participants (14 %), representing the *Task-oriented* pattern, played only slightly more than the low-intensity group, but the clusters differed both by game genre and motive. Members of cluster 2 focused solely on non-violent task performance type of games, like puzzles, platform, and edutainment. Their game motives involved both ritualized purposes and as social compensation.

Table 2. Cluster Means (Standard Deviations) for Digital Game Playing Variables (z-scores)

	Game playing cluster						
	1 Low intensity (n = 132)	2 Task oriented (n = 56)	3 Equipment (n = 7)	4 Violent imagination (n = 65)	5 Sports and racing (n = 85)	6 High intensity (n = 43)	
Variable	**M (SD)**	**M(SD)**	**M(SD)**	**M(SD)**	**M(SD)**	**M(SD)**	**F (5, 382)1**
Intensity of playing							
Game frequency	-0.45 (0.58)a	-0.14 (0.60)b	0.21 (0.84)	0.49 (0.61)c	0.81 (0.73)d	1.38 (0.77)e	74.69
Game time	-0.49 (0.47)a	-0.08 (0.62)b	-0.02 (0.79)	0.52 (0.56)c	0.61 (0.72)c	1.69 (0.86)d	95.58
Game genres							
Imagination	-0.58 (0.50)a	-0.33 (0.62)ab	0.14 (0.93)	1.21 (0.75)c	-0.09 (0.66)b	1.38 (0.98)c	100.18
Sports	-0.47 (0.57)a	-0.07 (0.90)b	0.17 (0.96)	-0.53 (0.68)a	1.16 (0.82)c	0.58 (0.98)d	61.23
Task performance	-0.12 (0.64)a	1.10 (1.10)b	0.42 (1.20)	-0.58 (0.68)c	-0.21 (0.83)ac	0.43 (1.36)d	26.98
Equipment	0.01 (0.72)a	-0.14 (0.72)ab	5.17 (1.68)	-0.12 (0.58)ab	-0.30 (0.53)b	0.17 (1.04)a	74.05
Game motives							
Instrumental	-0.73 (0.68)a	0.20 (0.87)b	0.59 (0.89)	0.62 (0.94)d	-0.11 (0.75)b	1.16 (0.64)c	53.32
Social compensation	-0.52 (0.59)a	0.51 (0.98)b	0.05 (1.17)	-0.06 (0.92)c	-0.07 (0.92)c	1.13 (1.10)d	28.64
Ritualized	-0.77 (0.69)a	0.61 (0.91)b	0.12 (0.75)	0.37 (0.87)bc	0.08 (0.88)c	0.83 (0.79)b	41.86
Violence in games	-0.57 (0.49)a	-0.44 (0.67)a	0.41 (1.40)	1.05 (0.88)b	0.46 (0.88)c	1.11 (0.84)b	67.78

[1] $p < .001$.

Note. The means within rows not sharing the same superscript differed significantly (Tukey HSD, $p < .05$) from each other. Due to the small number of members in cluster 3 Equipment this cluster was excluded from the ANOVA and is thus without superscripts.

Table 3. The Means (Standard Deviations) on Mood for Digital Game Playing Pattern and Non-Players

		Game playing patterns					
		1	2	3	4	5	6
Variable	Non-players (n = 41)	Low intensity (n = 132)	Task oriented (n = 56)	Equipment (n = 7)	Violent imagination (n = 65)	Sports and racing (n = 85)	High intensity (n = 43)
Depression-anxiety M (SD)	0.64 (0.39)	0.80 (0.59)	0.98 (0.64)	0.65 (0.50)	0.59 (0.52)	0.58 (0.39)	0.78 (0.66)
Positive feelings M (SD)	2.94 (0.55)	2.76 (0.81)	2.83 (0.78)	3.00 (0.97)	2.77 (0.85)	2.79 (0.80)	2.72 (0.68)

Digital Game Playing Patterns and Depressed Mood

To investigate how the groups representing different digital game playing patterns and the non-players would differ in their psychological distress and positive feelings, one-way ANOVAs with Tukey HSD comparisons ($p < .05$) were conducted (Table 3). Because of the small number of members in *Equipment* cluster 3 ($n = 7$) this cluster was excluded from the analyses. The results showed that the groups differed significantly according to depression and anxiety symptoms (F [5, 416] = 5.36, $p < .0001$) but non-significantly according to positive feelings (F [5, 416] = .44, $p = .824$). The mean of depression and anxiety symptoms was highest in the *Task-oriented* and lowest in the *Sports and racing* gamer group. The *Task-oriented* gamers had significantly higher levels of depression and anxiety symptoms than the non-players and the members in the *Sports and racing* and the *Violent imagination* gamer group. The mean of depression and anxiety symptoms in the *Sports and racing* gamer group was also significantly lower than the mean in the *Low-intensity* group.

To examine if the differences in depression and anxiety symptoms between the game playing patterns were explained by sex or age differences, we carried out ANOVA for depressive and anxiety symptoms in which sex and age were entered as covariates. The results showed that the group differences based on clusters and non-players remained about the same as in the preceding analysis (F [5, 414] = 4.01, $p = .001$).

We then conducted a second ANOVA for depressive and anxiety symptoms with sex and age as covariates, and with the inclusion of the missing group of game players who did not express any motives to play. This analysis revealed that the level of depression and anxiety symptoms in the *Task-oriented* cluster was also significantly (F [6, 468] = 3.51, $p = .002$) higher than in the missing group ($M = .76$; $SD = .61$; in planned comparisons $p = .009$).

Conclusion

The present study examined what kind of digital game playing patterns 10- and 13-year-old children and adolescents have and how the game playing patterns are associated with depressed mood. We identified six digital game playing patterns. The patterns differed significantly by sex and, as hypothesized, according to depressed mood.

Out of the six digital game playing patterns the low-intensity cluster was the largest, including one third of the respondents. It represented children and adolescents, mainly girls, who were not very inclined to playing. Although, in these respects the task-oriented cluster shared very similar features, these clusters differed essentially. While for members in the low-intensity group digital game playing was not important at all, members in the task-oriented cluster were inclined to task performance type of games and perceived ritualized motives and social compensation as important reasons to play. Interestingly, members in the task-oriented cluster expressed higher scores for depressed mood than any other gamers and non-players.

In the very small cluster of specialized gamers, the intensity of playing was quite low but they played new kinds of games which demanded additional equipment and skills. For instance, games using a dancing mat represent a novel and physically active form of playing and a special game culture has grown around the game (Höysniemi, 2006).

The remaining three clusters were predominantly male. The high-intensity cluster can be described as the opposite to the low-intensity cluster, and members in this group spent much time on playing. They were interested in all game genres but favoured especially violence and imagination. Their instrumental motives revealed that gaming was important in itself, but gaming was also a means for ritualized purposes, such as to pass time. A noteworthy finding was that, for the high-intensity gamers, the social meaning of digital game playing was more important than for any other group.

Members of the violent imagination game cluster played almost as much as the high-intensity gamers but differed from the latter cluster in their more restricted interest in only one game genre. Moreover, they used gaming for instrumental and ritualized purposes to a lesser extent and gaming did not have any social meaning for them.

Members in the sports and racing cluster played even more frequently than the violent imagination gamers. However, gaming did not seem to have any important motivational function in their lives.

The results showed that game playing patterns are differentiated by gender. Girls' repertoire is narrower than that of boys. Interestingly enough, a small proportion of girls was found in every male cluster, and vice versa, a small proportion of boys was seen in clusters with female majority, i.e. these boys and girls deviated from the stereotyped, gendered roles of game playing (Lucas and Sherry, 2004).

On the basis of earlier results we expected high levels of depressed mood to be related to high-intensity gaming (Durkin and Barber, 2002; Liu et al., 2001). Our results contradicted these findings showing that adolescents who expressed the most depressed moods played digital games quite infrequently.

We may speculate why depression was related to task-oriented type of games instead of another game genre. It is likely that task oriented games, such as puzzles, which involve e.g. thinking and problem solving fulfil the requirement of an effortful and rewarding activity, which has shown to be an effective technique to regulate mood (Fichman et al., 1999; Liu et al., 2001). Thus, our results concur with our hypothesis and earlier findings. Our results also support Bryant's and Davies' (2006) assumption that the more interactive a game is the more intervention potential it has to disrupt cognitive rehearsal and therefore alter the mood, at least temporary. Could the level of depressed mood be even higher in the task-oriented cluster if the children and adolescents did not play these digital games?

The boys and girls in the task-oriented cluster deviated from the other clusters not only by their higher levels of depressed mood but also by the games they played. These differed from what is typical of their own sex. Surprisingly, although girls in general were less motivated to play digital games than boys, those with higher levels of depressive and anxiety symptoms were interested in certain type of games, namely, task-oriented games. Equally interesting is the finding that boys high in depressive and anxiety symptoms preferred the same type of game as girls (task-oriented), although boys generally favoured violent game genres. Thus, task-oriented games seem to best fit the preferences of both boys and girls when experiencing depressed mood.

Our hypothesis that ritualized game motives are associated with depressed mood was substantiated in the task-oriented pattern of digital game playing. Motives such as to escape worries, recover or fill empty time reveal adolescents' striving to improve their condition to a more pleasurable one (Wallenius et al., in press). These motives fulfil the features of emotion-focused coping (Lazarus, 1993) and nichepicking by moving to virtual environments (Campos et al., 2004). Although this kind of passive avoidance, or escape (Min'er and Dejun, 2001; Silk et al., 2003), has been typically observed in depressed individuals, we do not know if there is any causal relationship in this study between ritualized motives and depressed mood.

The results also supported our hypothesis that higher levels of depressed mood are associated with lower levels of game violence. Perhaps violent games raise negative feelings, which individuals in depressed mood do not wish to experience or which do not serve to improve their mood (Zillmann and Bryant, 1985). Contrary to this, in the high intensity and violent imagination clusters boys and a small proportion of girls seemed to use violent games for the purpose of mood management as revealed by ritualized motives. It might be that violent games are suitable for emotion regulation in situations involving boredom or tiredness, but not depressed mood. Adolescents who played violent games, such as imagination and sports, tended to express the least depressed mood.

We furtherer hypothesized that adolescents higher in depressed mood would seek social compensation by digital game playing. Our results are in line with these expectations. Some reference to weaker peer relationships among adolescents higher in depressed mood can be seen in the observation that the children and adolescents representing the task-oriented pattern played least with their peers, and social compensation was an important motive for them to play. Social compensation can take two forms: gaming can be either a means of having company or compensation for lacking friends. Task-oriented gamers did not play alone more than did the members in the other clusters, but they seemed partly to replace peers by family members. Children and adolescents representing the high-intensity pattern emphasized the importance of social compensation as well. In their case, however, gaming clearly served as a means toward having companionship.

Because causal relations cannot be drawn from the cross-sectional data we have to consider other interpretations, too. Could assuming a game playing pattern atypical of one's own gender lead to depressed mood? Gender differences in social approval play an important role in digital game choices as well (Funk and Buchman, 1996). In general, digital game playing is characterized to represent the male culture, oriented primarily to meet male abilities and needs for social inclusion (Lucas and Sherry, 2004; Yates and Littleton, 1999). From the preschool age on, children identify and assume sex stereotyping of play (Carvalho, Smith, Hunter, and Costabile, 1990). Thereafter, gender-appropriate behaviour becomes central in social acceptance and encouragement (Moller, Hymel, and Rubin, 1992). A child who assumes gaming patterns of the opposite sex may, as a social cost, be rejected by peers (Lucas and Sherry, 2004; Yates and Littleton, 1999). Playing the opposite sex stereotyped games at the presence of schoolmates even raised the level of stress in adolescents (Cooper, Hall, and Huff, 1990). Thus, the higher level of depressed mood shown in the task-oriented cluster in our data might result from social rejection.

A third way to interpret our findings is that success in gaming counterbalances less successful peer relationships irrespective of their source. One of the uses and gratifications of digital games is the possibility to immerse in new worlds and realities, away from the real-life problems and worries. It could have been expected that children and adolescents would avail themselves of this possibility when in depressed mood. This did not happen, however. Instead, children and adolescents in the task-oriented cluster wanted to experience success. In Lucas and Sherry's (2004) study, challenge was equally important to both genders and ranked as the highest of all game gratifications. In our study motives such as not to feel lonely and to experience success loaded on the same principal component. Feelings of success and control in gaming might compensate for failings in social life, and as a consequence, help to regulate one's depressed mood. Moreover, it is possible that game playing pattern and depressed mood may both be due to a third factor, such as depressive personality style (Fichman et al., 1999).

To conclude, our findings lend themselves to the interpretation that children and adolescents use task performance type of gaming as a self-regulation strategy in psychological distress. In real-life situations, gaming could be classified as an emotional and avoidant coping strategy, albeit less effective than more active problem solving strategies (Lazarus, 1993). Children and adolescents may, however, have no real possibilities to alter their life situation, e.g. family conditions. Thus, altering mood instead of situation may be a more concrete way of coping. For a great number of children and adolescents digital games are easily accessible at home, even in their own room (Roberts, 2000).

This research has some limitations that have to be considered in any generalizations made on the basis of the study findings. First, the cross-sectional data do not allow us to make conclusions about the causal relations between digital game playing and depressed mood. The effectiveness of task-oriented games in alleviating depressed mood could be studied in an experimental design.

Second, only self-report measures were used. With regard to the intensity of digital game playing earlier findings show that survey estimates are moderately valid but they tend to overestimate the time spent on an activity when compared to diary measures (Greenberg et al., 2005; van der Voort and Vooijs, 1990). However, in correlative studies like the current study, the measures used do not necessarily need to reflect the absolute time spent but the correct order of the participants according to the amount of time spent in a specific activity (Nunnaly, 1978). The validities of weekdays/weekend estimates and the time-of-day (morning, afternoon, evening) estimates have been likewise compared (van der Voort and Vooijs, 1990), and the findings show that the two measures correlate strongly ($r = .72$) with each other and significantly with diary measures. The age differences in the validity are, however, smaller and non-significant when using the weekdays/weekend estimates compared to the time-of-day estimates. Intensity of playing could be measured more exactly by the diary method and the definition of the game genres would be more reliable when done by two trained persons on the basis of the game titles reported by the participants. In addition to subjective ratings, the mood of the child or adolescent could be rated by parents, teachers or peers.

The game motive structure shows stability over different samples (Wallenius et al., in press). Consistent with earlier results (Lucas and Sherry, 2004; Wallenius et al., in press) the overall level of motivation was higher in boys that in girls. Lucas and Sherry (2004) express a concern whether this is due to some methodological bias, such as general enthusiasm about game playing among males or underreporting among females. Repeated findings with different samples support, however, the interpretation that real gender differences exist in the level of game motivation.

Third, the age range in this study was quite narrow. This may explain why game playing patterns did not differ significantly according to age. A follow-up study is thus warranted to examine how stable the individual game playing patterns are in later adolescence. Replicability of the digital game playing patterns (Babaranelli, 2002) should also be studied using other samples.

Acknowledgements

This study was supported by the grants from the Academy of Finland (201669), the Information Society Institute of the University of Tampere and the Tampere University of Technology (16-01), and the Competitive research funding of the Pirkanmaa Hospital District (9G211). We are grateful to the schools for cooperation and to the children and adolescents who participated in the study. We thank Minna Rantanen, Riikka Haakana, Marja Vajaranta, Marjatta Radecki, Susanna Rainio, Lasse Pere, and Tomi Lintonen for assistance in data collection and Marjatta Radecki and Hanna Hölttö for coding the data. We also thank Mrs. Marja Vajaranta, University of Tampere, for revising the language.

References

Babaranelli, C. (2002). Evaluating cluster analysis solutions: An application to the Italian NEO personality inventory. *European Journal of Personality*, **16**, S43-S55.

Bartholow, B. D., Bushman, B. J., and Sestir, M. A. (2006). Chronic violent video game exposure and desensitization to violence: Behavioral and event-related brain potential data. *Journal of Experimental Social Psychology*, **42**, 532-539.

Birmaher, B. (1999). Psychometric Properties of the Screen for Child Anxiety Related Emotional Disorders (SCARED): A Replication Study. *Journal of the American Academy of Child and Adolescent Psychiatry*, **38**, 1230-1236.

Breckenridge, J. N. (1989). Replicating cluster analysis: Method, consistency, and validity. *Multivariate Behavioral Research*, **24**, (2), 147-161.

Bryant, J., and Davies, J. (2006) Selective exposure to video games. In: P. Vorderer and J. Bryant (Eds.), *Playing video games* (pp. 181-194). Mahwah, New Jersey: Lawrence Erlbaum.

Bryant, J., and Zillmann, D. (1984). Using television to alleviate boredom and stress: Selective exposure as a function of induced exitational states. *Journal of Broadcasting*, **28**, 1-20.

Campos, J. J., Frankel, C. B., and Camras, L. (2004). On the nature of emotion regulation. *Child Development*, **75**, (2), 377-394.

Carvalho, A. M. A., Smith, P. K., Hunter, T., and Costabile, A. (1990). Playground activities for boys and girls: Developmental and cultural trends in children's perceptions for gender differences. *Play and Culture*, **3**, 343-347.

Christakis, D. A., Ebel, B. E., Rivara, F. P., and Zimmerman, F. J. (2004). Television, video, and computer game usage in children under 11 years of age. *The Journal of Pediatrics*, **145**, (1), 652-656.

Colwell, J., Grady, C., and Rhaiti, S. (1995). Computer games, self-esteem and gratification of needs in adolescents. *Journal of Community and Applied Social Psychology*, **5**, 195-206.

Cooper, J., Hall, J., and Huff, C. (1990). Situational stress as a consequence of sex-stereotyped software. *Personality and Social Psychology Bulletin*, **16**, 419-429.

Csikszentmihalyi, M. (1988) The flow experience and its significance for human psychology. In: M. Csikszentmihalyi and I. S. Csikszentmihalyi (Eds.), *Optimal experience: Psychological studies in flow of consciousness*. Cambridge: Cambridge University Press.

De Cuyper, S., Timbremont, B., Braet, C., De Backer, V., and Wullaert, T. (2004). Treating depressive symptoms in schoolchildren. A pilot study. *European Child and Adolescent Psychiatry*, **13**, 105-114.

Diener, M. L., and Mangelsdorf, S. C. (1999). Behavioral strategies for emotion regulation in toddlers: Associations with maternal involvement and emotional expression. *Infant Behavior and Development*, **22**, 569-583.

Dodge, K. A., and Garber, J. (1991) Domains of emotion regulation. In: J. Garber and K. A. Dodge (Eds.), *The development of emotion regulation and dysregulation* (pp. 3-11). Cambridge, UK: Cambridge University Press.

Durkin, K., and Barber, B. (2002). Not do doomer: computer game play and positive adolescent development. *Applied Developmental Psychology*, **23**, 373-392.

Eisenberg, N., and Spinrad, T. L. (2004). Emotion-related regulation: Sharpening the definition. *Child Development*, **75**, (2), 334-339.

Ermi, L., and Mäyrä, F. (2003) Power and control of games: Children as the actors of game cultures. In: M. Copier and J. Raessens (Eds.), *Level up - Digital games research conference* (pp. 234-244). Utrecht: Universiteit Utrecht and Digital Games Research Association (DiGRA). Available also: http://www.uta.fi/hyper/gamelab/Ermi_Mayra_Power_and_Control_of_Games.pdf, 28.1.2005.

Estalló, J. A., Masferrer, M. C., and Aguirre, C. (2001). Efectos a largo plazo del uso de videojuegos (Long-term effects of the use of video games). *Apuntes de Psicologia*, **19**, (1), 161-174 (PsycINFO Database/abstract).

Fichman, L., Koestner, R., Zuroff, D. C., and Gordon, L. (1999). Depressive styles and the regulation of negative affect: A daily experience study. *Cognitive Therapy and Research*, **23**, (5), 483-495.

Funk, J. B., and Buchman, D. D. (1996). Children's perceptions of gender differences in social approval for playing electronic games. *Sex Roles*, **35**, 219-232.

Galambos, N. L., Leadbeater, B. J., and Barker, E. T. (2004). Gender differences in and risk factors for depression in adolescence: A 4-year longitudinal study. *International Journal of Behavioral Development*, **28**, 16-25.

Greenberg, B. S., Eastin, M. S., Skalski, P., Cooper, L., Levy, M., and Lachlan, K. (2005). Comparing survey and diary measures of Internet and traditional media use. *Communication Reports*, **18**, (1), 1-8.

Griffiths, M. D., and Hunt, N. (1998). Dependence on computer games by adolescents. *Psychological Reports*, **82**, (2), 475-480.

Hawthorne, G. (2008). Perceived social isolation in a community sample: its prevalence and correlates with aspects of peoples' lives. *Social Psychiatry and Psychiatric Epidemiology*, **43**, (2), 140-150.

Ho, S. M. Y., and Lee, T. M. C. (2001). Computer usage and its relationship with adolescent lifestyle in Hong Kong. *Journal of Adolescent Health*, **29**, 258-266.

Hoeksma, J. B., Oosterlaan, J., and Schipper, E. M. (2004). Emotion regulation and the dynamics of feelings: A conceptual and methodological framework. *Child Development*, **75**, (2), 354-360.

Höysniemi, J. (2006). Design and evaluation of physically interactive games. Academic dissertation in Interactive technology. *Acta Electronica Universitatis Tamperensis 544.* Retrieved August 19th, 2006, from http://acta.uta.fi

Kerr, J. H., and Tacon, P. (1999). Psychological responses to different types of locations and activities. *Journal of Environmental Psychology*, **19**, 287-294.

Kovacs, M. (1992). *Children's depression inventory.* New York: Multihealth Systems.

Kubey, R. W., and Csikszentmihalyi, M. (1990). Television as escape: subjective experience before an evening of heavy viewing. *Communication Reports*, **3**, (2), 92-100.

Lazarus, R. S. (1993). Coping theory and research: past, present, and future. *Psychosomatic Medicine*, **55**, 234-247.

Liu, X., Su, L., and He, B. (2001). Intelligence, personality, and behavior problems of children with video games dependence. *Chinese Journal of Clinical Psychology*, **9**, (4), 268-270.

Lucas, K., and Sherry, J. L. (2004). Sex differences in video game play: A communication-based explanation. *Communicaton Research*, **31**, (5), 499-523.

Min'er, H., and Dejun, G. (2001). Emotion regulation and depression of college students. *Chinese Mental Health Journal*, **15**, (6), 438-441.

Moller, L. C., Hymel, S., and Rubin, K. H. (1992). Sex typing in play and popularity in middle childhood. *Sex Roles*, **26**, 331-353.

Nunnaly, J. C. (1978). *Psychometric theory.* New York: McGraw-Hill.

Pennebaker, J. W., and Brittingham, G. (1982) Environmental and sensory cues affecting the perception of physical symptoms. In: A. Baum and J. E. Singer (Eds.), *Advances in Environmental Psychology* (Vol. 4, pp. 115-136). Hillsdale, NJ: Erlbaum.

Perse, E. M., and Rubin, A. M. (1990). Chronic loneliness and television use. *Journal of Broadcasting and Electronic Media*, **34**, (1), 37-53.

Potts, R., and Sanchez, D. (1994). Television viewing and depression: no news is good news. *Journal of Broadcasting and Electronic Media*, **38**, 79-90.

Punamäki, R.-L., Wallenius, M., Hölttö, H., Nygård, C.-H., and Rimpelä, A. (in press). The associations between information and communication technology (ICT) and peer and parent relations in early adolescence. *International Journal of Behavioral Development.*

Roberts, D. F. (2000). Media and youth: Access, exposure and privatization. *Journal of Adolescent Health*, **27**, (1), 8-14.

Rubin, A. M. (1993). Audience activity and media use. *Communication Monographs*, **60**, 98-103.

Rubin, A. M. (1994) Media uses and effects: a uses-and-gratifications perspective. In: J. Bruant and D. Zillmann (Eds.), *Media effects: Advances in theory and research* (pp. 417-436). Hillsdale, N.J.: Erlbaum.

Rubin, A. M., Perse, E. M., and Powell, R. A. (1985). Loneliness, parasocial interaction, and local television news viewing. *Communication Research*, **12**, 155-180.

Rutter, M., and Graham, P. (1966). The reliability and validity of psychiatric assessment of the child: I. Interview with the child. *British Journal of Psychiatry*, **114**, 563-579.

Selnow, G. W. (1984). Playing videogames: the electronic fiend. *Journal of Communication*, **34**, 148-156.

Silk, J. S., Steinberg, L., and Morris, A. S. (2003). Adolescents' emotion regulation in daily life: Links to depressive symptoms and problem behavior. *Child Development*, **74**, (6), 1869-1880.

Slater, M. D., Henry, K. L., Swain, R. C., and Andersson, L. L. (2003). Violent media content and aggressiveness in adolescents. A downward spiral model. *Commuication Research*, **30**, (6), 713-736.

Smith, S. L., Lachlan, K., and Tamborini, R. (2003). Popular video games: Quantifying the amount and context of violence. *Journal of Broadcasting and Elecronic Media*, **47**, 58-76.

Solantaus, T., and Toikka, S. (2005). *The Efficient Family: An Intervention Study on The Prevention of Mental Disorders in Children With Affectively Ill Parents.* Tampere: Juvenes Print.

Sproull, L., and Kiesler, S. (1991). *Connections: New ways of working in the networked organization.* Cambridge: MIT Press.

Staats, H., Gatersleben, B., and Hartig, T. (1997). Change in mood as a function of environmental design: Arousal and pleasure on a simulated forest hike. *Journal of Environmental Psychology*, **17**, 283-300.

Steinberg, L., and Morris, A. S. (2001). Adolescent development. *Annual Review of Psychology*, **52**, 83-110.

Twenge, J. M., and Nolen-Hoeksema, S. (2002). Age, gender, race, socioeconomic status, and birth cohort differences on the Children's Depression Inventory: A meta-analysis. *Journal of Abnormal Psychology*, **111**, 578-588.

Wallenius, M., Rimpelä, A., Punamäki, R.-L., and Lintonen, T. (in press). Digital game playing motives among adolescents. relations to school performance, family communication, sleeping patterns, and perceived health. *Journal of Applied Developmental Psychology*.

van der Voort, T. H. A., and Vooijs, M. W. (1990). Validity of children's direct estimates of time spent television viewing. *Journal of Broadcasting and Electronic Media*, **34**, (1), 93-99.

Wood, R. T. A., Gupta, R., Derevensky, J. L., and Griffiths, M. (2004). Video game playing and gambling in adolescents: Common risk factors. *Journal of Child and Adolescent Substance Abuse*, **14**, (1), 77-100.

Yates, S. J., and Littleton, K. (1999). Understanding computer game cultures. A situated approach. *Information, Communication and Sociey*, **2**, (4), 566-583.

Zillmann, D. (1988). Mood management through communication choices. *American Behavioral Scientist*, **31**, 327-340.

Zillmann, D., and Bryant, J. (1985) Affect, mood, and emotion as determinants of selective exposure. In: D. Zillmann and J. Bryant (Eds.), *Selective exposure to communication* (pp. 157-190). Hillsdale, NJ: Lawrence Erlbaum.

In: Computer Games
Editors: A. Soria et al, pp. 111-125

ISBN: 978-1-60876-658-1

Chapter 4

VIDEO GAMES FOR HEALTH: DESIGN STRATEGIES FOR MAXIMIZING LEARNING

Ivan L. Beale[1]
School of Psychology, University of New South Wales

Abstract

There is wide interest in the potential of 'serious' video games as vehicles for learning. Especially in the health education domain, there are now many reports of the use of video games intended to produce changes in players' knowledge, attitudes or behaviors that will transfer to 'real life' settings outside the context of the game. Real progress in this exciting field may be seriously limited by the lack of evidentially-based and theoretically driven models for creating learning strategies that can be incorporated in game design. In particular, there has been little published discussion of how learning strategies should be used in game design to maximize the achievement of learning objectives that are transferable to criterion settings outside the game. This chapter analyses the learning models implicit in health games described in the literature, and relates these to established learning models in order to illustrate the nature of the gaps between current game designs and relevant learning theory and technology. This analysis provides a systematic framework for identifying principles of game design that are soundly based both in theory and research evidence. Examples are provided from recent game designs.

---

[1] E-mail address: ibeale@bigpond.com, Ph: +61 2 95183060. Ivan L Beale PhD

Introduction

This chapter is a commentary on the design of video games intended or marketed as psychoeducational interventions for health problems. Psychoeducational interventions are interventions that focus on a learner's (usually a patient or health professional) acquisition of illness and/or treatment related knowledge and/or skills derived wholly or partly from that knowledge. Psychoeducational interventions in the form of video games for increasing knowledge, self-help skills and attitudes have been developed for a range of chronic diseases such as asthma (Lieberman, 2001), cancer (Dragone, Bush, Jones, Bearison, and Kamani, 2002; Kato, Cole, Bradlyn, and Pollock, 2008), obesity (Baranowski, Buday, Thompson, and Baranowski, 2008), cystic fibrosis (Duff, Ball, Wolfe, Blyth, and Brownlee, 2006), sickle cell disease (Yoon and Godwin, 2007) diabetes (Brown et al., 1997) as well as health preventive issues such as safe sex (Thomas, Cahill, and Santilli, 1997). These studies have generated some limited published evidence about the ability of such video games to bring about changes in health-related variables such as treatment expectations, treatment credibility and acceptability, treatment adherence, perceptions of internal states, pain management, participation in health care, decision making, risk judgments and risk behaviors.

Scope of this Chapter

There is not much research-based evidence on the efficacy of these health video games, that is, how efficacious they are in achieving outcome goals. Generally, the published evaluations of these health games do not meet criteria for systematic evaluation of computer-based interventions recommended in the literature (e.g., Beale, 2002; Spirito, 1999). In particular, research reports about the efficacy of health games contain little information about the learning theory and technology underpinning the design of the games, even though the learning design of a game is probably a critical determinant of its efficacy. This chapter attempts to provide an overview of what information currently is out there about learning design in health games. It includes a retrospective analysis of the published descriptions of the learning designs in a representative sample of health games and attempts to identify the sorts of theories, principles and technologies that game developers are using. The aim of this analysis to determine to what extent learning principles from psychology and education have been used appropriately and to make recommendations about how this might be improved to the benefit of future game designs.

Video Games for Learning

Much has been written about the great potential of the video game as a medium for learning (BECTA, 2007; Hansen, 2008; Mitchell and Savill-Smith, 2004; Prensky, 2001; Federation of American Scientists, 2006). Much also has been speculated about its limitations and its potential for harm (e.g., Carnagey and Anderson, 2005). The stimulus for all this attention seems to have arisen from fascination with the burgeoning success of video games as a form of recreation involving enthusiastic participation of an ever increasing demographic. Once the sole preserve of the 'Space-Invader'-addicted computer nerds of the 1970s, the video game now has reached us all, progressively invading our homes, workplaces, health and education institutions. It is inevitable that something so accessible and with such wide appeal, especially to the young, should raise questions about how it might best be harnessed to benefit society as a whole.

First developed and marketed almost exclusively as a form of entertainment, the video game has now been pressed into service in areas such as academic education, vocational training, health, social development and the creative arts. In adapting the video game to serve the purposes of these 'non-entertainment' domains, a fundamental challenge has had to be recognized and met. That challenge is how to adapt the structure of the video game to meet desired education or health objectives while still preserving those aspects of game structure that make it entertaining (Federation of American Scientists, 2006).

Educationists have long been interested in the use of computers to assist in meeting education objectives, well before the advent of the video game or even its humble predecessor, the computer game. This interest goes back at least as far as the concept of the 'teaching machine' popularized by B.F Skinner and his colleagues in the 1960s (Skinner, 1958). The extent of this interest is attested to by the number and longevity of the research journals about what is generally referred to as 'computer assisted instruction,' or CAI.

The approach exemplified by CAI is based on the recognition that computer programs could be designed that could simulate the actions of an expert teacher interacting with a learner. A program could represent an expert system that might help a learner to achieve specified education objectives by the most efficient route. For example, most of us have encountered the simple but effective programs that have been developed to teach chess, typing or word recognition without the direct involvement of a human teacher. The advantage is that the expertise resides in the program created by the teacher, so that many learners can be served by the one program, serially or concurrently, without the need for extensive hours of involvement of an always alert, expert teacher.

To the extent that some learners and teachers might regard some CAI programs as slogging and tedious, the appearance of video games on the entertainment scene has generated keen interest in the idea that maybe CAI learning principles could be moved across into video games. Maybe the fun and engrossing properties of the three dimensional video game could be combined with the CAI strategies to enable education objectives to be met in an entertaining environment. In the subsequent scramble to exploit the idea of using video games as a vehicle for education, it seems that the idea of building learning principles into game design has been largely neglected in favor of the more limited ideas of using educational content and making the games attractive. To a large extent, the 'education by video game' concept appears to have been hijacked by commercial developers more interested in selling a product than achieving educational objectives. Reviews of research on the efficacy of video games as education vehicles have shown only modest effects on learning, and education gatekeepers are becoming concerned with setting standards for design and efficacy of video games used in formal education settings (Kulik and Kulik, 1991; Federation of American Scientists, 2006).

Commentaries on educationists' approaches to the use of video games in academic education have noted that different philosophic camps in education have tended to take different directions in education game design. For example, instructionists have seen video games as an opportunity to apply a highly programmatic approach to more effectively teach specific academic content, whereas constructionists have seen video games as a vehicle for less-constrained learning by free exploration of a rich interactive environment (Gentile et al., 2009; Kafai, 2001; Reese, 2007). Such differences are based on philosophic differences about what formal education should best be trying to achieve; for example, a repertoire of specific mastered skills and knowledge versus generic creative and problem-solving abilities. These fundamental differences in education goals are of course reflected in substantive differences in approaches to game design.

Although this chapter is about video games for health rather than for academic education, even a brief consideration of the use of video games in academic education has heuristic value, because it refers to a wide theoretic and empirical literature base about whether and how video games generally can be designed to achieve specific kinds of learning. That literature encompasses everything from the most general philosophies of learning and theories of learning, to the more specific learning technologies and empirical evidence on the strategies and tactics of learning design. That literature also incorporates theory and research evidence about the psychology of learning, the knowledge domain about the intersection of the disciplines of psychology and education (Federation of American Scientists, 2006; Gentile et al., 2009;).

Video Games for Health

Video games for health belong to a multi-disciplinary domain at the intersection of health, psychology and education. Questions about the design and efficacy of video games for health may best be addressed by reference to relevant literature in all three domains. Currently, a major issue in the design of video games for health is that the design of the games is poorly referenced to the relevant literature. In the worst cases, there is simply no evidence at all that the game designers have looked to the psychology or education literature about learning, yet the developers are expending often substantial resources in money and human effort towards achieving educational or psychological goals. In the better cases, there are general references made to theories of learning, especially social learning, and to evidence or widely accepted beliefs about aspects of the technology of learning (e.g., Beale, Bradlyn, and Kato, 2003; Bradlyn, Beale, and Kato, 2003).

What is largely absent though, is detailed consideration of how the theories, principles and strategies of learning that have originated in research about real people learning in real environments can be validly transferred across to the learning contexts provided in a video game. It may be that the enthusiasm to create health applications of the video game model has resulted in a situation where game development and marketing has got well ahead of the research that arguably should have preceded it. In the absence of relevant research evidence, game designers have presumably made risky assumptions about the applicability of current evidence and theories that may or may not be applicable. Before exploring this issue in more detail, it is instructive first to consider some fundamental differences between learning goals in the education, vocation, and health domains.

Concrete Versus Conceptual Games

A video game provides a context in which the player can interact with objects in a simulated environment. The rules of the game determine the effects of the player's interactions with objects and with other characters in the game. These interactions enable the player to learn and perform to achieve some objective featured in the game.

Most commercial video games are just about the player learning to perform the skills required to succeed in the game. But some 'education' games set out to teach knowledge or skills that are transferable to real-life settings that are somehow represented in the game. Such games may represent the real-life situation concretely, while others may represent it only at a conceptual level.

An example of the concrete variety is the flight simulator used to train pilots in the skills needed to fly a particular type of aircraft. In this case the simulator provides an experience that closely approximates the real thing, and the trainee pilot acts in a 1st-person role. The simulator is a realistic model that allows the pilot to learn and practice in a safe environment. The motivation for the pilot to perform the skills learned in the simulator is a given. Not to perform them will have immediate adverse consequences. On the flight-deck, there are not alternative behaviors that might successfully compete with the learned behaviors required to fly the craft safely. There is no doubt that flight simulators are an effective component of flight training (Hayes, Jacobs, Carolyn, and Salas, 1992).

In the education domain, and in some health education applications, video games employing a concrete model are used as a vehicle for increasing the player's knowledge about something, maybe math or geography. In the course of the game, the player (or an avatar controlled by the player) responds to questions, explicit or implicit, and right or wrong responses have different consequences for the player's progress in the game. Such games generally are efficacious in increasing targeted knowledge both within the game and in settings outside the game.

Both in simulators and in education games employing the concrete model, the learning content within the game is the same as, or similar to, the content this represents in the real world. There seems to be no reason to look beyond current theories and technologies of learning to inform the design of such games, although new strategies may need to be developed to fit the flow of the game in which the learning is embedded.

On the other hand, the conceptual game presents some new challenges for the designer. A typical example of a conceptual game is a health-behavior game in which a player, who is a patient with a particular medical problem, learns to make health-promoting decisions on behalf of characters in the game that have the same medical problem as the player. In the game 'Packy and Marlon' (Brown et al., 1997) the diabetic player learns to control the diet of one of two diabetic elephants at a health camp. What is intended is that the player will learn health-management skills which he or she will then transfer to their own situation in real life. Notably, a study comparing the relative effects of playing Packy and Marlon or a control 'pinball' video game showed little difference in the effects of the two games on health behaviors or mediating variables, including knowledge.

What are the critical differences between concrete games and conceptual games like Packy and Marlon? In Packy and Marlon, there are likely to be alternative behaviors that will compete with the health-promoting behaviors learned in the game. Also, the real-life situation is unlikely to resemble closely the game environment in which the skills were learned, so this would impede transfer. The player does not actually perform the skills in the game, but rather chooses options for the 'actor' in the game who he or she chooses to play. In this sense, the game provides an opportunity for the player to gain relevant knowledge through experimentation with alternatives and observation of consequences. But the game does not teach the player to apply this knowledge to his or her own real-life health behaviors.

Learning Theory and Health Game Design

Researchers investigating the use of video-game based interventions for chronic health problems in children (e.g., Baranowski et al., 2008; Brown et al., 1997; Lieberman, 2001) have looked mainly to social learning theory (Bandura, 1977) for a theoretical basis for positive expectations. It has been argued that there is reason to expect a video-game intervention to produce increases in constructs such as self-esteem, self-efficacy and self-attribution. Moreover, changes in these mediating variables are seen as leading to improvements in real-life health behaviors, knowledge and communication.

The arguments that social learning theory would predict positive outcomes of video game interventions have not included any detailed analysis of how this would come about, except to note that there are some features of game design that seem to map onto variables that have been found to influence the development of self-efficacy. For example, video games frequently use models that may be seen to, and in the case of avatars, caused to, demonstrate appropriate behavior. Such models can have attributes that allow the player to 'identify' with them. Players may control the models, and so, by proxy, control the health outcomes. Players may observe the positive consequences of compliance with health-behavior imperatives. Also, there may be opportunities for extensive practice of desired behaviors, via a proxy character in the game.

Social learning involves the gaining of experience through observing or interacting with others sharing the same environment. In the case of video-game experience with health issues, the experience is vicarious in nature. It consists of the player observing models dealing with health threats by taking attitudes and behaving in certain ways, which lead to certain consequences. In some game formats (third person), the player may instigate the actions of the models, which heightens the player's attention to what the model is doing. Also, if a game has been designed so that the player's success in game-play depends on the outcomes of the model's behaviors, the player's attention will be drawn to the cause-and-effect association between the model's behaviors and their consequences. On the face of it, these are conditions that favor the development of social learning.

But all of this assumes that the modeling formats used in video games are equivalent to the modeling formats studied in social learning research. In fact, there are often some substantial differences that could well turn out to influence to what extent a particular learning model could facilitate learning by the player via vicarious experience. One notable departure from standard social learning paradigms is the 'third-person' model often used in health games, where the player participates in the game by controlling the behavior of an avatar in the virtual environment.

The Example of Re-Mission

An instructive example is provided by the health game Re-Mission (HopeLab, Palo Alto, CA), a video game designed to be played by young people undergoing treatment for cancer. The overall objective of the game is to change players' illness representations in order to promote adherence to self-care during treatment and to teach self care skills and related cancer knowledge. This video game in particular is appropriate for further analysis here, both because there is some published information about the learning design in the game, and because there are published analyses of a large randomized controlled clinical trial which indicate beneficial outcomes for patients, attributable to game play (Beale, Kato, Marin-Bowling, Guthrie, and Cole, 2007; Beale, Marín-Bowling, Guthrie, and Kato, 2006; Kato et al., 2008). Also, the author of this chapter was a member of the team that designed Re-Mission, jointly responsible with Pamela Kato for the identification of behavioral objectives and learning design strategies in the game.

This association provides detailed knowledge about the specifics of game design and how design decisions were made, as opposed to the limited information otherwise available in published reports.

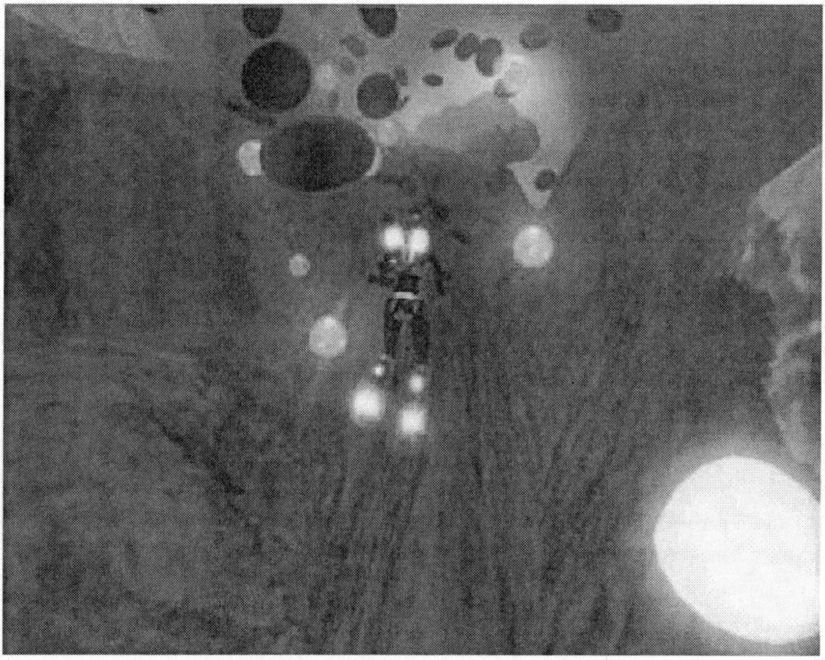

In Re-Mission, the avatar, controlled by the player, negotiates friendly and unfriendly cells while on a mission to address a cancer-treatment issue in the body of a virtual patient.

Re-Mission is a third-person action game in which the player can manipulate an avatar (a young humanoid robot character) on missions inside the three-dimensional (3-D) virtual bodies of 19 different young patients being treated for seven different cancers common in young people. The avatar is accompanied on these missions by a mentor robot who provides information, encouragement, warnings and prompts for appropriate actions. The game consists of two two-player missions and 20 single-player missions.

Players win by destroying cancer cells and other enemies in the body (e.g., bacteria, mucositis lesions, stool jags), but they need to be careful not to waste ammunition or cause secondary damage to the body. Players destroy enemies by using weapons armed with common treatments such as chemotherapy, radiation, and antibiotics. To complete mission goals, the player must use game elements called 'communication taps' to prompt the virtual patient to engage in positive self-care behaviors such as taking stool softeners to prevent colon tears, practicing good mouth care to combat mucositis, using relaxation techniques to reduce stress, communicating with the patients to take their medicine, or prompting the patient to eat and drink for more energy and to prevent dehydration. Re-Mission can be accessed at www.re-mission.com.

The game style, content and behavioral objectives are based on extensive research carried out with stakeholder groups in the U.S., including young people with cancer, oncologists and other physicians, psychologists and oncology nurses (Bradlyn, Kato, Beale, and Cole, 2004). The selection of self-care behaviors targeted in Re-Mission was based primarily on a survey of pediatric oncology nurses' judgments of relative importance of different behaviors (Baggott, Beale, Dodd, and Kato, 2003). Re-Mission was designed to be a learning environment that motivates, guides, and supports the learning of a set of behavioral objectives related to self care during treatment for cancer. To maximize its appeal to adolescent and young adult cancer patients, it has been given the look and feel of a high-quality commercial entertainment game, as opposed to an educational game. The learning curriculum and instructional components are present but integrated into the game-play agenda. Learning the underlying health-behavior objectives, although not essential to game play, enriches the game experience and facilitates achievement of mission objectives. The game provides opportunities to learn skills and knowledge content ranging from the very specific to more conceptual levels.

Symbolic Self Modeling in Re-Mission

As described in the published reports on Re-Mission, the theoretic basis for the expectation that the game will be an effective learning environment is a well-established extension of social learning theory known as 'self modeling' (Dowrick, 1999). The learning model used in Re-Mission is a novel, untested extension of the selective self modeling paradigm, for which the term 'symbolic self modeling' has been proposed (see Beale et al., 2007). The term 'symbolic' refers to the fact that the model is not the learner *per se*, but an avatar that the learner controls during game play in a virtual environment. In the current literature on vicarious learning, learners observe either another person (in reality, on tape, or imagined) or themselves (on tape or imagined) achieving some performance goal. The observational context in Re-Mission differs from standard vicarious learning paradigms in that the player observes the avatar, arguably an agent who represents the player, and controls the avatar. The design hypothesis is that the player will learn from observing the consequences (desired and undesired) of the avatar's actions, and hopefully will transfer what is learned to the player's own behavior in the real world.

Other Learning Principles in Re-Mission

Re-Mission was designed to include procedural features that have been found, in other contexts, to maximize the likelihood that such transfer of learning will occur. The game design is described as offering many features consistent with the concept of an efficacious learning environment. These include: self-selection of tasks from a menu of available activities; control and self-pacing of progress, with opportunities for exploration of the learning environment; and opportunities for incidental learning (Beale, 2005). Additional strategies used in Re-Mission to promote learning of behavioral objectives include the use of prompts, selectable task difficulty, immediate feedback for all alternative responses, unlimited opportunities for self-initiated practice and rehearsal, motivational relevance, and planned transfer of learning across situations and within response classes (Beale, 2005).

The fundamental procedural strategies relied on in Re-Mission for learning and transfer are based on those designated 'feedforward' and 'positive self-review' in theoretical accounts of self modeling (Dowrick, 1999). Feedforward occurs when the player views the virtual patient performing appropriate self-care behaviors (prompted by the avatar via the communication taps) and subsequently observes the desirable consequences of these behaviors. Positive self review occurs when the player sees the avatar prompting the virtual patient to perform the appropriate self-care behavior. However, while there is substantial empirical support for the heuristic value of self-modeling theory, it must be acknowledged that its extension to symbolic self modeling is based on untested assumptions.

Reliance on this unproven mechanism to achieve desired learning outcomes certainly involved significant risk. However, because a decision had previously been taken to design the game within the 'third-person shooter' genre, there were no feasible alternative learning models apparent to the design team. A decision was made to proceed with the chosen design, but to build into the game an extensive program of data collection that would enable subsequent analysis of game play at a detailed level sufficient to identify the efficacy of the learning strategies in the design. If sequential analysis of game play records showed that the particular learning design strategies promoted learning as intended, well and good. Such findings would support the validity of the theory on which the design was based. In the event that the data did not show evidence that the learning strategies were efficacious, there would at least be an evidential basis for changing the strategies and reconsidering the underlying theory.

In addition to the Social Learning Model, the design of Re-Mission is also referenced to the Illness Perception Model (see Kato et al., 2008; Tate, Haritatos, and Cole, 2009). The relevance of the Illness Perception Model (c.f., Cameron and Leventhal, 1995) is as follows. If social learning resulted in an increase in perceived self-efficacy to facilitate good treatment outcomes, the Illness Perception Model would predict changes in the patients' illness-related behaviors, such as treatment adherence. Notably, the randomized controlled trial of the efficacy of Re-Mission did find larger gains in cancer-related self-efficacy in the Re-Mission players, compared to the controls, as well as larger gains in medication adherence.

It must be emphasized here that while these results are consistent with efficacy of the learning models underlying the video game design, they are not to be taken valid evidence that the application of those models in Re-Mission were responsible for the positive effects of game play. That sort of inference would need to be based on analysis of the learning process that accompanied the game play of individual patients. Because Re-Mission was designed to collect detailed data on individual play, it will be possible to analyze the developmental trajectory of learning as individuals played the game. This may be the first health game to make provision for this type of analysis.

Conclusion

Detailed analyses of learning in the course of game play, especially those based on studies designed to test the efficacy of alternative learning strategies, are sorely need to provide a solid basis for the design of health games. Until this happens, the current model, which could fairly be characterized as 'develop-and-hope,' will continue to prevail as the default. As has been recommended elsewhere for the development of learning design in video games for education generally, there is a need for systematic research on theory and technology for learning design of games. Research programs need to be established where the activities are less driven by a need to 'get the game out there' and more oriented to understanding how to make learning principles and strategies work in the video game environment. In the case of health games where the focus is on changing health related attitudes and behaviors in the real world, there needs to be a focus especially on how to design games to maximize generalization of learning between the game and the real environment.

This chapter began with a brief discussion of the use of video games in academic education. The point was made that computer assisted learning has a long history in academic education and there has been significant research over several decades on how best to design games to maximize learning. Even so, recent summit conferences and white papers on the state of the art continue to identify a serious shortfall in the knowledge base (see Federation of Scientists, 2006). If that is the state of affairs in academic education, it is certainly worse in health, where serious research on learning processes in game design is just in its infancy. Before video games can be taken seriously as valid psychoeducational interventions for health problems, developers will themselves need to take seriously the question of how they can implement proven theories and technologies of learning in game designs. They could do worse that to follow recommended guidelines proposed for the formative evaluation, process evaluation and outcome evaluation of any games they develop, especially those guidelines that are focused on digital media (c.f., Beale, 2002).

References

Baggott, C., Beale, I. L., Dodd, M. J., and Kato, P. M. (2003). A survey of self-care and dependent-care advice given by pediatric oncology nurses. *Journal of Pediatric Oncology Nursing,* **21**(3), 1-9.

Bandura, A. (1977). Self-efficacy: Toward a unifying theory of behavioral change. *Psychological Review,* **84**(2), 191-215.

Baranowski, T., Buday, R., Thompson, D. I., and Baranowski, J. (2008). Playing for real: video games and stories for health-related behavior change. *American Journal of Preventive Medicine,* **34**(1), 74-82.

Beale, I. L. (2002). An evaluation model for psychoeducational interventions using interactive multimedia. *Cyberpsychology and Behavior,* **5**(6), 565-580.

Beale, I. L. (2005). Scaffolding and integrated assessment in computer assisted learning (CAL) for children with learning disabilities. *Australasian Journal of Educational Technology,* **21**, 173-191.

Beale, I. L., Bradlyn, A. S., and Kato, P. M. (2003). Psychoeducational interventions with pediatric cancer patients: Part II. Effects of information and skills training on health-related outcomes. *Journal of Child and Family Studies,* **12**(4), 385-397.

Beale, I. L., Kato, P. M., Marin-Bowling, V. M., Guthrie, N., and Cole, S. W. (2007). Improvement in cancer-related knowledge following use of a psychoeducational video game for adolescents and young adults with cancer. *Journal of Adolescent Health,* **41**(3), 263-270.

Beale, I. L., Marín-Bowling, V. M., Guthrie, N., and Kato, P. M. (2006). Young cancer patients' perceptions of a video game used to promote self care. *International Electronic Journal of Health Education,* **9**, 102-112.

BECTA. (2007). Computer games in education. *Emerging Technologies in Learning,* **2**, 47-63.

Bradlyn, A. S., Beale, I. L., and Kato, P. M. (2003). Psychoeducational interventions with pediatric cancer patients: Part I. Patient information and knowledge. *Journal of Child and Family Studies,* **12**(3), 257-277.

Bradlyn, A. S., Kato, P. M., Beale, I. L., and Cole, S. (2004). Pediatric oncology professionals' perceptions of information needs of adolescent patients with cancer. *Journal of Pediatric Oncology Nursing,* **22**(3), 1-8.

Brown, S. J., Lieberman, D. A., Gemeny, B. A., Fan, Y. C., Wilson, D. M., and Pasta, D. J. (1997). Educational video game for juvenile diabetes: results of a controlled trial. *Medical Informatics,* **22**(1), 77-89.

Cameron, L. D., and Leventhal, H. (1995). Vulnerability beliefs, symptom experiences, and the processing of health threat information: a self-regulatory perspective. *Journal of Applied Social Psychology,* **25**(21), 1859-1883.

Carnagey, N. L., and Anderson, C. A. (2005). The effects of reward and punishment in violent video games on aggressive affect, cognition, and behavior. *Psychological Science,* **16**(11), 882-889.

Dowrick, P. (1999). A review of self-modeling and related interventions. *Applied and Preventive Psychology,* **8**, 23-39.

Dragone, M. A., Bush, P. J., Jones, J. K., Bearison, D. J., and Kamani, S. (2002). Development and evaluation of an interactive CD-ROM for children with leukemia and their families. *Patient Education and Counseling,* **46**(4), 297-307.

Duff, A., Ball, R., Wolfe, S., Blyth, H., and Brownlee, K. (2006). Betterland: an interactive cd-rom guide for children with cystic fibrosis. *Paediatric Nursing,* **18**(7), 30-33.

Federation of American Scientists. (2006). *Harnessing the power of video games for learning*. Retrieved 13 June, 2009, from the World Wide Web: http://www.fas.org/gamesummit/Resources/Summit_on_Educational_Games.pdf

Gentile, D. A., Anderson, C. A., Yukawa, S., Ihori, N., Saleem, M., Lim Kam, M., Shibuya, A., Liau, A. K., Khoo, A., Bushman, B. J., Rowell Huesmann,

L., and Sakamoto, A. (2009). The effects of prosocial video games on prosocial behaviors: international evidence from correlational, longitudinal, and experimental studies. *Personality and Social Psychology Bulletin,* **35**(6), 752-763.

Hansen, M. M. (2008). Versatile, immersive, creative and dynamic virtual 3-D healthcare learning environments: a review of the literature. *Journal of Medical Internet Research,* **10**(3), e26.

Hayes, R. T., Jacobs, J. W., Carolyn, P., and Salas, E. (1992). Flight simulator effectiveness: a meta-analysis. *Military Psychology,* **4,** 43-64.

Kafai, Y. B. (2001). *The educational potential of electronic games: from games–to–teach to games–to–learn.* Retrieved June 13, 2009, from the World Wide Web: http://culturalpolicy.uchicago.edu/conf2001/papers/kafai.html

Kato, P. M., Cole, S. W., Bradlyn, A. S., and Pollock, B. H. (2008). A video game improves behavioral outcomes in adolescents and young adults with cancer: a randomized trial. *Pediatrics,* **122**(2), e305-317.

Kulik, C., and Kulik, J. (1991). Effectiveness of computer-based instruction; an updated analysis. *Computers and Human Behavior*, **7**(1-2), 75-94.

Lieberman, D. A. (2001). Management of chronic pediatric diseases with interactive health games: Theory and research findings. *Journal of Ambulatory Care Management,* **24**(1), 26-38.

Mitchell, A., and Savill-Smith, C. (2004). *The use of computer and video games for learning: A review of the literature.* London: Learning Skills and Development Agency.

Prensky, M. (2001). *Digital game-based learning*. New York: McGraw-Hill.

Reese, D. D. (2007). First steps and beyond: serious games as preparation for future learning. *Journal of Educational Multimedia and Hypermedia,* **16**(3), 283-300.

Skinner, B. F. (1958). Teaching machines. *Science,* **128**, 969-977.

Spirito, A. (1999). Introduction to special series on empirically supported treatments in pediatric psychology. *Journal of Pediatric Psychology,* **24**(2), 87-90.

Tate, R., Haritatos, J., and Cole, S. (2009). Hopelab approach to Re-Mission. *International Journal of Learning and Media,* **1**(1), 29-35.

Thomas, R., Cahill, J., and Santilli, L. (1997). Using an interactive computer game to increase skill and self-efficacy regarding safer sex negotiation: field test results. *Health Education and Behavior,* **24**(1), 71-86.

Yoon, S. L., and Godwin, A. (2007). Enhancing self-management in children with sickle cell disease through playing a CD-ROM educational game: a pilot study. *Pediatric Nursing,* **33**(1), 60-63, 72.

In: Computer Games
Editors: A. Soria et al, pp. 127-136
ISBN: 978-1-60876-658-1

Chapter 5

Dreams and Video Game Play[1]

Jayne Gackenbach, Beena Kuruvilla, Raelyne Dopko and Hau Le
Grant MacEwan University, Canada

Abstract

In a series of studies Gackenbach and colleagues have been investigating the relationship between video game play and dreams. Three lines of inquiry have been pursued, cognitive factors, emotional content and bizarreness in dreams associated with video game play. The question across studies being does hard core video game play change these fundamental qualities of dreams in the player? It has been found that gamers report more lucid/control type dreams, higher dream bizarreness and unusual reactions to nightmares. These findings are summarized in this chapter.

Introduction

Video game play has become so widespread that it rivals the other major entertainment industries. No longer only a child's toy, the average gamer is now in their late 20's and increasingly people of all ages and cultural backgrounds are enjoying gaming. Not surprisingly, the effects of such widespread immersion in

---

[1] This chapter is based upon a paper that was presented by the first author at the Toward a Science of Consciousness: Investigating Inner Experience Brain, Mind, Technology, Hong Kong, June, 2009.

these interactive immersive virtual worlds have become a focus of various research enterprises. Much attention has been on modeling of aggression findings although the potential for addiction, among other negative consequences of play, is also often discussed. Numerous positive consequences have also been found from practice in social realms to various improvements in cognitive skills. In this brief chapter we will summarize our research into the effects of game play on nighttime dreams.

Despite cultural stereotypes about dreams as meaningless internal experiences of the night, the research literature on dreaming function has clearly established that dreams are important for information and emotional processing. So the question posed in our laboratory is what is the effects upon the biologically constructed alternative realities of dreams by immersion in the technologically constructed worlds experienced during video game play?

Throughout these studies we generally defined the hard core gamer as someone who:

1) Plays video games on average several times a week,
2) Typical playing session more than 2 hours
3) Played 50 or more video games over their lifetime, and
4) Been playing video games since grade three or earlier.

The dream dimensions which we have examined thus far include lucid and control dreams, dreams where you know you are dreaming while the dream is ongoing and can have some control over the dream; bizarreness and creativity, the degree to which dreams are odd potentially due to the dreamer being creative; and nightmares and threat simulation, dreams that are so frightening that they wake the sleeper and the evolutionary function of dreams as rehearsal for potential threat.

Lucid – Control Dreams

In several studies we were able to show that high end gamers had more lucid and control dreams than those who rarely game (Gackenbach, 2006; 2009; Gackenbach & Kuruvilla, 2008a). Because in the previous studies the dream information was based retrospective reflections on dream history, we refined the methodology. We had not collected recent dream reports nor had we looked at other forms of electronic media use from the day prior to the reported dream. Thus Gackenbach (2009) administered an online questionnaire to Canadian college students where a dream report was gathered followed by a list of questions about the dreamers sleep the night of the dream and media use questions the day before the dream. Subjects were also asked various questions about the dream they reported. Data from subjects who reported normal sleep length, where they felt rested, was used from dreams that subjects reported had happened the night before they took the survey. Of the 800 plus respondents, only 152 fit these criteria. In a factor analysis of these dreams with dream type, media use and gamer history information, lucid and control dreaming were associated with high end gamer history and heavier media use the day before the dream.

Why might we expect this parallel between video game play and lucid-control dreaming? There are several reasons that support these findings. Video games are a technologically constructed alternative reality while dream worlds are biologically constructed alternative realities. One could argue that there is simply a practice effect. If you are in an artificial reality for hours a day is it any surprise that you recognize something similar when you are in another one at night? Video gaming has been associated with improved spatial skills as has lucid dreaming. A lack of proneness to motion sickness is needed to play these games a lot and lucid dreamers have better vestibular systems thus are not susceptible to motion sickness. Finally, the high attention and absorption reported by players and in research on gaming is reminiscent of the same qualities associated with meditation. Mediators' have been found to have very high levels of lucidity in sleep.

Hard Core Gamer Interviews

In order to get a clearer picture of the players experience both during gaming and afterward as a function of gaming, Gackenbach et al (2009) conducted hour long interviews with hard core gamers. Twenty-five men and two women answered an advertisement and fulfilled the criteria of being a hard core gamer. They were 25 years of age or younger (85%). Three types of questions were asked during the hour long interviews: experiences of self during play, video game dreams, and altered states of consciousness experiences related to play. These individuals provided a total of 56 dreams which were content analyzed using the Hall and Van de Castle Coding System (Hall & VandeCastle, 1966). In this system it is assumed that frequency equals intensity and thus it is a count of a variety of dream elements and events. It has been shown that this scale has high inter-rater reliability, well developed norms and has categories which are pertinent to waking concerns which may influence dreaming.

While there were a variety of significant differences for this group from the male norms, only a few will be mentioned herein. Of note were more dead or imaginary characters appearing in dream reports of these gamers relative to the norms (21% vs 0%). As one gamer pointed out, "why be human in a game? They have fewer powers than other types of creatures." Here is an example of one such dream with dead or imaginary characters, "I dreamt I was a character is Underworld 2, it was a werewolf character and then I became a 3rd person. It was the two main characters; it was the vampire girl and a hybrid werewolf character" (Subject 001- Dream 11). This finding was the impetus for subsequent inquires into bizarreness in gamers dreams which will be looked at shortly.

Another finding of interest and that has been pursued in subsequent research was with dream aggression. Gackenbach et al. (2009) found a smaller number of dreams with aggression (32% vs 47%) yet more intense aggression (namely physical aggression, 86% vs 50%) in those gamers dreams that did contain aggression. Here is an example of dream aggression;

> …so I went outside with my cat and shot these criminals that were trying to eat my dad and they were on top of my dad trying to eat his arms and he was fighting them off, and they were trying to hold him down and bite his shoulders and there was blood and stuff. And it was a very graphic shootout for a dream (Subject 002- Dream 6).

Potentially related to dream aggression was the category of dream misfortunes. We found fewer misfortunes (7% vs 36%) and fewer bodily misfortunes (0% vs 29%) for the gamers relative to the norms. These two findings of specific aggression and less misfortune combined to precipitate our follow-up investigation into threat simulation and nightmares.

Dream Bizarreness

In two studies Gackenbach, Kuruvilla, and Dopko (in press) and Dopko and Gackenbach (2009) investigated dream bizarreness and gaming. That dreams are bizarre is essentially an illusion according to Domhoff (2007) in a meta-analysis. He pointed out that dreams are more coherent, patterned and thoughtful than previously suggested. There is still some bizarreness in adult dreams, just far less than what was expected. In the first of these two studies (Gackenbach, Kuruvilla, & Dopko, in press) recent dreams were collected in an online questionnaire from college students. Various media use information was also gathered. Using the Revonsuo and Salmivalli's (1995) scale for dream content analysis, it was found that high-end gamers evidenced more bizarre dreams than low-end gamers in two of three types of bizarreness categories.

In the second study (Dopko & Gackenbach, 2009) a two week online dream diary was gathered from preselected research participants who varied on the four game play criteria mentioned earlier. This resulted in two groups, high and low end gamers. In addition to being an online dream diary study we also asked the research participants about features that were bizarre for subjects as well as various media use information. For those who fulfilled the criteria for the dream diary component of the research project, we also administered the Verbal and the Figural tests from the Torrance Tests of Creative Thinking (TTCT: Torrance 1966; 1974). The bizarreness dream content analysis was again done using Revonsuo and Salmivalli (1995) dream content analysis system. In an analysis of covariance with covariates of sex of subject, number of words in the dream, and number of hours of media used the day before the dream, a significant gamer group by bizarreness/nonbizarreness interaction was found. Specifically, it was found that high end gamers had more bizarre than nonbizarre dreams than low end gamers for the judges reports while the opposite was the case for nonbizarre dream elements. Here is an example of a dream rated as bizarre by the judges from a high end gamer:

> I remember being in a room with my brother and his friend, the room was filled with soft triangular blocks of different colors. They were transparent, and we talked about how the blocks might represent each of us. They thought i would be the orange blocks, though I though I was the green ones (Response 35, Subject 48).

It is important to point out that media use the day before was controlled, so a straight incorporation of bizarre game or other media elements into the dream would not appear to account for this finding.

At the end of the two week dream diary period two creativity tests were administered: Figural Torrance Test of Creative Thinking and the Verbal Torrence Test of Creative Thinking. Controlling for sex of subject, we found no significant difference for verbal test results, but significant differences for the figural test, favouring the high gamer group. Finally, when considering all three components; dream bizarreness, media use - history and creativity, in a factor analysis, support for our major hypothesis was found. That is, for high end gamers dream bizarreness, as evaluated by judges, was positively associated with creativity. As with the previous study, amount of media used the day before did not load with these variables. Thus we conclude that while this data is based upon only associations, none-the-less it appears that the bizarreness in gamers dreams may be due to gamers creativity and a history of media use in the form of gaming and not due to day before media use.

Nightmares and Threat Simulation

Due to our findings in the interview study mentioned earlier, we became curious about gamers nightmares. We explored this question with additional content analyses using the Hall and VandeCastle Scale (HVDC) scale but on larger samples of gamers dreams (Gackenbach & Kuruvilla, 2008a; Le & Gackenbach, 2009). When comparing the results of all three studies, the original interview study and the two additional ones, several variables were consistent across studies but of concern here are those potentially related to nightmares and threat simulation; e.g., aggression and misfortune. One study, in addition to the original content analysis, replicated the aggression finding and both replicated the misfortune finding. Thus two studies were undertaken to further examine these results. One explored threat simulation as an explanation for the aggression and misfortune findings (Gackenbach & Kuruvilla, 2008b) and the other compared nightmares to bad dreams (Le & Gackenbach, 2009).

Revonsuo (2000) argues that dreaming is an adaptive process with an evolutionary foundation. It allows us to simulate threatening situations in the safety of a virtual environment of dreams. This continued practice during dreaming would allow an individual to better prepare for these possibly dangerous instances, were they to arise in the waking world. Gackenbach and Kuruvilla (2008b) asked the question, given the higher specific aggression but less misfortune in gamers dreams, might gamers dreams be lower in threat simulation, because they have already practiced it in their game play during the day?

Using online questionnaires where only night before dreams were collected 98 participants dreams were gathered, 35 males and 63 females. Only dreams of 40 words or more were content analyzed using the Revonsuo and Valli (2001) method of content anlaysis examining threat simulation. In a factor analysis of media use (including gaming history), threat simulation content variables and various self report variables regarding dream content, we found that when high gamers reported playing a lot of games the day prior to a reported dream, that there was no threat associated with the dreams nor were they seen as nightmarish or scary by the dreamers, despite reporting that the dreams were violent. In contrast the low end gamers did not play games the day before the dream but did watch violent TV shows or movies and had dreams that were not only high in threat simulation but also in violence, nightmarishness and scariness. Thus we concluded, as hypothesized, that gaming was associated with less threat simulation in dreams.

In a second study Le and Gackenbach (2009) compared nightmares to bad dreams of high and low end gamers in order to try to answer the question, what is a nightmare for a gamer? In an online questionnaire participants', which included 231 low- and 222 high end gamers, filled out a media usage questionnaire and an impactful dreams questionnaire. In the latter we gathered information on four types of intensive dreams; lucid, nightmares, mystical, and bad dreams. The inclusion of the lucid and mystical dreams, was to obfuscate any stigma associated with the gathering only negative type dreams. In addition to a request for a recent dream of each type, we also asked the dreamer participants to evaluate each dream along several emotional dimensions. As before the Hall and Van de Castle method for content analysis of dreams (HVDC) was utilized. Here we will focus on the findings for aggression and misfortune. We used a sum score of all aggressive subscales and all misfortune subscales in subsequent analyses. In terms of the HVDC aggression and misfortune sum scores, there were significant interactions between type of negative dream (nightmare vs bad dream) and type of gamer (high vs low) when sex of subject and number of words in the dream were controlled. In terms of aggression, high end gamers were judged to have more aggression in their nightmares than their bad dreams, while there was not much difference between these types of dreams for the low end gaming group. Following the threat simulation study findings, misfortune scores were no different for the high end gamers across dream types, while for the low end gamers there was much more misfortune in bad dreams than in nightmares. So again we see gamers fighting off threat and thus not being victums to misfortune in their negatively toned dreams.

However, when we compared the dreamers self reported emotions during these two types of negative dreams to the judge's evaluations of their emotions, opposite pictures emerged. The low end gamers showed no differences in negative emotions between their nightmares and bad dreams either as self rated or judge rated. It was the high end gamers who self reported a different emotional reaction than the judges views of their dreams. Specifically, the high end gamers saw their own bad dreams as more negative emotionally than their nightmares, while the judges saw the opposite. That is, the judges saw the high end gamers nightmares as more negative than their bad dreams. Two interpretations are possible for these apparently contradictory findings, either high end gamers get stronger and are in more command during nightmares, as based on their self-report emotions, or alternatively they are experiencing nightmares more intensely with more negative emotions than their counterparts as viewed by the judges. The second interpretation is not consistent with the previous study on threat simulation where gamer emotional reactions to the dreams were also inquired about. There is precedence in the literature for this sort of mixed result regarding dream emotions. Shredle and Doll (1998) reported that judges evaluations resulted in more negative emotions of dreams while dreamer evaluations showed no preference for positive or negative emotions. They conclude this is due to underestimating positive emotions by the judges which could be a function of the scale used, the instructions given the judges, dream recall estimates, and/or dream intensity ratings.

Conclusions and Implications

Three general dream types have been examined in our program looking at the relationship between video game play and dreams. A participant - observer gamer in our research program illuminates our major findings; yes his dreams were lucid and bizarre and he sometimes has aggression in his dreams but rarely nightmares. Rather he pointed out that he was in the 3rd person in his dreams:

> I've just noticed that sometimes I'm just there as a hovering spirit watching things go on and I don't really have a role … I don't even pop up in my dreams, it's just like I'm watching a movie … I feel emotion definitely regardless of whether or not I'm the person involved (Jordan Olischefski; Gackenbach, et al, in press)

In this chapter we reviewed three major areas of inquiry into dreams of gamers: lucid/control dreams, bizarre dreams and nightmares. We have found higher lucid/control dreams in gamers and wonder if this is indicative of improved metacognition in dreams. Increased bizarreness in gamers might imply that gamers are capable of improved "novel adaptive responses" as per the Global Workspace theory of consciousness. Finally, in terms of aggression/misfortune in dreams, we found some association between gaming serving a Threat Simulation function in waking and potentially a protective function regarding nightmares, if not bad dreams. While not entirely clear taken together it seems that a case can be made that larger neuronal assemblies in sleep are associated with video game play while awake.

References

Domhoff, G.W. (2007). Realistic simulation and bizarreness in dream content: Past findings and suggestions for future research. In D. Barrett and P. McNamara (Eds.), *The New Science of Dreaming: Content Recall, and Personality Characteristics*. (Vol 2, pp. 1-27). Westport, CT. Praeger Press.

Dopko, R. and Gackenbach, J.I. (2009, June). *Video Game Play, Dream Bizarreness and Creativity*. Paper presented at the annual meeting of the International Association for the Study of Dreams, Chicago, ILL.

Gackenbach, J.I. and Kuruvilla, B. (2008a). Video game play effects on dreams: Self-evaluation and content analysis. *Eludamos. Journal for Computer Game Culture*. **2**(2), 169-186.

Gackenbach, J.I. and Kuruvilla, B. (2008b). The relationship between video game play and threat simulation dreams. *Dreaming*, **18**(4), 236-256.

Gackenbach, J.I. (2006). Video game play and lucid dreams: Implications for the development of consciousness. *Dreaming*, **16**(2), 96-110.

Gackenbach, J.I. (2009) Electronic media and lucid-control dreams: Morning after reports. *Dreaming*, **19**(1), 1-6.

Gackenbach, J.I. (2009). Video Game Play and Consciousness Development: A Replication and Extension. *International Journal of Dream Research*, **2**(1), 3-11.

Gackenbach, J.I., Kuruvilla, B. and Dopko, R. (in press). Video game play and dream bizarreness. *Dreaming*.

Gackenbach, J.I., Matty, Ian, Kuruvilla, Beena, Samaha, Ashley Nicole Zederayko, A., Olischefski, J. and Von Stackelberg, H. (2009). Video game play: Waking and dreaming consciousness. Stanley Krippner (Ed.), *Perchance To Dream*, Hauppauge, NY: Nova Science Publishers, p. 239-253

Gackenbach, J.I., Matty, I., Kuruvilla, B., Samaha, A.N., Zederayko, A., and Olischefski, J. (in submission). Video Game Play: Waking and dreaming consciousness explored through interviews of hard core players. *International Journal of Dream Research*.

Hall, C., and Van de Castle, R. (1966). *The content analysis of dreams*. East Norwalk: Appleton Century-Crofts.

Le, H. and Gackenbach, J. (2009). *Nightmares of Video Game Players: What do They Look Like?* Paper presented at the annual meeting of the International Association for the Study of Dreams, Chicago, ILL.

Revonsuo, A. (2006). *Inner Presence: consciousness as a biological phenomenon*. Cambridge, Massachusetts: MIT Press.

Revonsuo, A. and Salmivalli, C. (1995). A content analysis of bizarre elements in dreams. *Dreaming*, **5**(3), 160-187.

Shredle, M. and Doll, E. (1998). Emotions and diary dreams. *Consciousness and Cognition*, **7**(4), 634-646.

Torrance, E. P. (1966). *The Torrance Tests of Creative Thinking - Norms-Technical Manual Research Edition - Verbal Tests, Forms A and B - Figural Tests, Forms A and B*. Princeton NJ: Personnel Press.

Torrance, E. P. (1974). *The Torrance Tests of Creative Thinking - Norms-Technical Manual Research Edition - Verbal Tests, Forms A and B - Figural Tests, Forms A and B*. Princeton NJ: Personnel Press.

In: Computer Games
Editors: A. Soria et al, pp. 137-142
ISBN 978-1-60876-658-1

Chapter 6

RACING GAMES

Vladimir Gurvich*
RUTCOR, Rutgers University,
640 Bartholomew Road,
Piscataway NJ 08854-8003

Abstract

I would like to suggest a family of computer games which modify (in fact generalize) some well-known games: such as Chess, Checkers, Go, Go-Moku, Reversi, etc. The main idea is simple: **do not wait for your turn**, move as soon as you wish and can. However, to realize a move you need to define it by your cursor. This takes time, since there are six main parameters of the game: handicap delay, move delay, cursor movement delay, and the same three parameters (which might take different values, yet) are defined for the opponent. These six parameters can be chosen in such a way that the Racing and Standard versions of a game become (almost) equivalent. On the other hand, if all delays are small enough then it becomes more important to make a fast move than clever one. In Racing games, speed and brains can be traded. Moreover, in general, whether a move is smart or not will depend on the parameters.

Racing Chess, Go, and Go-moku were realized in the late 80s by Vladimir Oudalov and Andrei Vasiliev from Moscow. This program works on any IBM/PC compatible with CGA, EGA, VGA or Hercules. Although, this version can hardly be of any use now, since it works only

*E-mail address: gurvich@rutcor.rutgers.edu.

with DOS and no "windows version" was ever written. Yet, if somebody will find such a task interesting then the following notes might help.

Key words: Racing Chess, Go, Go-Moku, Reversi.

1. Do Not Wait for Your Turn

This is the main principle of Racing Games.

Two players (or one and a computer) are playing chess according to the standard rules with only one exception: each player can move any time, it is not necessary to wait for your turn.

For example, if you are quick enough you can move three times while your slower opponent is making only one move. It would be hardly possible to realize such a modification on a standard chess-board, but playing with a computer (or with a human by means of a computer) the idea of racing is easily implementable.

Your goal is to take opponent's King before he takes yours. Strictly speaking, the standard rules of Chess should be modified a bit. Such standard chess concepts as "mate" or "stale mate" are eliminated. One can play until his King is on the board, otherwise the opponent wins.

Confess that playing the standard quick chess you would like to move several times in a row. However, the opponent would object. In Racing Chess it is an absolutely legal option.

In Racing Go-Moku we can keep all rules except alternating. The aim of White (Black) is to put five White (Black) stones in a row: horizontal, vertical, or diagonal.

Similarly, we can introduce Racing Go, Checkers, Reversi, Back-Gammon, Domino, or even Billiard, etc.

2. Players

There are two players WHITE (W) and BLACK (B) and four options for each one, to play with: (L) Left keys, (R) Right keys, (M) Mouse, or (C) Computer. For example, W = C and B = M means that you (Black) are playing with the mouse against computer (White).

Let us remark that combinations B = L, W = L; B = R, W = R; B = M, W = M are forbidden, while B = C, W = C (computer with itself) is possible; moreover, it can be quite interesting and educational.

3. Cursor Control

First of all, let us note that there are TWO cursors: the black and white ones. A cursor can be moved by one movement from a current square to one of 8 of its neighbors (2 horizontal, 2 vertical and 4 diagonal). Respectively, Left keys are Q W E A D Z X C and ENTER to mark, while Right keys are 1 2 3 4 6 7 8 9 and INSERT to mark.

Notice that such choice is natural for a 20-year-old keyboard but not for a modern one.

4. How to Move

In Go-Moku, you just fetch your cursor to the square you are going to occupy and mark it.

In Chess, every move consists of two parts: first, you fetch your cursor to the piece you are going to move by, and mark this piece, then, you fetch your cursor to the square you are going to move on and mark this square, too.

Let us note that, while you perform all these operations, the position on the board might change, because in the same time the opponent could make some move(s). Moreover, as a consequence, your move might become illegal.

All illegal moves are just ignored, no other punishment. Let us note that the rules "how to move" differ for the different games. For example, Go-Moku, Go, and Reversi are similar, while Chess, Checkers, Domino and Back Gammon differ from them and one from another.

5. Parameters

The whole family of Racing Games is based on a few parameters.

5.1. Time Delays

This is the most important group of parameters.

(A) MOVE DELAY. After each move, cursor disappears for TM seconds.

(B) MOVEMENT DELAY (or CURSOR DELAY). After each movement (to a neighbor square) cursor disappears for TC seconds.

Since these delays are introduced for White and Black, we obtain TMW, TMB, TCW, TCB.

Let us remark that for small delays it is more important to be ”quick” than ”clever” while for larger delays, it is vice versa. In Racing Games players easily can trade Brains for Reaction by adjusting parameters.

Finally, let us introduce one more parameter:

(C) HANDICAP DELAY. White cursor appears TH seconds ahead of the Black one, where TH may be positive or negative.

For example, let us choose TMW = TMB = 1000, TCW = TCB = 0, and TH = 500. It is easy to understand that the obtained Racing version will be very close to the Standard one. Indeed, two players will take turns unless one of them will think MUCH LONGER than the opponent.

5.2. Cursor Modes

After each move cursor disappears for TM seconds. Where does it appear then? There are several options. Two of them are deterministic:

(S) Cursor appears at the same square and (F) Cursor appears at a fixed square,

while five others are stochastic, namely cursor jumps with the same probability to each square of a given set of squares from the following list:

(A) all, (B) occupied, (I) occupied by the own pieces, (O) occupied by opponent's pieces, and (F) non-occupied squares.

For example, MCW = S, MCB = A means that White cursor always appears at the same square (where it disappeared), while the Black cursor can be expected at any square with the same probability. Obviously, such parameters are favorable for White in Chess and, especially, in Go-Moku.

6. Variety of Racing Games

By playing with parameters, we can realize a great variety of games. If we choose some very big move delays and some very small cursor delays, for example, TCW = TCB = 0; TMW = TMB = 10 ; TH = 5. The obtained game is rather similar to the standard one, quick Chess or quick Go-Moku. Just time control looks rather special (like "biomi" in Japanese games). Only if your opponent is too slow, you might occasionally move twice in a row but usually you will take turns.

If we choose TCW = 0.2, TCB = 0.3; TMW = 3.0, TMB = 0.5; TH = 0 (MCW = MCB = A) then the obtained game will differ a lot from the standard one but still some common features remain. Yet, if we fix something like TCW = 2.0, TCB = 1.0; TMW = 0.07, TMB = 0.1; TH = 7 (MCW = MCB = A) then it will be something totally different. Indeed, standard values of moves are changed by the racing. By rough estimate, to obtain the "racing value" of a move we should divide its "standard value" by its "performance-time". Obviously, the good and the bad moves will be mixed by this transformation. Let us notice that there are more accurate ways to approximate the "racing value" of a move. These ways are realized in the Oudalov and Vasiliev codes.

7. Adjustment of Parameters

By playing with parameters, we can realize a great variety of racing games. Yet, they rarely will be interesting if we choose parameters at random. An adjustment is necessary to get equal chances with a stronger or weaker opponent, or with the computer.

Let us choose, for example, Chess or Go-Moku. For the beginning, let computer plays for both, White and Black. Now, let us fix some modes for both cursors MCW and MCB. For example, let MCW = MCB = A, that is both white and black cursors after each move jumps to any square with the same probability.

Then, let us fix the delays. For the beginning, we will not use the handicap delay, so let us set TH = 0. The most important is adjusting the move and delays for White and Black (TMW, TCW and TMB, TCB). Let us fix, for example, TMW = 1.41, TMB = 3.14, and TCW = TCB = 0.2, then start the game and we will see that White easily win. So let us increase TCW and/or decrease TCB until we get an equal game.

Later we can introduce some positive or negative TH as well as we can use other modes of cursor behavior.

Let us also note that different modes are not equivalent. For example, the modes MC = S, cursor appears at the same square, and MC = I, cursor appears randomly but only at squares occupied by player's own pieces, give advantage in Chess and, especially, in Go-Moku. Of course, this advantage can be compensated by time delays or by the level of the opponent.

8. Computer Plays with Itself

It might be very useful (and quite exciting) just to watch the computer playing for both, White and Black. Doing so you can learn some hidden options of Racing. Try for example Go-Moku with parameters: MCW = MCB = A; TMW = 0.3, TMB = 3, TCW = 1.0, TCB = 0.1. Once we watched a "BICYCLE SURPLUS" in Go-Moku. Black and White cursors just wandered around some important place on the board for a long time and made no moves. We can explain this phenomenon but we did not expect it.

In: Computer Games
Editors: A. Soria et al, pp. 143-166
ISBN 978-1-60876-658-1

Chapter 7

PREDICTING FOREIGN EXCHANGE TIME SERIES WITH AN EXTENDED ISING MODEL

Christopher A. Zapart[*]
The Graduate University for Advanced Studies,
Department of Statistical Sciences,
The Institute of Statistical Mathematics,
4-6-7 Minami-Azabu, Tokyo, Japan

Abstract

The chapter investigates the use of an extended Ising spin glass prior in predicting financial time series. It introduces a probabilistic model consisting of a large number of computational agents (small neural networks and fuzzy logic systems) acting as nodes in a two-dimensional Ising spin glass. The research has been inspired partly by earlier applications of Minority Games (Lamper, D and Howison, S and Johnson, 2001, "Predictability of large future changes in a competitive evolving population", Advances in Condensed Matter and Statistical Physics) in predicting financial time series. In addition the chapter also investigates whether or not there are any benefits in using an intrinsic time scale when forecasting high-frequency foreign exchange time series. The method converts a constant frequency at which financial time series are sampled into a variable intrinsic trading frequency of real stock markets. This so-called intrinsic trading time may be more suitable when dealing with market models in which internal agents trade at fixed regular intervals.

[*]E-mail address: czapart@ism.ac.jp

Key words: econophysics, Ising model, minority games, high-frequency financial time series, time series prediction, foreign exchange currency markets, intrinsic trading time

Pacs: 89.70.Cf, 89.65.Gh, 89.75.-k

1. Introduction

Forecasting financial time series such as foreign exchange rates or stock market indices is recognised to be unreliable and difficult, as evidenced by poor out-of-sample performance of econometric models yielding apparently good in-sample fits [1]. Established forecasting techniques typically involve finding a linear or non-linear regression function $f(\cdot)$ that takes as arguments past values of econometric time series $x(t)$:

$$x\left(t+\Delta T\right)=f\left(x\left(t\right),x\left(t-1\right),x\left(t-2\right),\ldots,x\left(t-p+1\right)\right)+\varepsilon \qquad (1)$$

with ε accounting for noise and p denoting the number of predictor variables. However, in cases where observed time series $x(t)$ come from financial markets, for example foreign exchange currency returns, the equation (1) may not be able to capture sufficiently the underlying time series generator and its often non-stationary nature. Because of the difficulties experienced by conventional approaches [1], over the past decade there has been considerable interest expressed by the research community in applying Minority Games to study financial time series. The use of the Minority Game Theory in financial markets can be traced back to a seminal paper [2] published in 1997. Readers unfamiliar with minority games may find the following references [3] and [4] useful. A more detailed explanation of how to build realistic market models within the context of minority games is provided in [5].

At the root of all minority game theory models lies a simple observation: for a given level of risk in financial markets no single investment strategy or a trading system remains "excessively"[1] profitable in the long term. In other words, stock markets tend to be mean-reverting. As soon as a highly successful investment strategy is discovered, increasing numbers of traders tend to adopt it. When a majority of market participants start using it, the profitability of such a

[1] "Excessive" profits can be thought of as being above the long-term growth rate of the economy.

strategy gradually diminishes. The only entities that benefit from the profitable strategy are early adopters able to take advantage of it in early stages when only a small minority of traders are aware of it. This results in a minority of traders benefiting at the expense of the losing majority. In most types of minority games there are N binary computational agents that buy or sell imaginary shares in a competitive setting. At each time step, of those N agents N_+ will be found placing buy orders and N_- will be sellers. From a physics perspective minority games resemble a spin glass — a disordered magnetic material with a high level of frustration. By frustration one usually means the inability of a system to remain in the lowest energetic state. The "buy" decisions are equivalent to an "up" magnetic spin orientation, and "sell" operations correspond to the "down" spin.

Although very good forecasting results from minority games were reported earlier in [5, 6], other authors have also encountered somewhat less positive experience [7]. Hence the probabilistic model described in this chapter does not attempt to follow strictly minority games. Financial time series arise directly as a result of interactions between a large number of traders. As an alternative to equation (1), from a physics point of view a much more attractive proposition is to try to approximate the underlying processes responsible for generating the time series in the first place. In the probabilistic model presented in this chapter individual traders are represented by simple computational agents (neural networks, fuzzy logic systems [8]). Although these agents take trading decisions primarily based on the equation (1), they are also influenced in a minority game-like fashion by actions taken by other agents. The minority-like behaviour is enforced by placing computational agents in nodes of a two-dimensional grid that behaves like a probabilistic Ising spin glass. Such an approach attempts to mimic the real world in which speculative traders analyse past data looking for patterns and trends whilst at the same time trying to guess the reactions of other market participants.

2. Probabilistic Computational Agents

This section introduces a probabilistic multi-agent forecasting model — inspired by the minority game theory — where the prior probability of "buy" and "sell" states is given by an extended Ising model. Initially a short introduction to the Bayes formulæ will be given.

Given two sets of events A and B, the Bayes formulæ can be used to express the conditional probability of an event B given A:

$$P(B_i|A) = \frac{P(A|B_i)P(B_i)}{\sum_{i=1}^{N} P(A|B_i)P(B_i)}. \tag{2}$$

In statistical modelling the Bayes formulæ, given in its standard form by equation (2), is often used to combine information from two distinct sources of information: i) model parameters derived purely from observational data and ii) prior (often subjective) expectations of the practitioner about the general structure of the model and/or nature of the experimental data. For example one could impose a prior expectation that experimental data conform to a somewhat truncated Gaussian distribution. The cut-off (truncation) could be due to a physical constraint such as limitations of the measuring device etc.

From a non-statistician physicist point of view, in the context of a certain physical system capable of assuming states S_i Bayesian analysis can be interpreted in the following way:

$$P(S_i|\theta) = \frac{P(\theta|S_i)P(S_i)}{Z} \tag{3}$$

where θ is a vector of some internal parameters and Z is a normalising constant to ensure $P(S_i|\theta)$ is a proper probability (i.e. $0 \leq P(S_i|\theta) \leq 1$ and $\sum_i P(S_i|\theta) = 1$). For completeness $Z = P(\theta) = \sum_{i=1}^{N} P(\theta|S_i)P(S_i)$. From equation (3) it is clear that the probability of a system being in a state S_i given the internal configuration θ is influenced by two factors: i) the prior probability $P(S_i)$ of the state S_i and ii) the probability $P(\theta|S_i)$ of the internal parameters θ given the specific system state S_i. The system will be found in a state S_i with a high probability only when both these factors coincide (in regions where they both exhibit high probabilities) since the resulting $P(S_i|\theta)$ will also be high. However, if one of the factors has a low probability, it will automatically lead to a reduced probability of the state S_i. The term $P(\theta|S_i)$ can be derived from experimental observations. The prior $P(S_i)$ is either assumed based on a subjective (but hopefully well-informed) choice made by an experimenter or, as is the case in *Empirical Bayes Analysis*, it is also derived directly from experimental data. Non-Bayesian statisticians and some physicists in particular may have serious reservations about the use of the Bayes formulæ as per equation (2). In statistics the choice of the prior probability $P(B_i)$ (or $P(S_i)$ in equation (3)) is often highly subjective, subject to interpretation, and hence it is possible to come up with differing formulas for modelling the same physical phenomenon, which is somewhat disturbing to the author. One way to avoid the controversy would be to let the prior reflect the underlying physics governing the problem at hand. For example, the prior expectation could be that entropy of a closed and isolated physical system tends to increase. Therefore the states S_i leading to a lower net entropy would be prohibited (physically impossible).

Within the context of computational agents acting as nodes in an Ising spin glass, to calculate the posterior probability $P(S = S_i|x(t), \theta)$ of an agent being in a state S_i given an observed data sequence $x(t)$ and model parameters θ, the Bayes formulæ could be applied in the following manner:

$$P(S = S_i|x(t), \theta) = \frac{P(x(t), \theta|S = S_i)P(S = S_i)}{Z} \tag{4}$$

where $P(x(t), \theta|S = S_i)$ is the conditional probability of the state S_i making a contribution towards the outcome $x(t)$. The calculation of this conditional probability will be discussed in the subsection 2.2.. Prior probabilities of states $S = S_i$ are provided by an extended Ising model, as described in the subsequent subsection. In [9] Sornette discusses the use of an Ising model in financial markets. The dynamics of spin glass-like evolutionary minority games was also studied in [10]. The Ising spin glass can also be interpreted as a form of a Majority Game with a strong element of local imitation. Traders check the trading decisions made by other agents in the immediate neighbourhood and formulate their output as a weighted average of other traders' decisions. As opposed to Minority Games, traders here attempt to follow the herd, the prevailing majority of agents. In [9] an argument has been made for using majority behaviour to model trend-following financial time series. On the other hand, there exists a body of evidence from econophysics [6] for using the Minority Game Theory to explain large moves in the stock market. Fortunately, both the majority and minority views can be accommodated by the Ising model. To this end we introduce the concept of a *Local Majority/Global Minority* Ising prior. On a global scale agents would try to adopt positions different from their competitors in order to gain competitive advantage, in order to differentiate their strategies. However, within their local neighbourhood agents would tend to imitate neighbouring strategies in an attempt to follow trends of the stock market.

2.1. Extended Ising Prior

In the original Ising spin glass model the state of a local node S_i is a function of states of other nodes S_j, $j \in N_i$ from the immediate neighbourhood N_i of

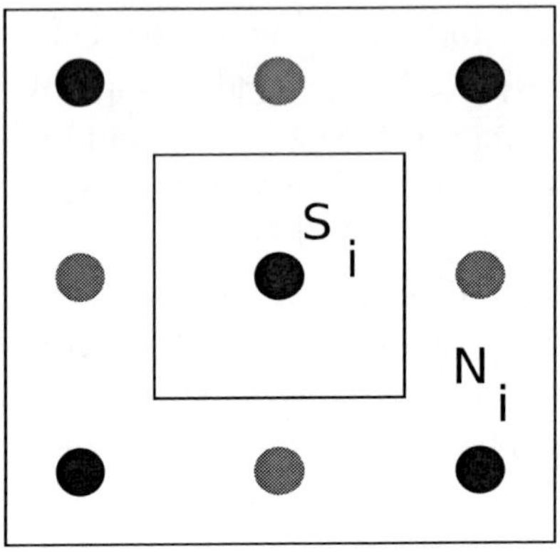

Figure 1. A local neighbourhood N_i for a node S_i in a 2D Ising model. The red colour denotes the four nodes used in the original 2D lattice Ising spin glass.

S_i and the connection strengths $J_{i,j}$ linking the S_i node to S_j, as shown in an example 2D rectangular lattice in figure (1). The node S_i can be found in two possible states: "-1" or "$+1$" with probabilities given by

$$P\left(S_i = -1\right) = \frac{\exp\left(-\beta\theta_i\right)}{\exp\left(-\beta\theta_i\right) + \exp\left(\beta\theta_i\right)} \tag{5}$$

$$P\left(S_i = +1\right) = \frac{\exp\left(\beta\theta_i\right)}{\exp\left(-\beta\theta_i\right) + \exp\left(\beta\theta_i\right)} \tag{6}$$

$$P\left(S_i\right) = \frac{\exp\left(\beta S_i\theta_i\right)}{\exp\left(-\beta S_i\theta_i\right) + \exp\left(\beta S_i\theta_i\right)},\ \theta_i = \sum_{j\in N_i} J_{i,j}S_j \tag{7}$$

where β is a constant parameter governing the global characteristics of the model[2] and θ_i expresses the level of interaction between the node S_i and all the other nodes belonging to the neighbourhood N_i. Typically the connection strengths $J_{i,j}$ are all set to the same constant value of for example $+1$. It can be observed that for $J_{i,j} > 0$ (corresponding to a ferromagnetic state) the Ising model takes on a form of a probabilistic imitation (or majority) game. The agents (nodes on a 2D lattice) assume the prevailing state of their neighbours

[2]For certain values of β the Ising model can exhibit interesting unstable behaviour. It can constantly keep switching between two regimes: one dominated by most agents being in a "+1" configuration and another one with a dominant "-1" state.

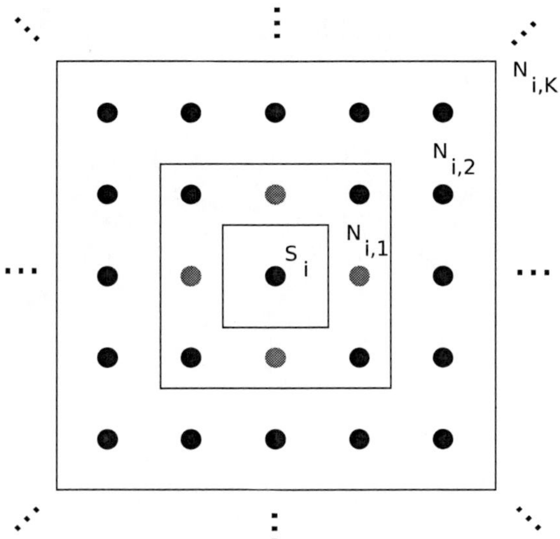

Figure 2. Multiple-level neighbourhoods $N_{i,K}$ for a node S_i in an extended Ising model. The neighbouring nodes from the original 2D Ising model are shown in red.

with the probability proportional to the average state of the neighbouring nodes. This is equivalent to positive correlations between states S_i and S_j. However, in the opposite case of $J_{i,j} < 0$ (analogous to an antiferromagentic state) the model exhibits a local minority game behaviour. In the extreme variant where the "local" neighbourhood N_i includes all the remaining nodes S_j, $j \neq i$, one would obtain a global probabilistic minority game where agents attempt to adopt a state opposite to the prevailing (majority) view.

One can exploit the ability of an Ising model to represent both majority and minority games in order to try to reconcile the seemingly opposite views of how to model behaviour of financial markets. Hence in an extended Ising model used in this chapter we define multiple levels K of neighbourhood $N_{i,K}$ to make a smooth transition between a local majority behaviour for small K (corresponding to $J_{i,j} > 0$, $j \in N_{i,\text{small } K}$) and a global minority game for all the other levels (corresponding to $J_{i,j} < 0$, $j \in N_{i,\text{large } K}$) (see figure (2)). The equation (7) needs to be modified to take into account multiple levels K of

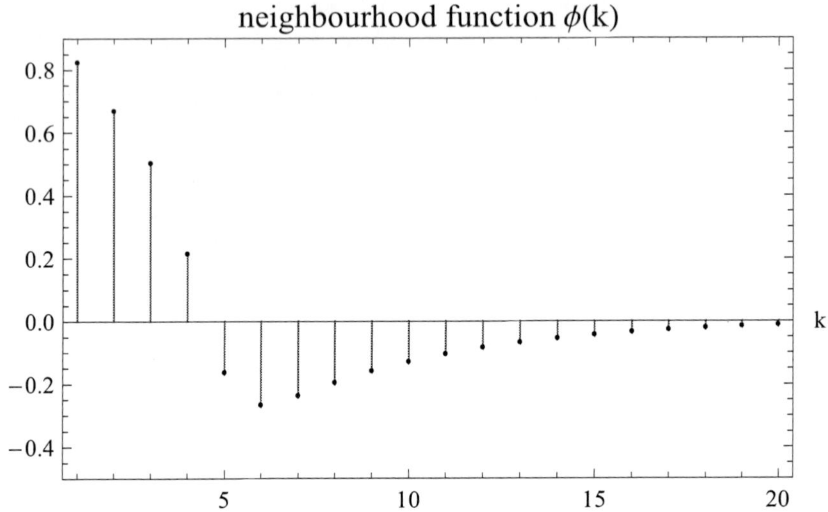

Figure 3. A hyperbolic tangent neighbourhood function $\Phi\left(N_{i,k}\right)$, $\omega = 4.5$, $\rho = 1$, $\tau = 5.0$ for a node S_i used in an extended Ising model as it asymptotically approaches 0 for large k.

neighbourhood $N_{i,K}$:

$$\theta_i = \sum_{k=1}^{K} L_k \left(\Phi\left(N_{i,k}\right) \sum_{j \in N_{i,k}} J_{i,j} S_j \right) \tag{8}$$

where $L_k = 1/k$ is the scaling coefficient to compensate for the increasing number of nodes in the successive neighbourhoods $N_{i,k}$[3]. For convenience we set $J_{i,j} = 1$ for all nodes and instead use the neighbourhood function $\Phi\left(\cdot\right)$ to change the sign (vary the character of the game) from local majority to global minority as the neighbourhood index increases. Figure (3) shows one example of a such a neighbourhood function provided by a hyperbolic tangent with an exponential decay envelope:

$$\Phi\left(k\right) = -\tanh\left(\frac{k-\omega}{\rho}\right)\exp\left(-\frac{k}{\tau}\right) \tag{9}$$

[3]The number of nodes in each successive neighbourhood is directly proportional to the neighbourhood index k.

where ω denotes the point where the game changes character from majority to minority, ρ controls the steepness of the transition and τ governs the exponential envelope as it decays asymptotically to zero.

It is worth noting that a mirror image opposite model is also possible: a *Local Minority/Global Majority* Ising prior by inverting the sign of the neighbourhood function $\Phi(k)$.

2.2. Inference

Suppose that a time t a node S_{ij} indexed by $\{i, j\}$ on a 2D $size \times size$ lattice is found initially in a state $S_i \in \{-1, +1\}$. Given the past price history until x_t, in the inference process we seek the probability $P(S_{ij} = S_i|x_t)$ of the node S_{ij} remaining in the state S_i during the transition from t to the next time step $t + 1$. Intuitively it corresponds to stock market traders (represented here by nodes S_{ij}) taking directional views on the future moves of the stock market.

At the beginning of section 2. an intuitive physicist's interpretation of Bayes was given in which the probability $P(S_i|\theta)$ depended on two factors: the prior probability $P(S_i)$ of the current state S_i and the conditional probability $P(\theta|S_i)$ of a model given the state S_i. In the right circumstances where these two probabilities coincide the prior tends to reinforce (or reconfirm) the model. In keeping with a spirit of this interpretation the probability $P(S_{ij} = S_i|x_t)$ is modeled in this chapter as a product of two factors: the **prior** $P(S_i)$ and the probability $P(y_{ij} \Rightarrow S_i|x_t)$ of the **model** y_{ij} implying the current state S_i:

$$P(S_{ij} = S_i|x_t) \propto \text{model} \times \text{prior} \tag{10}$$

$$P(S_{ij} = S_i|x_t) \propto P(y_{ij} \Rightarrow S_i|x_t)P(S_{ij} = S_i) \tag{11}$$

where $y_{ij} \in [0, 1]$ is an output from a non-linear model (fuzzy logic or neural networks) associated with the node S_{ij}. Computational agents are trained to predict the sign of the next one-step-ahead price return x_{t+1} based on m previous returns: $y_{ij} = y_{ij}(x_t, x_{t-1}, x_{t-2}, \ldots, x_{t-m+1})$. The output $y_{ij} \in [0, 1]$ is then interpreted as a probability of the next move x_{t+1} being "+1": $P(y_{ij} \Rightarrow +1|x_t) = y_{ij}$. In order to introduce a certain degree of diversity to the population of agents, each model is randomly assigned a training dataset of a varying length $T \in [T_{min}, T_{max}]$. Hence in the proposed probabilistic model simple computational agents placed in the nodes of a 2D extended Ising spin glass act as diverse "intelligent traders". At first the following equation was considered as a formal way of combining the model with the prior:

$$P(S_{ij} = S_i|x_t) = \frac{P(y_{ij} \Rightarrow S_i|x_t)P(S_i)}{\sum_k P(y_{ij} \Rightarrow S_k|x_t)P(S_k)}. \tag{12}$$

However, after some preliminary experimentation with the model it became clear that equation (12) could not cope adequately with very large or very small probabilities coming from the model or the prior. As a workaround a small neural network function $\mathrm{f_n}$ has been implemented to yield

$$P(S_{ij} = S_i|x_t) = \mathrm{f_n}\left(P\left(y_{ij} \Rightarrow S_i|x_t\right), P\left(S_i\right)\right). \tag{13}$$

This is illustrated in figure (4) with the training data set provided in the table (1). The next states $S_{ij}(t+1)$ for all agents are randomly selected according

Table 1. A small training data set used to initialise the neural network posterior mapping given by equation (13).

model	prior	$P(S_{ij}\|x_t)$	model	prior	$P(S_{ij}\|x_t)$
1.0	1.0	1.0	0.25	0.25	0.25
0.0	0.0	0.0	0.75	0.75	0.75
1.0	0.0	0.5	0.25	0.5	0.5
0.0	1.0	0.5	0.5	0.25	0.5
0.5	0.5	0.5	0.75	0.5	0.5
0.75	0.25	0.5	0.5	0.75	0.5
0.25	0.75	0.5			

to the posterior probabilities $P(S_{ij} = S_i|x_t)$. In a deliberate departure from the original Ising spin glass, the selected states $S_{ij} \in \{-1, 1\}$ are further weighted by the *confidence to trade* coefficient c_{ij}:

$$S_{ij}(t+1) = \frac{S_{ij}}{1 + \exp(-\mu c_{ij})} \tag{14}$$

where $\mu > 0$ controls the steepness of the sigmoid function. Therefore the final selections are allowed to assume continuous values $-1 < S_{ij}(t+1) < +1$. After the arrival of a new price return $x(t)$ (also denoted by x_t) the confidence c_{ij} is updated individually for each node through an exponentially-weighted moving average:

$$c_{ij} = \kappa \,\mathrm{sgn}(x_t)\,\mathrm{sgn}(S_{ij}) + (1-\kappa)\,c_{ij} \tag{15}$$

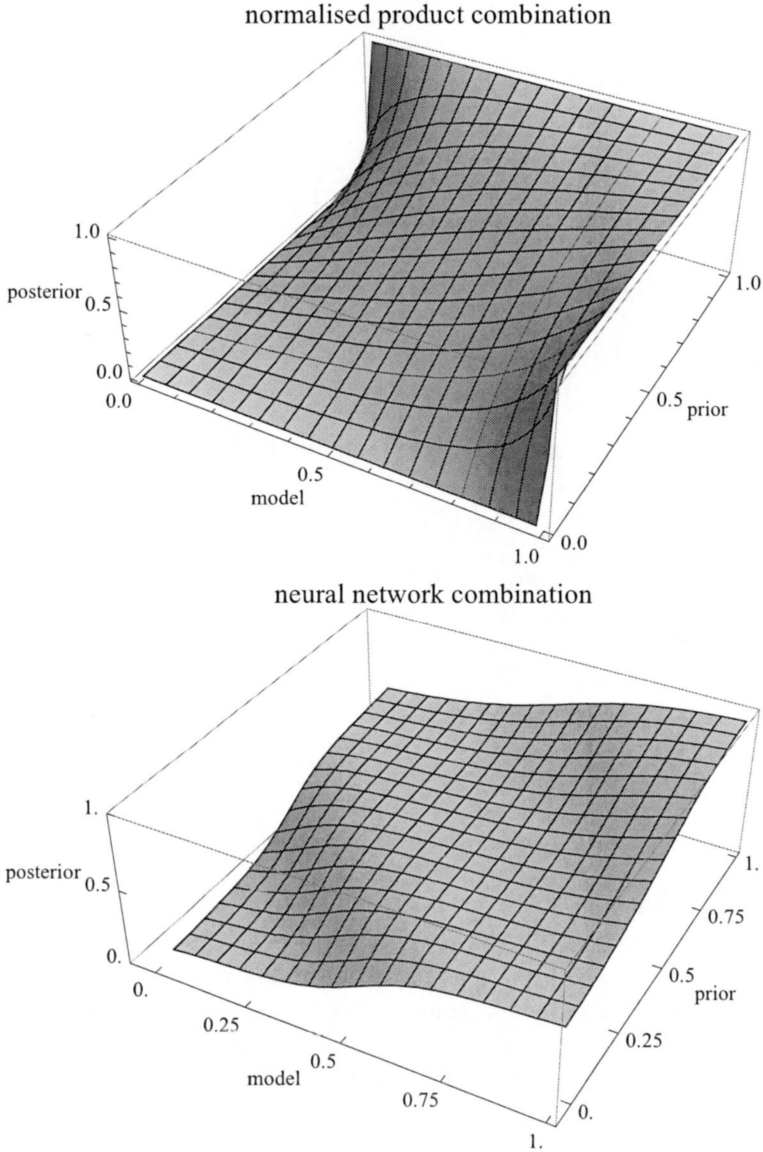

Figure 4. A normalised posterior mapping $P(S_{ij}|x_t)$ given by equation (12) (top) versus an alternative mapping provided by neural networks (bottom) as per equation (13).

with an exponential smoothing coefficient κ. Subsequently the model forecast $y(t+1)$ for the next return $x(t+1)$ is obtained by averaging the newly-selected states S_{ij}:

$$y(t+1) = size^{-2} \sum_{i=1}^{size} \sum_{j=1}^{size} S_{ij}(t+1). \tag{16}$$

3. Model Parametrisation

There are a number of parameters controlling internal dynamics of the proposed probabilistic forecasting model:

- ρ, ω and τ in the neighbourhood function $\Phi(k)$
- temperature β in the prior $P(S_i)$
- κ and μ in the *confidence to trade c*
- the number of past returns m used to estimate x_{t+1} by computational agents
- the range $[T_{min}, T_{max}]$ for the duration of training sets used by those agents
- dimensions of the 2D grid.

Choosing the right set of parameters adequate for modelling given financial time series does not seem straightforward. The most important parameter that regulates the amount of "randomness" exhibited by the model is the temperature β. Altering the three parameters from the neighbourhood function Φ can completely change the character of the probabilistic model from a minority game-like behaviour to a majority game. Another choice to be made is deciding whether to use small neural networks or fuzzy logic models as computational agents. Utilising small artificial neural networks as grid nodes potentially offers superior modelling accuracy. However, fuzzy logic systems offer a speed advantage since during tuning they require only one pass through the entire training dataset as opposed to multiple passes involved in slow gradient-based training of neural networks. As at each time step t all agents are fully retrained, a fuzzy logic model has been chosen for use in the simulations described in section 5..

3.1. Choosing β

The dynamics exhibited by an Ising model strongly depends on the choice of the temperate parameter β. A close look at equations (5) and (6) reveals that as $\beta \rightarrow 0$ both $P(S_i = -1)$ and $P(S_i = +1)$ approach the value of 0.5, at which point the model behaves in a totally random way with nodes being independent of each other. On the other hand, a very large β results in a deterministic oscillatory behaviour between the two states of "-1" and "+1" due to $P(S_i = -1)$ or $P(S_i = +1)$ approaching either 0.0 or 1.0. In an Ising model β controls the amount of randomness present in the dynamics of the model. This is further illustrated by the figure (5) where information-theoretic Shannon entropy H, defined for the extended Ising prior as

$$H = -\sum_{i=1}^{size}\sum_{j=1}^{size}\sum_{k=1}^{2} p(S_{ij} = S_k)\log p(S_{ij} = S_k), \tag{17}$$

approaches its maximum theoretically possible value H_{MAX} as $\beta \rightarrow 0$[4]. For large β randomness entirely disappears and the prior becomes deterministic. It is not clear at all how much randomness one should be deliberately inducing into a financial model through the modified Ising prior. In physics one often seeks to identify phase transitions in dynamical systems for which a certain parameter exhibits a maximum sensitivity to, for example, temperature β. The original 2D Ising lattice experiences phase transitions at a critical value β_C. Intuitively, by a loose analogy to physical phase transitions one could set β heuristically to such a β_C for which the entropy H experiences maximum sensitivity to β. This corresponds to an inflection point in the entropy curve fitted experimentally to

$$H(\beta) = \frac{H_{MAX}}{1 + \beta^a b}. \tag{18}$$

From the bottom plot in figure (5), and from numerically finding the root of $\frac{\partial^2}{\partial \beta^2}\frac{H(\beta)}{H_{MAX}}$ one can identify the inflection point at a critical temperature $\beta_C \approx 0.3$. This value will be used in the initial experiments with the probabilistic forecasting model.

[4]For a two-state Ising model maximum entropy H_{MAX} occurs when $P(S_+) = P(S_-) = 0.5$.

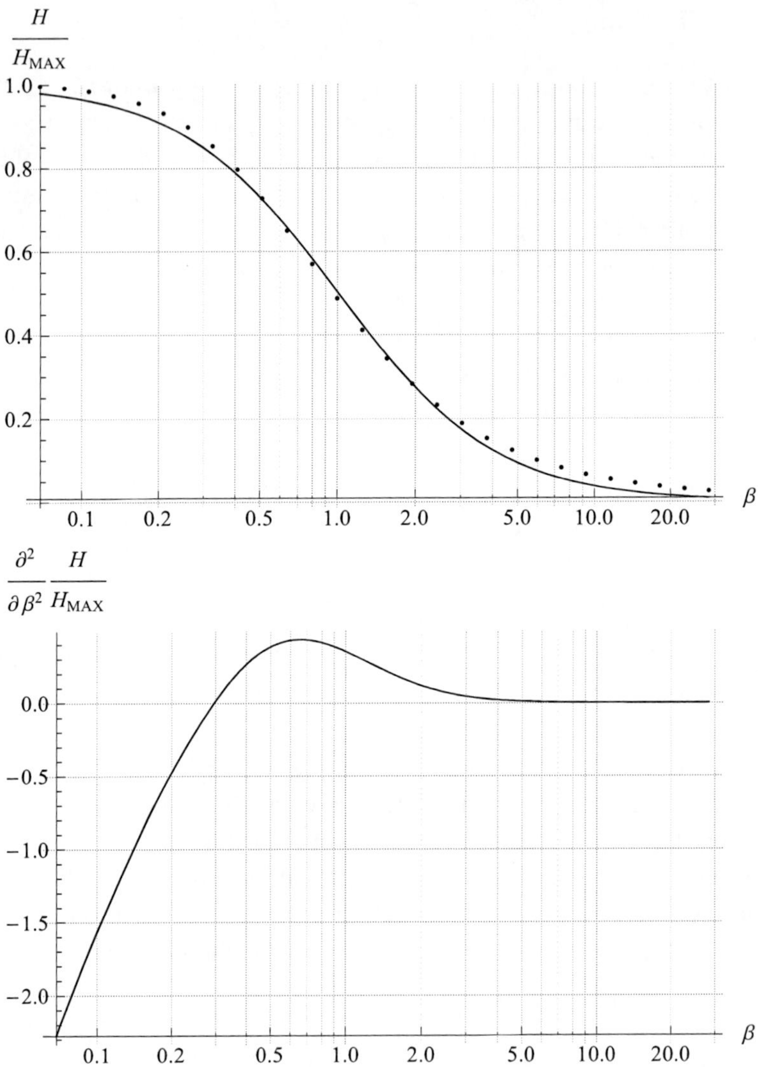

Figure 5. Entropy H as a function of β obtained for an extended Ising prior on a 2D 30x30 grid (top). The bottom plot shows the second partial derivative $\frac{\partial^2}{\partial\beta^2}\frac{H}{H_{MAX}}$ which is used to infer an inflection point (or a critical temperature β_C) at $\beta \approx 0.3$. The solid line represents the least-squares fit with a sigmoid-derived function $\frac{H}{H_{MAX}} = 1/\left(1+\beta^a b\right)$.

3.2. Other Parameters

The remaining model parameters have all been set heuristically to the following values: $\rho = 1.0$, $\omega = 4.5$, $\tau = 5.0$, $\kappa = 0.1$, $\mu = 10.0$, $m = 3$, $T_{min} = 25$ and $T_{max} = 125$. These represent plausible values based on prior experience of the author with financial time series prediction and minority games. The size of the 2D grid was set to 30×30 which is similar to grids used in [10].

It is unreasonable to expect that the same set of parameters would facilitate successful prediction of a wide range of different financial time series. Instead some numerical optimisation procedure should be employed to fine-tune the model settings. Gradient-based maximum-likelihood techniques cannot be easily applied because of the difficulty in calculating analytically the gradients of any assumed error cost function. Bayesian statisticians would strongly favour setting up a Bayesian inference framework for inferring automatically the parameters. However, first, there is a split in the statistics community between those favouring maximum likelihood and those in favour of Bayesian inference — in other words using Bayesian methods is highly contentious. Second, after performing some simple computer experiments with one-dimensional Bayesian modelling the author cannot place full trust in Bayesian inference. The method seems subjective because of using an arbitrary prior. Furthermore, it introduces an artificial bias through a prior[5] and is computationally expensive. Although a more established alternative maximum likelihood parameter estimation method is not without its problems (for example sensitivity to outliers), in the toy experiments performed by the author it managed to recover the true one-dimensional model parameter with a greater accuracy and speed.

The personal preference of the author would be to employ either Simulated Annealing [11] or preferably an optimisation technique borrowed from machine intelligence: Genetic Algorithms [12]. As a fitness function to optimise one could choose to maximise the correlation between predicted and true returns on a training dataset. However, irrespective of the chosen optimisation method one would still need to evaluate the probabilistic model a large number of times with different sets of parameters. Despite using a SONY PlayStation 3 containing a fast SONY/IBM/Toshiba CELL processor in some experiments[6] (the software

[5]The bias introduced by the prior only disappeared when a very large number of data points was used. However, given a large data sample the more established maximum likelihood approach consistently produced more accurate results.

[6]SONY PlayStation 3 was used in initial simulations not involving the neural network mapping given by equation (13). This is due to a difficulty porting the external FANN neural networks

architecture is shown in figure (6)), this computationally expensive evaluation process is still too slow to allow a full numerical optimisation of all the parameters within a reasonable time frame. For this reason in the subsequent section an

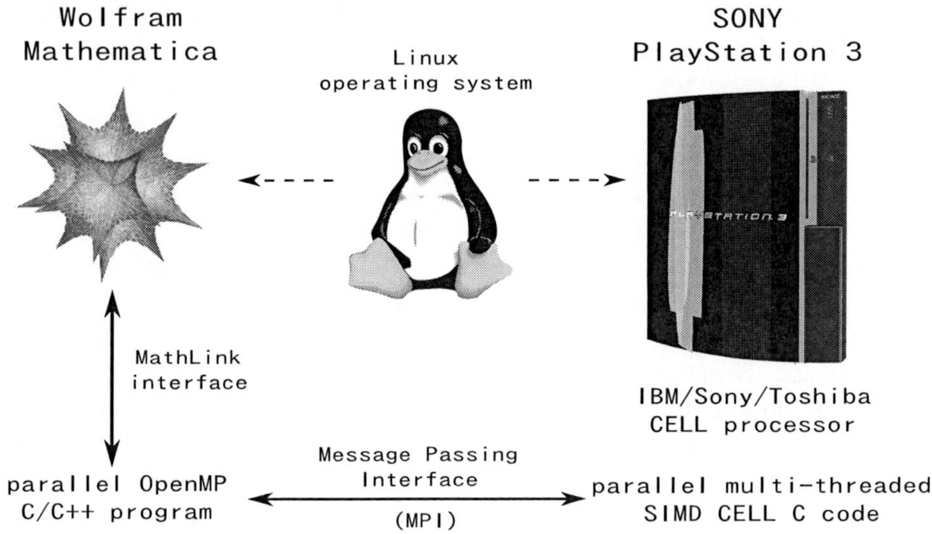

Figure 6. Software architecture involves linking Wolfram Mathematica running on a desktop Linux workstation with Sony PlayStation 3 also running a Gentoo Linux operating system.

experimental demonstration of the forecasting model will be restricted to using heuristic parameters only.

4. Intrinsic Time Scale

When forecasting financial time series researchers usually tend to work with data sampled at regular intervals, for example one day or one hour. In case of high frequency time series this means that equal importance is attached to samples corresponding to both quiet times with little trading activity (night time)

library (http://leenissen.dk/fann/) to run efficiently across the CELL Synergistic Processing Units (SPUs). The Fuzzy Logic implementation was developed internally by the author to execute fast on CELL SPUs.

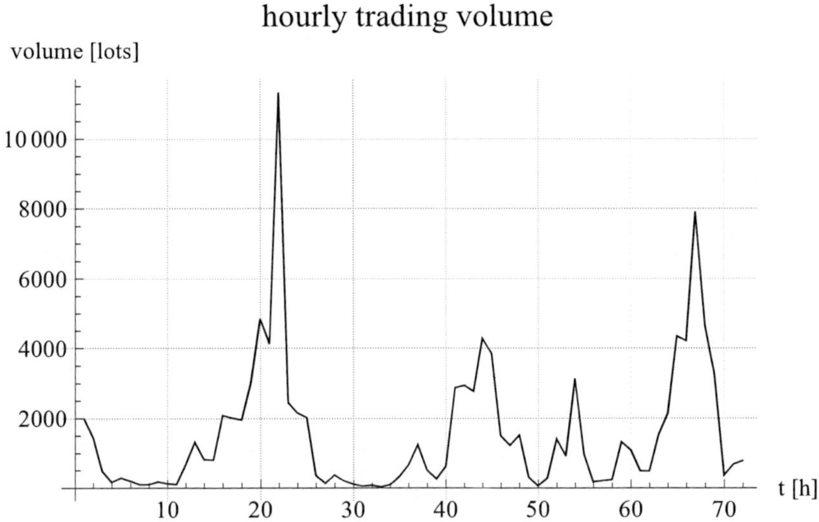

Figure 7. The number of futures contracts traded in one-hourly intervals during the last three days of December 2005.

as well as daytime business activity. The figure (7) illustrates this fact by plotting the hourly trading volume (number of lots)[7] of the Japanese Yen/US Dollar exchange rate futures at the end of December 2005. One can notice repeating spikes of high activity interspersed with quiet periods. Unsurprisingly, a simple Fourier analysis of the entire year 2005 volume time series reveals a well-defined (see figure (8)) fundamental frequency that corresponds to the period of 24 hours, with the second harmonic frequency corresponding to a period of 12 hours. It can be speculated that the shorter 12-hour period is caused by a late secondary spike in activity due to American investors trading in yen. In [13], and more recently in [14] it has been argued that instead of working with high-frequency time series sampled at regular intervals (i.e. one hour), the sampled time series should follow a non-linear intrinsic trading time. Accordingly such a trading time scale attempts to compress quiet passages whilst expanding high-activity periods of time. One practical implementation of an intrinsic trading time involves modelling the functional relationship between either the

[7]The number of traded lots is extracted from the *volume* column of the GLOBEX tick-by-tick historical futures data.

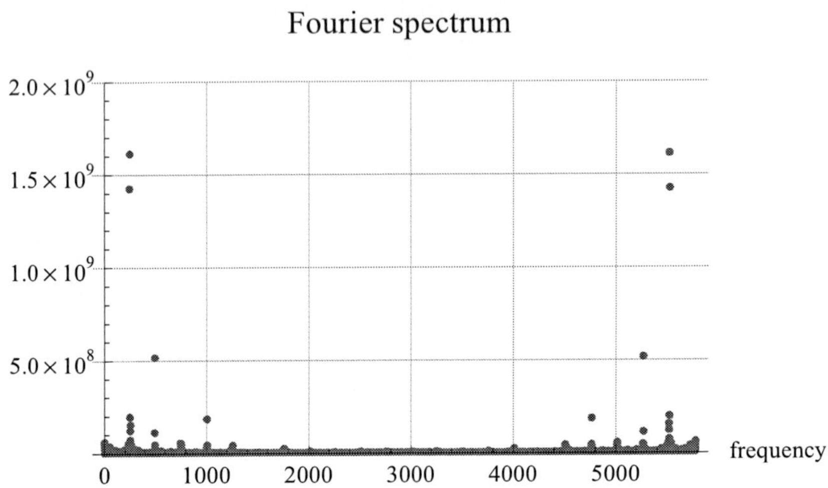

Figure 8. A Fourier spectrum of the one-hourly trading volume during year 2005. At least three well-defined harmonic components can be deduced with periods approximately 24, 12 and 6 hours.

mean volatility (used in [13]) or the mean trading volume V (proxied in [14] by counting the number of ticks) and the sampling interval ΔT according to the power scaling law:

$$\langle V \rangle = A \Delta T^B. \tag{19}$$

The constants A and B are estimated experimentally from a double-logarithmic plot of $\langle V \rangle$ as a function of ΔT, shown for the year 2005 in figure (9). Given a high frequency (tick-by-tick) time series $x(t)$ and a reference fixed sampling interval $\Delta T = 1$ hour, the goal is to estimate the intrinsic time scale $\upsilon(t)$ at time t. Values $\upsilon > 1$ correspond to faster flowing time; $\upsilon < 1$ corresponds to time flowing slower in comparison with a fixed sampling interval ΔT. The intrinsic time scale $\upsilon(t)$ is given by the following equation:

$$\upsilon(t) = k \exp\left(\frac{\log V(t) - \log A}{B}\right) / \Delta T, \tag{20}$$

where $V(t)$ is the trading volume measured over an interval ΔT ending at time t and the constant k is used to adjust the overall average flow of time. For simplicity k is set to 1 in this chapter. When sampling from the tick-by-tick

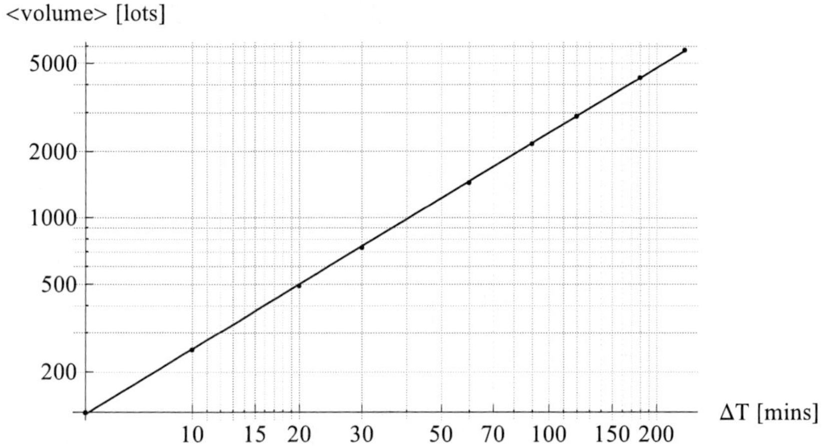

Figure 9. A double-logarithmic plot of average trading volume as a function of a sampling interval (shown here between 5 and 240 minutes). The solid line shows a least-mean squares fit with the power law as per equation (19). The average volumes were calculated from the year 2005 Japanese Yen/USD exchange rate futures time series.

data, the time intervals $\delta t_i = t_i - t_{i-1}$ between two adjacent samples $x(t_{i-1})$ and $x(t_i)$ are rescaled by $v(t_i)$: $\delta t_i^* = v(t_i)\delta t_i$. As can be observed in figure (7) the trading volume time series is very noisy. Therefore the logarithm of $V(t)$ used in equation (20) has been pre-filtered using a discrete Fourier transform, as shown in figure (10).

5. Simulations

In the experimental part of the chapter the probabilistic model is applied to short-term (one-step ahead) prediction of the Japanese Yen/US Dollar exchange rate futures collected by the author from the GLOBEX FTP historical download service during the years 2005, 2006 and 2007. The raw tick-by-tick dataset is sampled at one-hourly intervals to yield regularly-spaced time series. For comparison the raw data is also transformed using the intrinsic time scale compressing quiet periods and expanding times of increased activity. For simplicity and partly in order to avoid the so-called "curse of dimensionality", fuzzy logic

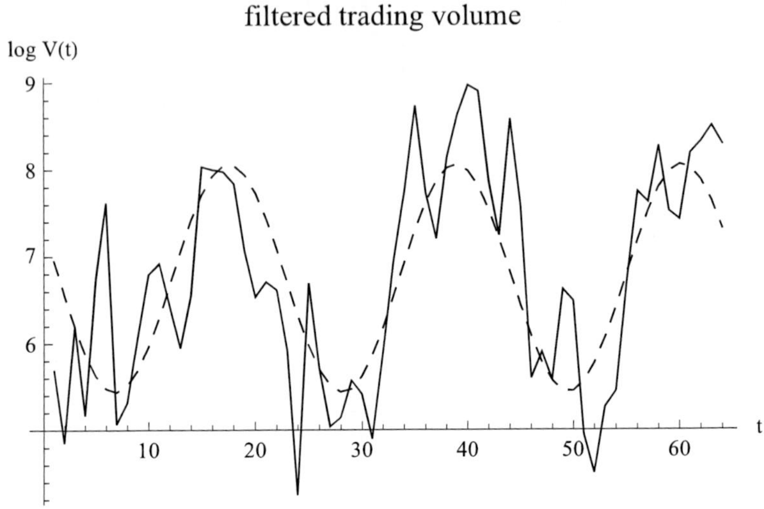

Figure 10. Trading volume time series $\log V(t)$ (solid line) filtered with a discrete Fourier transform (dashed line). Only the first fundamental harmonic frequency is used in the reported experiments.

computational agents use only two fuzzy sets to encode returns $x(t)$: "POSITIVE" and "NEGATIVE".

The next figure 11 shows internal snapshots of agents' current states, the extended Ising prior, outputs from fuzzy logic models and the combined "posterior" probabilities. The profit/loss graphs obtained from hypothetical trading of one futures contract during the years 2005 — 2007 are shown in figure (12). Given the probabilistic nature of the model, simulations were repeated 100 times with the model outputs averaged to form a single forecast. Transaction costs were not taken into account in this preliminary investigation. Compared with the baseline "buy-and-hold" strategy, most of the time the performance of the agent-based model using a normal time scale was competitive. However, more satisfactory trading profits were realised only after utilising the intrinsic time scale. A further investigation is needed to ascertain whether or not different filtering schemes for the volume time series $\log V(t)$, for example linear models or simple neural networks, lead to further improvements in the forecasting performance.

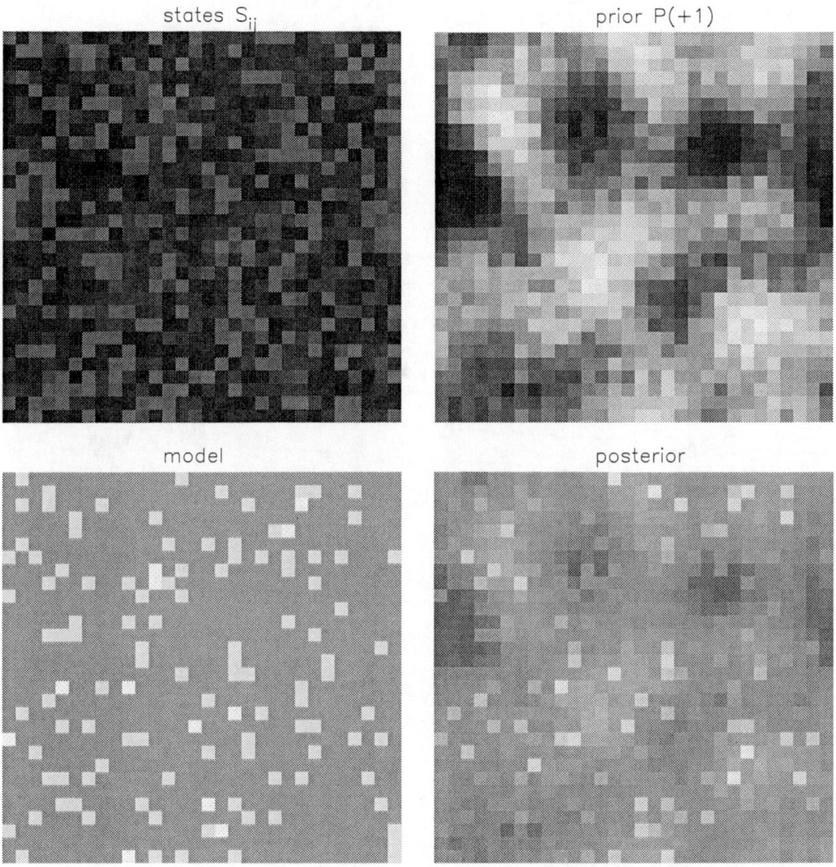

Figure 11. Example output from simulations. The top left chart visualises current states S_{ij} of models distributed on a 2D grid. The various shades of blue represent positive states $S_{ij} > 0$ whereas the red colour corresponds to $S_{ij} < 0$. The posterior probability (bottom right) is influenced by both the prior (top right) and the model (bottom left). The prior reflects the probability $P(S_{ij} = +1)$ whilst the model array visualises the probability $P(y_{ij} = +1|x_t)$.

6. Conclusions

Established statistical time series forecasting techniques, both linear regression and non-linear neural networks, do not take into account the generative aspect of financial time series. Such time series arise directly as a consequence of inter-

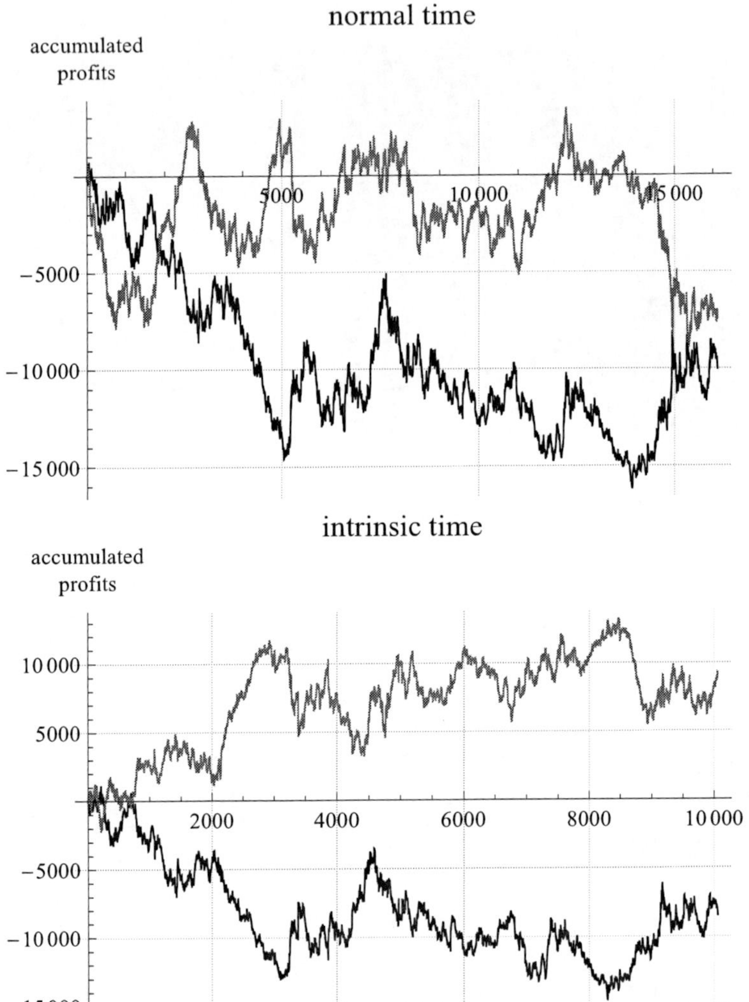

Figure 12. Profit/loss plots for the years 2005 — 2007 comparing the normal time (top) versus the intrinsic time scale (bottom). The black curve represents profits accrued by the baseline "buy-and-hold" strategy. The performance of the proposed probabilistic model is denoted with the red colour.

actions between a large number of often irrational traders. In contrast, computational agent-based models attempt to recreate some aspects of these interactions, which from a physics point of view is a much more attractive proposition.

The chapter introduced a new agent-based forecasting model that utilises an extended Ising model. After applying the method to forecasting intra-day Japanese Yen/US Dollar exchange rate returns, encouraging experimental results have been obtained. The unoptimised version of the probabilistic model has been found capable of offering above-average (better than chance) forecasting performance. Although at present the relatively large computational requirements render impractical an attempt at automatic parameter optimisation, it is anticipated that future advances in computing facilities will lift this limitation. The study presented in this chapter also examined whether or not there is an advantage to be gained from sampling high frequency financial time series according to its intrinsic time scale. The time transformation attempts to under-sample quiet periods and over-sample busy periods of time. Experimental results obtained using the intrinsic trading time have been shown to benefit from this non-linear time scale.

The results from preliminary experiments serve as an encouragement for expending further time and effort into developing a fully optimised version of the proposed model.

Acknowledgements

The author would like to acknowledge financial support received from the Japanese Ministry of Education, Culture, Sports, Science and Technology.

References

[1] M P Clements, P H Franses and N R Swanson, Forecasting economic and financial time-series with non-linear models, *International Journal of Forecasting,* **20/2**, 2004, 169–183

[2] Emergence of Cooperation and Organisation in an Evolutionary Game, D Challet and Y C Zhang, *Physica A,* **246**, 1997, 407

[3] *The Minority Game: an introductory guide*, E Moro, Advances in Condensed Matter and Statistical Physics, February 2004

[4] *Minority Games: Interacting Agents in Financial Markets (Oxford Finance)*, D Challet, M Marsili and Y Zhang, Oxford University Press, 2005

[5] P Jeffries, M L Hart, P M Hui and N F Johnson, From market games to real-world markets, *European Physical Journal B - Condensed Matter and Complex Systems,* Springer, 2001, 493–501

[6] D Lamper, S Howison and N F Johnson, Predictability of large future changes in a competitive evolving population, *Advances in Condensed Matter and Statistical Physics*, 2001

[7] J V Andersen and D Sornette, A mechanism for pockets of predictability in complex adaptive systems, *Europhysics Letters,* **70 (5)**, 2005 697–703

[8] *Neural Networks and Fuzzy Systems: A Dynamical Systems Approach to Machine Intelligence*, B Kosko, Prentice Hall, 1991

[9] *Why Stock Markets Crash: Critical Events in Complex Financial Systems*, D Sornette, Princeton University Press, 2003

[10] E Burgos, H Ceva and R P J Perazzo, Order and disorder in the local evolutionary minority game, *Physica A,* **354**, 2005, 518–538

[11] C R Reeves, *Modern Heuristic Techniques for Combinatorial Problems*, Halsted Press, 1993

[12] *Adaptation in Natural and Artificial Systems*, J H Holland, University of Michigan Press: Ann Arbor, MI, 1975

[13] U A Muller, R Dacorogna, R D Davé, O V Pictet, R B Olsen and J R Ward, Fractals and Intrinsic Time - A Challenge to Econometricians, *Opening address of the XXXIXth International Conference of the Applied Econometrics Association (AEA), Real Time Econometrics – Submonthly Time Series,* Ascona, Switzerland, 1993

[14] E Derman, The Perception of Time, Risk and Return During Periods of Speculation, *Quantitative Finance*, **2**, 2002, 282–296

In: Computer Games
Editors: A. Soria et al, pp. 167-191
ISBN 978-1-60876-658-1

Chapter 8

EXPLORING THE EDUCATIONAL POSSIBILITIES OF COMPUTER GAMES FOR 7TH GRADE MATH

Hillevi Gavel* ***and Kimmo Eriksson***†
School of Education, Culture and Communication
Department of Applied Mathematics
Mälardalen University, Sweden

Abstract

Computer games constitute an important part of young teenagers' life in Sweden. This paper reports on our exploration of whether computer games can be put to good use for mathematics educational purposes for this age group. First, we discuss which positive role computer games could potentially play; in brief, we think that computer games can be used as a complement for making routine practice more varied, more enjoyable and more effective. Second, we describe a game that we have developed for practising the arithmetic of fractions. An important module of this game is built on our novel specification of how to automatically generate sensible problems of well-defined difficulty, which is the third point. Fourth, we report how the game has been evaluated by users (students and their teachers). Fifth, we present results of diagnostic tests given before and after playing this game, indicating a positive effect on learning. Last, we discuss what we have learnt from this study.

*E-mail address: hillevi.gavel@mdh.se
†E-mail address: kimmo.eriksson@mdh.se

Key Words: educational computer games, computer generated problems, arithmetic of fractions

AMS Subject Classification: 97U70

1. Introduction

The aim of this study is to explore the educational possibilities of computer games in mathematics for 13-year-old students. Bluntly speaking: Can computer games be any good at all in math class, and if so, how? Since this is an explorative piece of work, we tell the story as it unfolded. This means that we report, for each stage of the project, on the deliberations made at that stage.

We begin with some background on the use of of computer games in education. In section 3. we then describe how we, from sound didactical principles, have tried to create a computer game that could fill a niche in math education for Swedish 7th grade students.

For reasons to be explained, we chose the topic to be the arithmetic of fractions. A particular challenge was to generate a large set of sensible problems of well-defined difficulty. We think that our solution to this problem is the most important contribution from this project and will prove to be useful also in other settings. We describe it in detail in section 4..

The game has been extensively user tested, both with students and their teachers. Section 5. presents the procedures and results of these user-tests. In brief, user comments have been generally very positive. Many constructive ideas for improvements have also been given, several of which are implemented in the present version of the game.

Of course, in order to deserve being used in math class, the game must be more than a positive experience; it must be educationally effective. In section 6. we describe a procedure for testing the effectiveness of playing the game. Preliminary results indicate that the game does indeed have some effects of the desired kind. We discuss how a large-scale study could be carried out and what parameters would be interesting to investigate.

We conclude with our own critical assessment, summarizing our answer to the research question posed above.

2. Background: Computer Games in Education

Games have been used for educational purposes for a long time, but the use has increased during the last 50 years. This is connected to the rapid growth of the computer gaming industry and to the many educational reforms starting in the 1960s. In Sweden, the whole school system was re-organised (Skolöverstyrelsen [15], Marklund [10]), and much effort put into getting away from "old-fashioned" teacher-centred instruction. In the USA the "new math" (Bosse [2]) was introduced, and it was quickly adopted in Sweden as well.

There are several reasons for using educational games (Sandford and Williamson [13], Shaftel et al. [14]). In our area, these are the most important ones:

- Since children like games, and often play them in their spare time, giving them a game with educational contents can be a simple way of getting some extra learning into the daily life.
- Since playing games is entertaining, a game may be used for longer time and with greater attention than a traditional school task with similar contents. Even when the game setting is less efficient, considered from a "material learnt per unit of time" perspective, the game may still be more effective if it is sufficiently engaging to be used for longer periods of time.
- The occasional use of games can make the school situation more varied, and thus more interesting.

Games that are to be used in schools have to be selected with the same care as any other teaching materials, and their use carefully planned and evaluated (Shaftel et al. [14]). The present study contributes to a growing body of research on educational computer games (Amory et al. [1], Zavaleta et al. [18], Rieber [12], Prensky [11]).

Games can be divided into "classical" games (e.g. board games) and computer games, but that is not the only way of classifying them, nor the most useful, because the medium does not say much about the game as such. It is more informative to classify them according to *style* (cf. Tveit and Tveit [16]). For example, games can be single- or multi-user; they can be fast paced or demand considerable deliberation; they can include chance to a greater or lesser extent; etc. When we study *educational* games, we also have to analyse their educational value.

Educational games are supposed to have some educational contents. These can be more or less integrated in the whole. If you regard chess as an educational game (teaching logic, strategy, planning and so on), the whole game is a teaching experience. On the other end of the spectrum are games where the reward for a correctly solved educational problem is some "fun" gaming. A game can be highly educational but still not very good regarded as a *game*, meaning that it is not fun to play. And since the whole point of using a game as a means to an educational end is that it should be fun, that makes them pointless. A good educational game has to be both educational and fun. Gough [7] gives a very good summary of mathematical games (computer and traditional, fun and not-so-fun).

Not all educational games have as a goal to actually *teach* new things. In many cases the aim is to practice things already learned. Learning involves several steps, going from a first understanding to a deeper understanding. In mathematics, learning includes practising, to help memorisation and develop the conceptual awareness. This practice can be quite boring. Klawe [8] states that computer games have been found quite effective in making such practice more engaging.

Educational *computer* games have some advantages over ordinary games. A problem with many educational games is that the number of questions or problems is limited. A child who likes the game will learn them all by heart. A computer game can be loaded with a very great or virtually infinite number of problems. It is also usually impossible to cheat. Then, there are practical aspects. Computer games do not contain any small parts that get broken or lost, and they do not take up much space. (These aspects are important elementary schools and day-care centres.)

A disadvantage is that you need a computer, which puts restrictions on when and where they can be used. Computers are found in most schools, where they have many other uses than just being play-stations (cf. Cuban [4]). They can be used for text editing, information seeking, and so on, and there also exist much educational software that are not games. Laborde [9] gives a good description of one such product. An advantage of educational games as compared to other educational software is that good games are self-motivating; you want to keep on using them. That decreases the need for supervision (to check that the students are doing what they are supposed to do), and since the computers often are placed outside the class-rooms, this is an important aspect.

3. The Math Game

In 2003, we submitted a project proposal to an advanced course in computer programming at the Royal Institute of Technology (KTH). In this course, groups of students had to run big programming projects under realistic conditions.

Our proposal was named "A game for learning mathematics". The description was not very detailed, leaving the greater part of the design to the students. The most important points we made were:

1. The game should be an easily installed single-user game. A game of this kind will probably be used in a school (or an afternoon day-care) setting, and the computer resources and competence can vary widely. Some schools have a separate computer room, others have one or two computers in each class-room. A game connecting several computers can be more interesting to play, but only a few schools would be able to use it. The game should run under MS-Windows, since that is the most widely used operative system.

2. The game should be extendible. The programmers should provide a platform, that we (or anyone) could fill with contents.

3. The game should be entertaining enough to make it probable that children would actually play it (at least if is the only game available and/or the alternative is normal school work).

4. The educational value should be so apparent that teachers, who sometimes are very negative to computer-games (cf. Sandford and Williamson [13], p. 8), would be prepared to let their students spend time using it.

The students used many resources (one of them younger siblings, who were interviewed and asked for input on the suggested design). The end result was a "Super-Mario"-inspired platform game. The player negotiates a labyrinth-like obstacle course, jumping hurdles, climbing ladders, avoiding monsters, while trying to find treasures. The treasures are hidden in boxes waiting to be opened by the player. Some boxes contain extra lives, some contain bonus points, some contain questions. The end user can add game courses and questions.

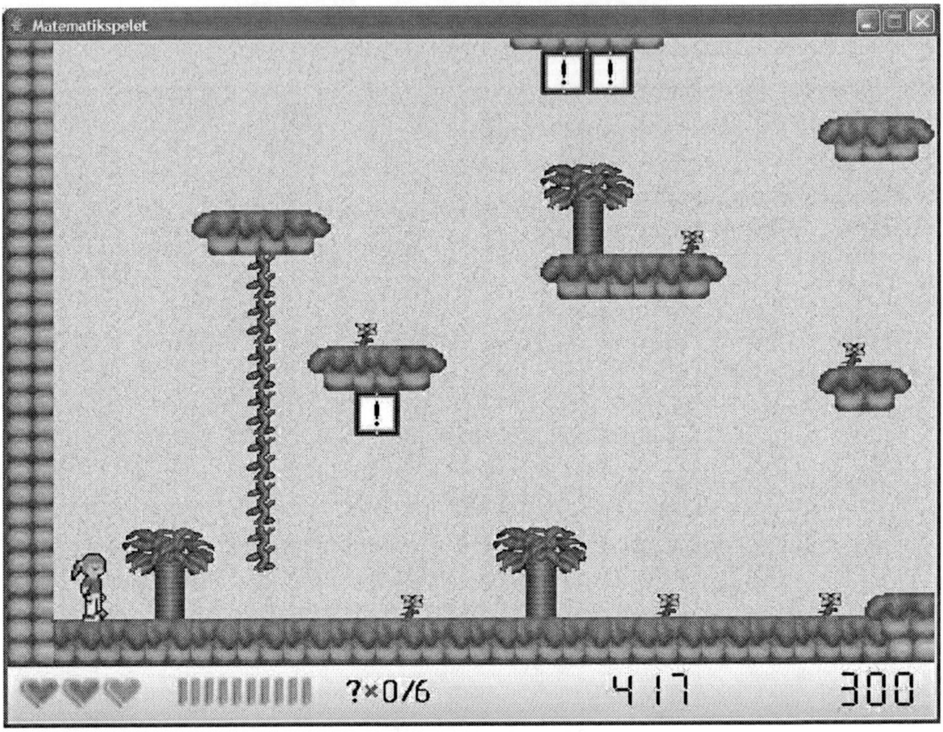

Figure 1. Start at the first course at level 1. The player has chosen to be a girl. The "treasures" are found in the white boxes marked with an exclamation mark. The player jumps and hits the boxes with her head to open them. The hearts (the first two are red and the last one gray) indicates that the player has already spent one out of three available "lives". The bars indicates health in the current life. (You loose some health every time you touch a monster, and can regain health by eating fruits. When you have spent all your health, you loose a life.) The "? × $0/6$" does not mean anything at this course; at other courses it tells how many questions you need to answer to get a key to open a more convenient door than the default one. "417" is the number of seconds you have left to complete this course. "300" is the number of points you have.

3.1. The Game Setting

This is a description of the version of the game used at the last user evaluation, after several modifications based on user input given at the earlier trials.

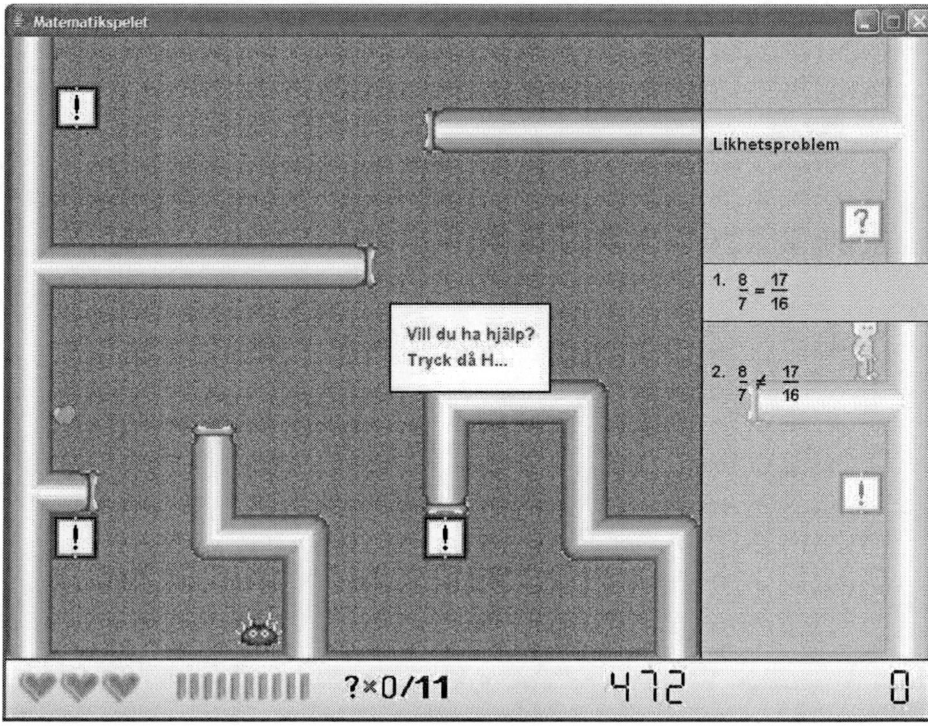

Figure 2. A question at the second course at level 1. The player has chosen to be a boy. (He can be seen behind the question; the opened question box has changed to an question mark. An empty box is marked with an ×.) The text in the middle translates to "Do you want help? Then click H. . . ". The point of this question (does $\frac{8}{7}$ equal $\frac{17}{16}$?) is that *adding* the same number to the numerator and the denominator does *not* mean that the value is unchanged. (A common mistake is to overgeneralise "multiplying the numerator and the denominator with the same number does not change the value" to "doing the same thing—no matter what—in the numerator and the denominator does not change the value".)

After choosing a game character, you arrive at a room with several exits, one for each difficulty level. Manipulating the character using the key-board, you choose a door to walk through, and arrive at the first course at the chosen level. Figure 1 shows a player at the start of level 1. The goal is to open all boxes at

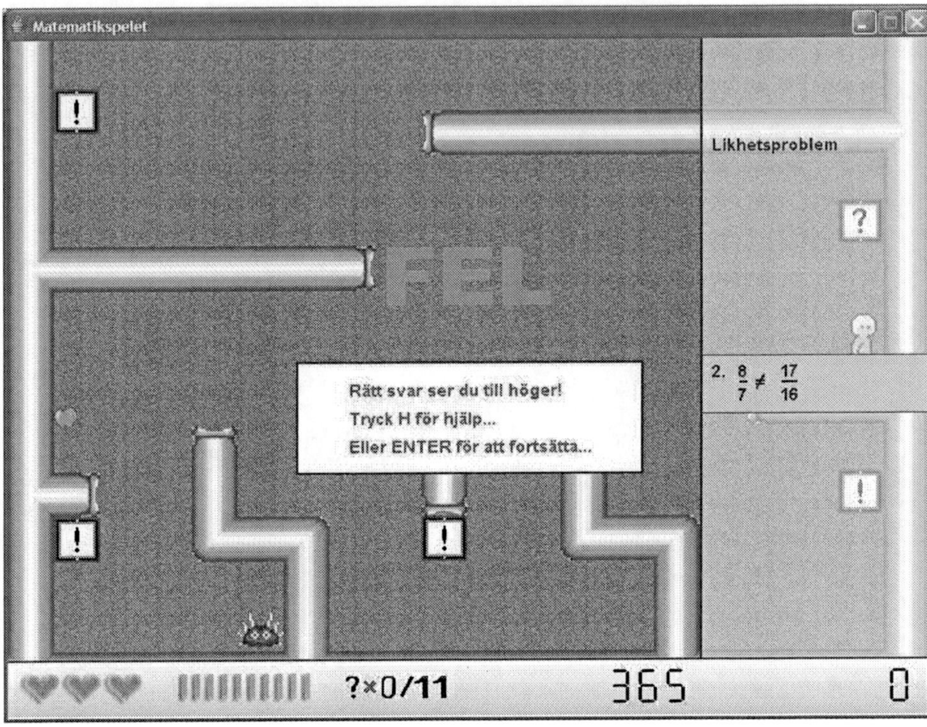

Figure 3. What happens if you choose the wrong answer. The text reads "WRONG. The right answer is shown to the right! Press H for help... Or ENTER to continue...".

the course before passing through the door to the next course. The time to do this is limited; when the clock reaches zero, you are dead.

When the head of the character hits a question-box, the question pops out, as shown in Figure 2. The clock ticks on, but movement is impossible until you have answered the question. You can ask for help. Then the clock stops, and a helptext pops out. (Two examples of helptexts are shown in Figures 4 and 5 in section 4.3..) You have to close the helptext before choosing your answer. If the answer is correct, you get 100 points, and can resume the game. If the answer is wrong (shown in Figure 3), the correct answer is displayed and you are asked if you want to read the helptext.

As long as you do not have a question opened, it is possible to halt the game, stopping both the clock and the play. This makes it possible to go and ask someone for help, and then resume the game without any penalties.

Sometimes during play a kind of porcupine-like monsters appear, moving randomly. One of those can be seen in the lower left part of Figure 2. They are poisonous to the touch, and affect your health. If your health drops to zero, you die, and have to start this course from the beginning (but keeping the points you have gained this far). If you use up all your lives, the game terminates, and if you want to keep on playing you have to start from the beginning, with zero points.

The contents of the boxes are different every time you start a certain course. The designer specifies how many of the boxes that are to contain extra lives and bonus points, and from which sets of questions the boxes are to be filled, and the program assigns these contents randomly to the boxes when the course is opened.

When you have passed through all courses at one level, you are brought back to the starting room, and are free to choose any level you want.

3.2. The Mathematics Contents of the Game

Developing the math contents of the game involved considerations at various levels.

3.2.1. Practical Considerations

First, we had to decide what kind of tasks made sense in the context given by our platform. Long complicated problems do not integrate well in this setting; they interrupt the flow of the game. So it seemed that questions that could be worked out in the head were the kind that had to be used. Furthermore, the questions had to be multiple choice. Parsing written answers can be difficult, and an answer can be correct but not in the format expected, and thus incorrectly classified as wrong. *Writing* an answer requires removing the hands from their positions on the key-board and the gaze from the screen. Multiple choices can be made using the same keys as used elsewhere in the game, and thus integrate well with the game.

3.2.2. A Suitable Topic

After analysing the *kind* of questions that would work, we had to decide on some first topic (of course, new topics can be added at any point). The game seemed suitable for children in elementary school; high school students would probably find it a bit below their dignity. We decided to work with *fractions*. This subject is learnt around the age of 12, and practised yearly from then on.

We know from own teaching experience that many people find working with fractions difficult, and many students arrive at university not knowing how to do tackle fractions. Therefore, we think anything that might help developing understanding in this area is worth exploring.

The subject of fractions also has the advantage that it has clear bounds and a reasonable size. This made it possible to cover the whole subject in the game prototype, with enough different questions to make the game challenging.

A closer discussion on the design of the questions is given in section 4..

3.3. Evaluation of the Design from a Didactical Perspective

We now make a first evaluation of the game, connecting to the discussion on games given in section 2..

This game does not have its mathematical contents highly integrated, but seems to fall into the category that Gough [7] classifies as "dressed-up work sheets". We think that those too have a place in education. Some types of problems require lots of practice, but large work sheets with problems can be discouraging. Teaching aids that make it possible to practice enough without being bored to death seem like a good idea, and the more of them there are, the more varied you can make the lessons.

The game is somewhat discontinuous in that you switch back and forth between game and math, but the two activities mix fairly well, as they are both about making fast decisions. However, we also want to point out an educational advantage from the discontinuous game setting. When you first focus on the game, then focus on the math, then return to the game, etc., you must go through lots of refocusing on the math. Conventional teaching materials do not provide this kind of training. During a normal lesson or home-work session, you put yourself in "math-mode" and try to stay there, because it seems to take many children a substantial effort to switch over to math-mode — but this may be a problem for the general utility of their math skills. Many persons associate math solely with school lessons, and have great trouble using it in other circumstances, even when their actual knowledge of the subject is sufficient (Wistedt et al. [17]). The training on refocusing on math provided by the setting of our game may potentially make such refocusing easier in the long run, also outside the game.

The mixture of different types of questions may force players to *analyse* the problems. In school, students often work with one kind of problem at a time, and many of them work according to the principle "all right, all problems on this page should be solved by approach X". It is not uncommon that you can use the approach without really reflecting on the problems. If it is possible to finish the set task without such reflection, that is what many students will choose (cf. Geary [6]).

Another advantage of this game setting is the effort needed to get to the questions. If you have spent a lot of trouble to reach the place where the question-box is, it may feel stupid not to put at least some effort into doing something sensible with the contents.

Lastly, the fact that the game is possible to extend and modify increases its usability. A teacher can tailor the game contents to the needs of his/her pupils, and does not have to accept the game as it is.

4. The Design of the Questions

The approximately 20 000 questions that are loaded into the game were computer generated, since this was the most efficient way of getting a large amount of material. Here we describe our approach to this automated question design.

4.1. Determining the Difficulty Level

Most math problems are worked out step by step:

- $\frac{1}{5} + \frac{2}{5} = \frac{3}{5}$
- $\frac{3}{5} + \frac{4}{5} = \frac{7}{5} = 1\,\frac{2}{5}$
- $\frac{2}{5} + \frac{5}{2} = \frac{4}{10} + \frac{5}{2} = \frac{4}{10} + \frac{25}{10} = \frac{29}{10}$

Here we show examples of questions that take between one and three steps to solve. More steps than three may be unreasonable for most children to keep in their head. We use the number of steps needed as a basis for classification of question difficulty in three levels.

One complication with this classification is that many problems can be solved in several different ways, requiring different numbers of steps. For instance, to determine which is greater, $\frac{3}{4}$ or $\frac{6}{5}$, you can either convert them to a common denominator and compare them (takes 4 steps) or realise that the first one is less than one and the second one greater than one. These two insights combined give the answer. The first way is likely to be chosen by someone who is good at the mechanics but does not think too deeply, the second by those who have a good understanding of what they are doing and by those who do not know how to do it according to the first method. It is usually the case that the shorter solution only works in special cases, while the longer one works for all problems of a given type. Some persons prefer to stick to the universal method and avoid the "choose an appropriate method" step, others enjoy finding short-cuts. We think that the "finding short-cut" approach should be encouraged, since the short-cuts depend on understanding what you are doing. Therefore, the problems were classified according to the solution method requiring the least number of steps, and coupled to a helptext explaining this method but with links to texts describing the more general cases.

Another complication is that in some cases determining that a statement is false takes more steps than checking an equivalent true statement. These questions were classified according to the difficulty level of the true statement.

To keep the arithmetic operations (like addition and multiplication) as one-step operations, the numbers involved had to be restricted. The children are supposed to learn the times tables up to 10×10 by heart, so all multiplications and factor extractions were kept within that range. There do not seem to be any strict rules regarding addition, but we judged that additions where the answer is at most 30 and additions of a single digit number to a two digit number without carry are simple enough to count as "one-step".

4.2. Question and Number Formats

We have used three different question formats:

- *Comparison problems*, where you get two numbers and have to choose between "less-than" and "greater-than". All these problems have "less" as first choice, since we hoped that this standard way of stating the problems would make focusing on the contents easier. In 50 % of the cases, "less" is the correct choice.

- *Equality problems*, where you get two numbers and have to choose between "equal" and "not equal", "equal" given as first choice. Figure 2 shows a problem of this type. These problems concern simplification and changes between improper fractions and mixed fractions. Since there is an infinite number of correct ways of writing a fraction it did not seem right to state these problems as a choice between three alternatives, since that seems to imply that there can only be *one* correct solution. For every correct statement, there is a similar incorrect one (where e.g. the simplification has been incorrectly done, as in Figure 2). This means that "equal" is correct in 50 % of the cases.
- *Computational problems*. Here, a question and three alternative answers are given, and you have to choose the right one. The first, second and third alternatives are correct equally often.

All questions and answers are given with all fractions maximally simplified, and either all numbers involved are given mixed, or none of them are (unless the whole point of the question is about changing the format).

4.3. Example of a Problem Type Definition

After the considerations described in the previous section, we had to specify the question types in detail. Here is a description of how one of the types was defined. A complete list of the problem types is given in Appendix A..

The definition of *First-level addition problem* is:

> Addition of two maximally simplified (not necessarily proper) fractions, same denominator, answer cannot be simplified. Numerators in the questions in the range 1–10, denominators in the range 2–10.

Figure 4 shows the helptext belonging to this kind of problem. A concrete example of such a problem and its solution is

$$\frac{2}{7} + \frac{3}{7} = \frac{5}{7}$$

Addition och subtraktion av bråk: Samma nämnare

Hur gör man?

Addera eller subtrahera täljarna och låt nämnaren vara som förut.

$$\frac{2}{7}+\frac{3}{7}=\frac{2+3}{7}=\frac{5}{7}$$

$$\frac{8}{5}-\frac{4}{5}=\frac{8-4}{5}=\frac{4}{5}$$

Om nämnarna inte är lika, läs här.

Varför?

Då man adderar och subtraherar måste sakerna som man räknar med vara av samma sort. Två kronor plus tre kronor är fem kronor, sju bananer minus två bananer är fem bananer. Då är det bara att addera eller subtrahera antalen. Däremot blir det ganska konstigt om man försöker dra kronor från bananer!

Om vi ska addera eller subtrahera två bråk och bråken har samma nämnare så har vi saker av samma sort. Då räknar vi ihop antalen, och sorten förblir densamma:

$$\frac{1}{7}+\frac{3}{7}=\frac{1+3}{7}=\frac{4}{7}$$

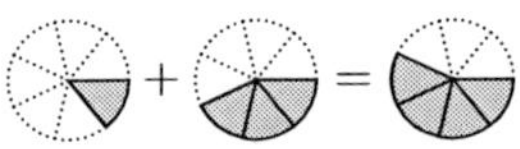

En sjundedel plus tre sjundedelar är fyra sjundedelar.

Figure 4. A sample of a helptext from the third course at level 1. (Addition and subtraction, no other complications.) The text links to a vocabulary, defining the words *täljare* (numerator) and *nämnare* (denominator), and also to the helptext describing the simplest case of addition when the denominators are not equal. The first section describes how to do it, the second why this gives the correct answer.

This is a one-step problem, because the only necessary computation is to add the numerators. (It is not necessary to check that the fraction cannot be simplified when you can compare the answer to three given alternatives.)

There exist exactly 167 problems conforming to this specification, and if you exchange the first term and the sum, you get another set of subtraction

Addition och subtraktion av bråk: Förkortning av svaret

Hur gör man?

Addera eller subtrahera bråken på vanligt sätt. Förkorta sedan svaret så mycket som möjligt.

$$\frac{2}{9}+\frac{4}{9}=\frac{2+4}{9}=\frac{6}{9}=\frac{\cancel{3}\cdot 2}{\cancel{3}\cdot 3}=\frac{2}{3}$$

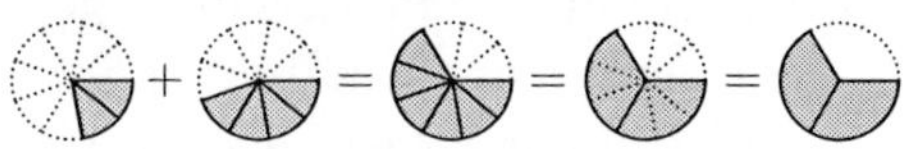

Varför?

Man förkortar eftersom svaret blir lättare att hålla reda på då.

Figure 5. A sample of a helptext from level 2. (Addition and subtraction, followed by simplification.) The text links to the text describing addition without complications, shown in Figure 4, and to a text explaining simplification.

problems of the same difficulty:

$$\frac{5}{7}-\frac{3}{7}=\frac{2}{7}$$

Problems where the answer *can* be simplified belong to another category, classified as two-step (the steps being the addition and the simplification). Their helptext is shown in Figure 5. Problems where the fractions in the question are proper but the sum is improper can be transformed into another kind of two-step problems, with the answer given in mixed form.

4.4. Design of the False Alternatives

The problems had to be coupled to incorrect answer suggestions, and that took some care to avoid any false alternatives that can easily be ruled out. Our questions are designed to make the most common tricks impossible.

- *Pattern recognition:* If you have to solve many problems designed by the same person, you can learn to recognise the false alternatives from their form. To avoid this possibility, every kind of question has several types of false alternatives. We have used four errors for each question type. In the three-alternative questions, the six possible combinations of error types are equally common.

- *Voting for the majority:* If you give three alternative answers, one correct, one with one kind of error and one with another kind of error, it is often possible to make an educated guess as to which answer is correct. As an example, if the suggested answers to a question are (a) $\frac{6}{7}$, (b) $\frac{6}{8}$, (c) $\frac{5}{8}$, then voting for the majority would give the answer $\frac{6}{8}$, which is correct. To avoid this possibility, it is better to make one alternative with one of the errors and one with both. (This takes some extra care when working with mathematics, since it is possible that the errors will cancel each other.) Combining a common error in reasoning with an arithmetic error is an option if the common errors cannot be combined.

- *Voting for the middle:* The answer $\frac{6}{8}$ to the above question is suggested also by another heuristic: vote for the middle. When one designs questions it easily happens that one erroneous alternative has the answer too big and another one has it too small. When generating questions, we ensure that the middle alternative is the correct one in only one third of the cases.

- *"Randomness"* A person making a multiple choice test usually tries to make a random pattern out of the correct alternatives. A random pattern generated by a human is usually much more "random" than a real random pattern (where nothing stops you from getting the same value ten times in a row). This makes it possible to check that the answer distribution looks likely, and double-check the answers that seem to skew it, but computer-generated randomness avoids this possibility.

5. User Testing

We have made three user trials, with students from neighbouring schools as study participants. After the first and second trial, we redesigned parts of the game, based on user input. The third trial was a first test of the usefulness of the game as a teaching tool.

5.1. The First Trial

This was a small "pilot test", with six students (three girls and three boys). The participants were given a diagnostic test. Then they ran the game for about 30 minutes in our game laboratory. Afterwards they were interviewed.

Based on their comments, we made some major extensions of the game. The most important ones from an educational point of view were the addition of helptexts; the display of the correct answer when a question is incorrectly answered; and a redesign of the assignment of bonus points, to encourage the players to put a serious effort into answering the questions correctly.

5.2. The Second Trial

This time, we had a whole form (28 students, divided into two groups) of 7th-graders as study participants. In line with recommendations on research practice (Cohen et al. [3]), we had previously visited them at their school, and then explained what we were doing.

First, they were given a diagnostic test and a demonstration on how to run the game. Then, they were given half an hour to play. Computer gaming is a highly social activity among children (Facer et al. [5]). The players maintained contact, called to each other, asked about their friends' progress, asked for hints on tricky places, and so on.

After the gaming session, the participants were given a questionnaire on the game experience. Based on the questionnaires, we made some changes in the game. The most important one was to make the helptexts available after an incorrect answer. The helptexts were also completely redesigned, for easier reading.

5.3. The Third Trial

The third trial was performed with a new form of 25 pupils from grade 7. The main objective of this trial was to run diagnostic tests both pre-trial and post-trial, to see if test results showed any improvement after the game.

The trial started out in a class-room, where the diagnostic pre-test was given. After that, we went to the laboratory and ran the game for about 45 minutes. Then, we returned to the class-room, where the diagnostic post-test was given, followed by the questionnaire.

6. Results

These are the results from the third trial.

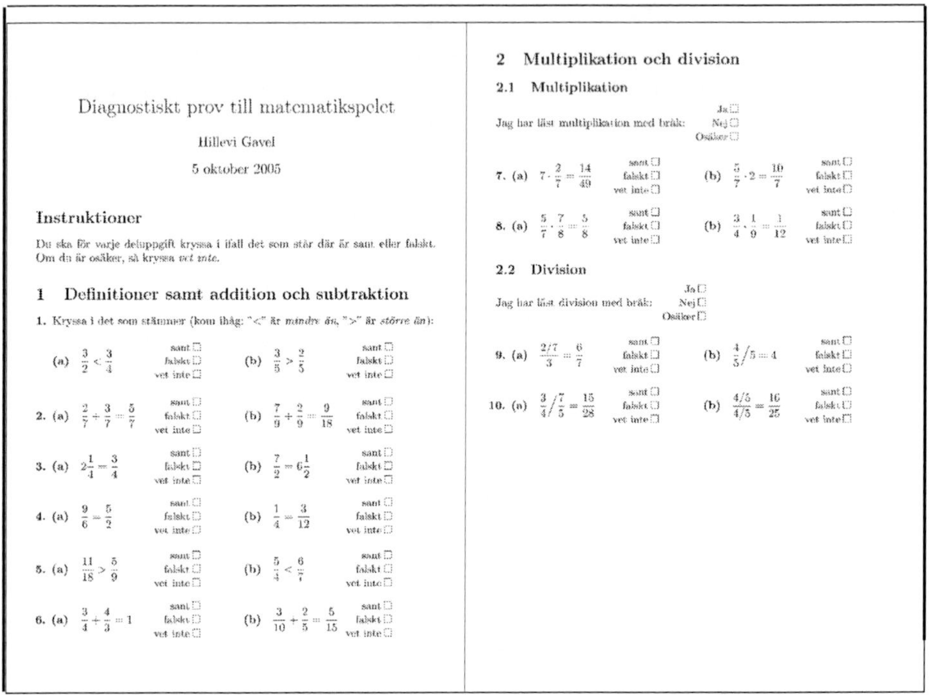

Diagnostiskt prov till matematikspelet

Hillevi Gavel

5 oktober 2005

Instruktioner

Du ska för varje deluppgift kryssa i ifall det som står där är sant eller falskt. Om du är osäker, så kryssa *vet inte*.

1 Definitioner samt addition och subtraktion

1. Kryssa i det som stämmer (kom ihåg: "<" är *mindre än*, ">" är *större än*):

(a) $\frac{3}{2} < \frac{3}{4}$ sant ☐ falskt ☐ vet inte ☐ (b) $\frac{3}{5} > \frac{2}{5}$ sant ☐ falskt ☐ vet inte ☐

2. (a) $\frac{2}{7} + \frac{3}{7} = \frac{5}{7}$ sant ☐ falskt ☐ vet inte ☐ (b) $\frac{7}{9} + \frac{2}{9} = \frac{9}{18}$ sant ☐ falskt ☐ vet inte ☐

3. (a) $2\frac{1}{4} = \frac{3}{4}$ sant ☐ falskt ☐ vet inte ☐ (b) $\frac{7}{2} = 6\frac{1}{2}$ sant ☐ falskt ☐ vet inte ☐

4. (a) $\frac{9}{6} = \frac{5}{2}$ sant ☐ falskt ☐ vet inte ☐ (b) $\frac{1}{4} = \frac{3}{12}$ sant ☐ falskt ☐ vet inte ☐

5. (a) $\frac{11}{18} > \frac{5}{9}$ sant ☐ falskt ☐ vet inte ☐ (b) $\frac{5}{4} < \frac{6}{7}$ sant ☐ falskt ☐ vet inte ☐

6. (a) $\frac{3}{4} + \frac{4}{3} = 1$ sant ☐ falskt ☐ vet inte ☐ (b) $\frac{3}{10} + \frac{2}{5} = \frac{5}{15}$ sant ☐ falskt ☐ vet inte ☐

2 Multiplikation och division

2.1 Multiplikation

Jag har läst multiplikation med bråk: Ja ☐ Nej ☐ Osäker ☐

7. (a) $7 \cdot \frac{2}{7} = \frac{14}{49}$ sant ☐ falskt ☐ vet inte ☐ (b) $\frac{5}{7} \cdot 2 = \frac{10}{7}$ sant ☐ falskt ☐ vet inte ☐

8. (a) $\frac{5}{7} \cdot \frac{7}{8} = \frac{5}{8}$ sant ☐ falskt ☐ vet inte ☐ (b) $\frac{3}{4} \cdot \frac{1}{9} = \frac{1}{12}$ sant ☐ falskt ☐ vet inte ☐

2.2 Division

Jag har läst division med bråk: Ja ☐ Nej ☐ Osäker ☐

9. (a) $\frac{2/7}{3} = \frac{6}{7}$ sant ☐ falskt ☐ vet inte ☐ (b) $\frac{4}{5}/5 = 4$ sant ☐ falskt ☐ vet inte ☐

10. (a) $\frac{3}{4}/\frac{7}{5} = \frac{15}{28}$ sant ☐ falskt ☐ vet inte ☐ (b) $\frac{4/5}{4/5} = \frac{16}{25}$ sant ☐ falskt ☐ vet inte ☐

Figure 6. Test A. Used as pre-test by the first group and as post-test by the second group in the third user trial. The alternatives are *true*/*false*/*don't know*. We thought that the *don't know*-alternative would give a clearer picture of the participants' actual knowledge. We also emphasised that we really wanted them to check this if they were unsure. Since the Swedish school usually encourage the students to "at least try", the participants seemed to find this quite unusual.

6.1. The Questionnaires

According to the questionnaires, the majority of the participants liked math and did not find the subject difficult. Their gaming habits varied. Some played computer games daily, others hardly ever. Most of them gave this game a rating of "could be worse" or "fun". Eight (out of 25) of them would definitely not play it if they had many other games to choose from, the rest said that they might choose it.

Asked if the questions did fit in well in the game or if they felt like an interruption, four checked "interruption" and eight that they fit in well. The rest

Diagnostiskt prov till matematikspelet

Hillevi Gavel

5 oktober 2005

Instruktioner

Du ska för varje deluppgift kryssa i ifall det som står där är sant eller falskt. Om du är osäker, så kryssa *vet inte*.

1 Definitioner samt addition och subtraktion

1. Kryssa i det som stämmer (kom ihåg: "<" är *mindre än*, ">" är *större än*):

(a) $\frac{7}{6} < 1$ sant ☐ falskt ☐ vet inte ☐ (b) $\frac{14}{5} < 3$ sant ☐ falskt ☐ vet inte ☐

2. (a) $\frac{1}{4} + 4 = 4\frac{1}{4}$ sant ☐ falskt ☐ vet inte ☐ (b) $\frac{4}{5} - \frac{1}{5} = \frac{3}{0}$ sant ☐ falskt ☐ vet inte ☐

3. (a) $3 = \frac{6}{3}$ sant ☐ falskt ☐ vet inte ☐ (b) $\frac{7}{5} = 1\frac{2}{5}$ sant ☐ falskt ☐ vet inte ☐

4. (a) $\frac{6}{18} = \frac{3}{9}$ sant ☐ falskt ☐ vet inte ☐ (b) $\frac{9}{4} = \frac{3}{2}$ sant ☐ falskt ☐ vet inte ☐

5. (a) $\frac{8}{9} < \frac{9}{10}$ sant ☐ falskt ☐ vet inte ☐ (b) $\frac{7}{3} > \frac{9}{4}$ sant ☐ falskt ☐ vet inte ☐

6. (a) $\frac{5}{6} - \frac{1}{6} = \frac{2}{3}$ sant ☐ falskt ☐ vet inte ☐ (b) $\frac{4}{5} + 1\frac{2}{5} = \frac{7}{5}$ sant ☐ falskt ☐ vet inte ☐

2 Multiplikation och division

2.1 Multiplikation

Jag har läst multiplikation med bråk: Ja ☐ Nej ☐ Osäker ☐

7. (a) $\frac{2}{7} \cdot \frac{1}{3} = \frac{2}{21}$ sant ☐ falskt ☐ vet inte ☐ (b) $2\frac{1}{4} \cdot 3 = 6\frac{3}{4}$ sant ☐ falskt ☐ vet inte ☐

8. (a) $\frac{7}{8} \cdot \frac{4}{9} = \frac{63}{32}$ sant ☐ falskt ☐ vet inte ☐ (b) $2\frac{1}{5} \cdot \frac{1}{3} = 2\frac{1}{15}$ sant ☐ falskt ☐ vet inte ☐

2.2 Division

Jag har läst division med bråk: Ja ☐ Nej ☐ Osäker ☐

9. (a) $5/\frac{1}{4} = 20$ sant ☐ falskt ☐ vet inte ☐ (b) $\frac{7}{1/5} = 35$ sant ☐ falskt ☐ vet inte ☐

10. (a) $\frac{2}{3}/\frac{3}{2} = 1$ sant ☐ falskt ☐ vet inte ☐ (b) $\frac{4/7}{5/9} = \frac{20}{63}$ sant ☐ falskt ☐ vet inte ☐

Figure 7. Test B. Used as pre-test by the second group and as post-test by the first group.

were in-between. Most of them did care about the points, so they seem to be an important incentive.

Everyone believed that you could learn at least something from playing a game like this. If given a choice between the game and similar work in a text-book, two would choose the book and four said that it did depend; the rest would choose the game. Most would also be prepared to play it during a week-end, if the teacher issued a high-score challenge (it did depend a bit on other things).

6.2. The Diagnostic Tests

Here, we used the diagnostic tests shown in Figure 6 and 7.

Only three out of the 25 participants checked "yes" on the question "I have studied multiplication of fractions" (and one of them added "but it was a long time ago"), so it did not seem to be any point in including the results on those questions in the statistics.

Table 1. Results from the diagnostic tests in the third trial. The data used is from questions 1–6 on the tests (see Figure 6 and 7). Score is defined as number of correct answers minus number of incorrect answers. Standard deviation in parenthesis.

	Pre-test	Post-test
Answered	86 %	84 %
Correct/answered	69 %	76 %
Mean score	3.8 (5.1)	5.2 (4.6)

A compilation of the results is shown in Table 1. The number of answered questions actually decreased slightly. This is not necessarily a bad effect, because it could indicate an increased awareness of what problems one does not master. The proportion of correctly answered questions increased, which suggests a positive effect of the game. The average score (with minus points for incorrect answers) increased from 3.8 points to 5.2 points. For each participant we computed the game effect as the difference between the post-test score and the pre-test score. The average effect (1.8, with standard deviation 2.4) is significantly greater than zero ($p < 0.01$, t-test).

7. Conclusion

Here we would like to return to our original question from the introduction: Can computer games be any good at all in math class, and if so, how? For us, the main question is "how". Given the huge range of possibilities for computer games, it would be sensational if there were absolutely no good use for them at all in math class.

In this study, we identified a couple of things that computer games would seem to be good for: to generate large numbers of varied kinds of problems on a given topic, and to encourage pupils to practice on such problems. We also identified a topic in need of such an educational device: 7th grade arithmetic with fractions.

Above we have described how we developed and tested such a game. Questionnaire results suggest that many pupils find a game like this reasonably fun and effective, and results from diagnostic tests indicate that the game has a positive educational effect. Thus, we believe it is worthwhile to test games like these also in the classroom.

We see two important directions for future research. The first question is how much time in math class is optimally spent on a game like this. This issue coud be investigated through large-scale tests over an entire semester, with several participating groups spending varying amounts of time at the game. The second question is what other effects games like this have on math skills. In particular, we speculated in section 3.3. that playing a game that involves repeated refocusing on mathematics will make it easier to use mathematics outside math class. To the best of our knowledge, there exists no research bearing on this issue.

Acknowledgements

We would like to thank the student group at KTH, who implemented the original game: Delby Arrospide, Niloofar Ghassemino, Lars Helander, Taghrid Hodroj, Magnus Johansson, Caroline Koch, Erik Larsson and Helena Nilsson, with an extra thanks to Lars Helander and Erik Larsson, who added the modifications. Also Alvin Gavel, who designed several courses for the game and gave important input on the design of the game editor. UVEN and Wallenberg Foundation for partial financial support. Max Scheja, for useful input on this text. And finally the teachers and students at Viksängsskolan and at St Iliansskolan, who participated in this project.

A. A Complete List of the Question Types

Here is a summary of the descriptions of the question types used at the user trials, with a typical question of each type.

In all the question types, the size of the numbers are restricted. In most cases, denominators in the questions are kept in the range 2–10. No multiplications involve numbers greater than 10. In the additions, either the sum is at the most 30 or one of the terms is a one digit number and the addition can be carried out without carry. Subtractions are defined in a similar way.

Since multiplication and division appear later in the curriculum than addition and subtraction, these problems are kept separate.

Level 1	
Comparison problems	
Two fractions with a common denominator.	$\frac{7}{8} > \frac{5}{8}$
Two fractions with a common numerator.	$\frac{3}{8} < \frac{3}{5}$
A fraction and the number 1.	$\frac{6}{7} < 1$
Equality problems	
Extending/simplifying a fraction.	$\frac{1}{2} = \frac{3}{6}$
Writing an improper fraction as a mixed fraction.	$\frac{5}{4} = 1\frac{1}{4}$
Computational problems	
Addition/subtraction, common denominator, no complications.	$\frac{4}{9} + \frac{7}{9} = \frac{11}{9}$
Level 2	
Comparison problems	
Fractions close to 1, same side.	$\frac{7}{6} > \frac{9}{8}$
Fractions close to 1, different sides.	$\frac{5}{4} > \frac{4}{5}$
Fractions, extend one to get a common denominator.	$\frac{3}{8} < \frac{1}{2}$
A fraction and an integer (not 1).	$\frac{41}{6} < 7$
Equality problems	
Simplifying two fractions.	$\frac{2}{6} = \frac{3}{9}$
Computational problems	
Addition/subtraction, common denominator, simplifying answer.	$\frac{3}{8} + \frac{1}{8} = \frac{4}{8} = \frac{1}{2}$
Addition, common denominator, mixed answer.	$\frac{3}{5} + \frac{4}{5} = \frac{8}{5} = 1\frac{3}{5}$
Subtraction, common denominator, one term mixed.	$1\frac{1}{7} - \frac{5}{7} = \frac{8}{7} - \frac{5}{7} = \frac{3}{7}$
Addition/subtraction, common denominator, mixed form, the whole parts and the fraction parts can be handled separately.	$1\frac{3}{5} + 2\frac{1}{5} = 1 + 2 + \frac{3}{5} + \frac{1}{5} = 3\frac{4}{5}$
Addition/subtraction, one term has to be expanded.	$\frac{1}{3} - \frac{1}{6} = \frac{2}{6} - \frac{1}{6} = \frac{1}{6}$

Level 3 *Computational problems*	
Addition/subtraction, denominators relatively prime.	$\frac{3}{5} - \frac{1}{2} = \frac{6}{10} - \frac{5}{10} = \frac{1}{10}$
Addition/subtraction, common denominator, mixed form, the whole parts and the fraction parts cannot be handled separately.	$2\frac{4}{7} + 2\frac{5}{7} = 2 + 2 + \frac{4}{7} + \frac{5}{7} = 4 + \frac{9}{7} = 5\frac{2}{7}$
Addition/subtraction, finding lowest common denominator, numerator $= 1$.	$\frac{1}{6} - \frac{1}{8} = \frac{4}{24} - \frac{3}{24} = \frac{1}{4}$
Multiplication *Computational problems*	
Multiplying a fraction and an integer, no simplification.	$\frac{3}{4} \cdot 5 = \frac{15}{4}$
Multiplying a fraction and an integer, integer result.	$\frac{7}{8} \cdot 8 = 7$
Multiplying two fractions, no simplification.	$\frac{3}{5} \cdot \frac{6}{7} = \frac{18}{35}$
Multiplying two fractions, some part completly cancelled.	$\frac{9}{2} \cdot \frac{5}{3} = \frac{15}{2}$
Division *Computational problems*	
Dividing a fraction by an integer, no simplification.	$\frac{7}{10}/3 = \frac{7}{30}$
Dividing a fraction by an integer, some part completly cancelled.	$\frac{5}{3}/10 = \frac{1}{6}$
Dividing an integer by a fraction, no simplification.	$5/\frac{3}{4} = \frac{20}{3}$
Dividing an integer by a fraction, some part completly cancelled.	$14/\frac{7}{2} = 4$
Dividing a fraction by a fraction, no simplification.	$\frac{10}{7}/\frac{3}{5} = \frac{50}{21}$
Dividing a fraction by a fraction, some part completly cancelled.	$\frac{5}{2}/\frac{10}{3} = \frac{3}{4}$

References

[1] A. Amory, K. Naicker, J. Vincent, and C. Adams. The use of compter games as an educational tool: Identification of appropriate game types and game elements. *British Journal of Educational Technology*, **30**(4):311–321, October 1999.

[2] M. J. Bosse. The NCTM standards in light of the New Math movement: A warning! *Journal of Mathematics Behavior*, **14**(2):171–201, June 1995.

[3] L. Cohen, L. Manion, and K. Morrison. *Research Methods in Education*. RoutledgeFalmer, 2000.

[4] L. Cuban. *Oversold and Underused: Computers in the Classroom*. Harvard University Press, 2003.

[5] K. Facer, R. Sutherland, and R. Furlong. *ScreenPlay: Children and Computing in the Home*. RoutledgeFalmer, 2003.

[6] D. C. Geary. *Children's Mathematical Development: Research and Practical Applications*. American Psychological Association, 1994.

[7] J. Gough. Mathematics games that really teach mathematics, 1995. http://education.deakin.edu.au/resources/maths_ed/StaffPages/Gough/ articles/mathsgamesreallyteach.pdf

[8] M. M. Klawe. When does the use of computer games and other interactive multimedia software help students learn mathematics?, 1998. http://mathforum.org/technology/papers/papers/klawe.html

[9] C. Laborde. Designing tasks for learning geometry in a computer-based environment. In L. Burton and B. Jaworski, editors, *Technology in Mathematics Teaching*, pages 35–68. Chartwell-Bratt, 1995.

[10] S. Marklund. *Skolsverige 1950–1975*, volume 2. Liber Utbildningsförlaget, 1982.

[11] M. Prensky. *Digital Game-based Learning*. McGraw-Hill Education, 2001.

[12] L. P. Rieber. Seriously considering play: Designing interactive learning environments based on the blending of microworlds, simulations, and games. *Educational Technology Research & Development*, **44**(2):43–58, 1996.

[13] R. Sandford and B. Williamson. Games and learning. Handbook, NESTA Futurelab, 2005.

[14] J. Shaftel, L. Pass, and S. Schnabel. Math games for adolcents. *TEACHING Exceptional Children*, pages 25–30, Jan/Feb 2005.

[15] Skolöverstyrelsen. *Läroplan för grundskolan: Lgr69*. Svenska Utbildningsförlaget Liber AB, 1969.

[16] A. Tveit and G. B. Tveit. Game usage mining: Information gathering for knowledge discovery in massive multiplayer games. In *Proceedings of the International Conference on Internet Computing (IC'2002), session on Web Mining*. CSREA Press, June 2002.

[17] I. Wistedt, G. Brattström, and C. Jacobsson. Att vardagsanknyta matematikundervisningen. Report, Stockholms Universitet, Pedagogiska institutionen, 1992.

[18] J. Zavaleta, M. Costa, M. T. Gouvea, and C. Lima. Compter games as a teaching strategy. In *Fifth IEEE International Conference on Advanced Learning Technologies (ICALT'05)*, pages 257–259, 2005.

INDEX

A

B

E

F

G

H

I

L

M

T

V

W

Y

Z